Tanky Challenor

Tanky Challenor

SAS & THE MET

Ex-Detective Sergeant
HAROLD CHALLENOR, MM

with ALFRED DRAPER

LEO COOPER

First published by Leo Cooper 1990

Leo Cooper is an independent imprint of the
Octopus Publishing Group, Michelin House,
81 Fulham Road, London SW3 6RB

LONDON   MELBOURNE   AUCKLAND

A CIP catalogue record for this book
is available from the British Library

ISBN 0 85052 1246

Printed in Great Britain by St Edmundsbury Press Ltd, Bury St. Edmunds
and bound by Hunter & Foulis Ltd, Edinburgh

Illustrations

Foreword

by Major Roy Farran
DSO & Bar, MC & 2 Bars, French Croix de Guerre
and American Legion of Merit

Harold 'Tanky' Challenor is a friend of mine. Years ago when the world was in turmoil, I just knew him as a corporal under my command in the Special Air Service.

We had countless adventures on operations in Sicily, Italy and France. And he was always a resolute soldier, ready to brighten up our darkest moment with the quick smile and ready wit of a Londoner.

In a type of warfare where there was little distinction between officers and men, we all loved Tanky.

We knew we could rely on him in a pinch and that he would never let down the team. He came to us from the Commandos and was totally in his element in the SAS where the lives of men in a small group depended so much on the actions of each other.

Tanky was adept on foot or in a boat, walking, swimming or parachuting, but his real element was the jeep. He loved his jeep as much as a cavalryman loves his horse.

In June, 1980, I made a flying trip to meet our old comrades of the French Resistance in Burgundy. As I went from one village to another and through the forests in which we had lurked in days gone by, everyone enquired about 'Challenor'. He was the one personality all could remember.

Then in August, 1980, the former Maquisards launched a great reunion with the SAS in numerous villages across France. I received newspaper clippings in distant Canada and was delighted to see that the processions were led by a replica of Challenor's jeep, suitably titled 'Little Tanky'. The French had remembered. And to my joy I saw that

Tanky himself was aboard and that he looked remarkably young for his years.

I remembered then his troubles after the war when, as a highly successful Police Officer, he had met a personal disaster.

Tanky always gave everything he had in whatever he did. After all his hair-raising exploits in wartime, it was understandable that he should have regarded law-breakers as an enemy. He did marvellous work, I am told, against gangsters from his base in the West End Station of the Metropolitan Police.

Then the strain of so many years of active service began to catch up with him. His health broke down and he began to confuse his police work with wartime SAS operations. Finally he committed a serious error during a London riot when he made a wrong assumption that certain innocent persons were guilty.

His friends in the Metropolitan Police and his old comrades in the SAS understood. Through all his tribulation, they did not forsake him. They knew that every man had his breaking point and that when it is reached his actions may not be rational.

Tanky Challenor is now fully recovered.

He served his country well as both soldier and policeman. And I am glad to be called his friend. With a few more Challenors, the war would have been over sooner.

Roy Farran

Chapter One

Members of the criminal fraternity are not renowned for the unanimity of their opinions, but on one thing they are in total agreement: all policemen are illegitimate – but the sentiment is expressed a little more forcefully in the argot of the underworld. Far from being offended, policemen take it as a compliment; it means they are doing their job. Although no one would have dared say so to my face, I know that in the sordid world of Soho's gangland I was frequently referred to as "that bastard Challenor".

The more respectable residents of that cosmopolitan square mile of London who simply wanted to lead an honest and industrious life saw me as a friend and a dedicated detective who was doing his best to stamp out organized crime.

Later it was claimed that I had delusions of having been appointed the "saviour of Soho", and the crooks who had planned to 'frame' me in order to get me transferred to another Division because I was such a thorn in their flesh, latched on to the description and used it to denigrate me and my record as a crime-buster.

It is said that the whores danced in the street outside the Old Bailey when Oscar Wilde was jailed, glad to see a menace to their profession out of the way. I'm pretty certain that though there may not have been quite such an exuberant display of relief when I was publicly disgraced, a few glasses were raised in the clip-joints and strip clubs by the men who controlled organized crime and prostitution in the West End. I had got what they would have described as my come-uppance.

It arose out of what has come to be known as the "Brick Case" when I was accused of planting pieces of brick on innocent demonstrators.

I have done a lot of things I can be reasonably proud of, and a few of which I am ashamed, but one thing I will never be allowed to forget – my downfall. It will follow me to the grave and any obituary notice I might get will certainly harp on it, because it has been mentioned

1

in those of other people. I was reminded of this when the eminent psychiatrist Doctor William Sargant died in August, 1988, at the ripe old age of 81. His obituary in the *Daily Telegraph* was spread over three columns and included this paragraph:

"The numerous cases in which he was involved included the trial in 1964 of Det. Sgt. Harold Challenor (accused of planting pieces of brick on demonstrators) who was found unfit to plead. Sargant told the subsequent inquiry that although Challenor was medically 'as mad as a hatter' he was completely sane and responsible for his actions."

Make sense of that if you can, coming as it did from the brother of Tom Sargant, the founder of the organization Justice.

I do not *want* to be remembered as Challenor "the bent copper", but if I have to be I would like the public to know there is a possible explanation for it. What is known in legal circles as a plea of mitigation. Perhaps they will then begin to understand if not forgive.

I'm prompted to write about it a quarter of a century later because more recent wars than the one I fought in have made people more responsive to the problems of the returning warrior and the invisible scars they often bear. This especially applied to Vietnam which left in its wake the wreckage of many young Americans who had been taught to kill in the most stealthy and barbaric manner, and who had served their country well. Some veterans managed to rehabilitate themselves, others could not adjust and resorted to living a solitary existence in self-imposed exile in the mountains, sustained by the special skills they had been taught.

At the end of the last war I was somewhat in the same category. I was a member of that military elite, the SAS, who fought their battles behind the enemy lines and were licensed to kill in the most unorthodox ways. But I did not run away, I sought to take my place in society and serve it. For a considerable time I succeeded, then I failed and paid the price, and twenty-five years later I'm still not sure if I've managed to come in from the cold.

When I began writing this book I intended to confine it to my war-time experiences with the Special Air Service; I could not bring myself to think, let alone write about, the events which brought about my disgrace. I wanted to draw a veil over it and tell people what a brave soldier I had been, and how later in civvy street, I became the scourge of criminals in the twilight world of Soho. Like Othello I wanted to remind everyone that I had done the State some service. The reader could form his own conclusions about the allegations of framing people.

I showed what I had written to Tom Sandrock, an old friend and formerly the Crime Correspondent of the *Daily Telegraph*, and asked for his opinion. Tom read it and was as frank and honest as I knew he would be. "Like it or not, Harry, in spite of all you did during the war and as a police officer, and both those phases of your life are on record, it was the 'Brick Case' which put your name before the general public. You must, however painful or difficult it might be, include in your story all you can recall about it."

It was sound advice, and in my heart of hearts I have always wanted to explain, if not justify, my fall from grace, but I had never been able to bring myself to face up to the realities of what brought it about. The mere effort of trying to recall exactly what had happened on one fateful night made me physically ill. But I knew it was an ordeal I would have to endure if this book was to have any merit.

My problem was that, no matter how hard I tried, I would never be able to hold the New Testament in my right hand and solemnly swear to tell the truth, the whole truth and nothing but the truth, for the simple reason that there are still blank areas in my memory where the "Brick Case" is concerned. To let it rest there would appear too much like a glib evasion of unpalatable truths, so I have interspersed what I can recall with the transcripts of the Court hearings, and the official inquiry that followed. (Even that proved too great a strain and I was ill again for the first time for a considerable period and had to undergo further treatment before I could continue.)

On 4 June, 1964, I sat in the dock of Number One Court in the famous Old Bailey wedged between two prison officers. Many notorious criminals had sat in the same seat behind the glass surround – Crippen; Christie, the necrophiliac mass killer; Ruth Ellis, the last woman to hang; Smith, the brides in the bath murderer; Thompson and Bywaters; traitors, gangsters, fraudsters, conmen and arsonists.

I suppose I had something marginally in common with Christie. He was an ex-policeman and I was certainly a mass killer, although I had the blessing of the State at the time.

It was certainly no place for a detective sergeant who had gained a reputation for being a first class copper and the wielder of the iron fist which had become feared and detested by the criminal elements in Soho.

There was a certain amount of irony in the situation, for I was no stranger to the famous courtroom. I had appeared there many times in the past, but then I had played the role of prosecutor and my evidence from the witness box had sent many a lawbreaker to prison. Now I was the accused.

I had been branded a "bent copper", the greatest stigma that can be levelled at a serving officer of the Metropolitan Police which prides itself, quite rightly, on being the finest force in the world.

Maybe I was not the model CID officer. Perhaps I retained too many of the qualities which had served me so well in the SAS. I was rough, tough, coarse and often profane. I did not meditate over a meerschaum; I mixed. I walked the dimly lit streets and visited the sleazy haunts where crime was incubated. I could drink all night and still retain, sponge-like, what booze-loosened tongues were saying, and next morning I could appear in Court looking as fresh as a man who had slept the clock round.

In my wallet I kept a scrap of paper on which I had written a couplet from Kipling's "If":

> If you can wait and not be tired by waiting,
> Or being lied about, *don't deal in lies*.

The words meant a great deal to me, and I had always made the young detectives placed under my jurisdiction read them. Now I was going to be made to eat each of those words letter by letter and exposed as a hypocrite, a man from whose lips lies slipped like syrup from a spoon.

I could expect no mercy if I was found guilty, for the public place great faith in the custodians of law and order, and anyone who betrays that trust cannot expect any leniency. The gamekeeper turner poacher asks for all he gets. I was a man who had made a mockery of the lady holding the scales of justice on top of the enormous dome above me. If I was found guilty the judge would make an example of me. But before that could happen the jury had to decide whether I was fit to plead or whether I was mad.

The yardstick by which insanity is judged in our courts are the McNaghten Rules which had their beginning in 1843 when Daniel McNaghten set out to shoot the Prime Minister, Sir Robert Peel, but shot the wrong man, Edward Drummond, Peel's secretary. At his trial the defence pleaded that he suffered from acute persecution mania, the judges acquitted him, and he was committed to a lunatic asylum. As a result the House of Lords questioned the judges about their decision and the outcome was the McNaghten Rules which declared that a man could not be condemned if, at the time of the crime, he was suffering from a defect of reason such as to make him unaware of the nature of the act, or that he was doing wrong.

The rules have often been strongly criticized on the grounds that their too strict interpretation has led to miscarriages of justice, especially in murder cases, but so far no one has managed to come up with a better alternative.

Their main drawback is that it is up to the defence to prove insanity, and as the accused can hardly be expected to argue his own madness, reliance has to be placed on the evidence of medical experts who have an unfortunate tendency to disagree. Normally the prosecution can produce six witnesses to the defence's four.

In my case there was no conflict of opinion. A formidable array of experts were called to say how mad I was: Doctor William Calder, Principal Medical Officer at Brixton Prison; Doctor Niall Farnan, Consultant Psychologist at Netherne Hospital; Doctor William Sargent, Head of the Department of Psychological Medicine at St. Thomas's Hospital. I could have saved the State a lot of money because I knew in my lucid moments I had been mad for a long time, but I had been too scared to admit it for fear of the consequences, and in any case the moments of lucidity were becoming fewer and fewer, and I was gradually descending into a Walter Mitty world where I could not distinguish between fantasy and reality.

The law, like God, moved in a mysterious way, and although I was incarcerated in what is euphemistically called the "funny farm" on the recommendation of mental experts, they could not say I was unfit to stand trial. That could only be decided by a jury after they had heard the medical evidence.

As the experts gave their diagnoses I was certainly not "all there" in the physical as well as the mental sense. My head was bowed as if in penance, or so it must have seemed to the people in the crowded public gallery. In reality my eyes were fastened on the gleaming black shoes of the prison officer sitting beside me, and I was transported back in time to when I was a prisoner. Only then the circumstances were somewhat different; I was a POW and doing my utmost to withstand the brutal interrogations of the German SS who wanted details about the secret mission I had been parachuted into Italy to carry out. They too had worn shiny black shoes. I relived those moments of terror, memories of which still wake me in the night sweating and shaking.

I forced myself to return to the present. I looked up and fixed my eyes on the formidable figure of Mr Justice Lawton in his scarlet robes sitting on a dais below the Sword of Justice hanging

5

on the oak-panelled wall behind him. It reminded me of the sword of Damocles.

I saw the judge lean forward and peer over the top of his half-moon spectacles at the man in the witness box whom I recognised as Doctor William Calder, who had examined me in Brixton Prison. I realized they were talking about me, but in a rather detached manner, as if I were not there. I could not grasp everything that was being said because of the continuous ringing in my ears, like an incessant alarm clock. I turned my head from side to side, hoping that one ear might pick up what the other had missed, cursing the deafness which had become progressively worse over the past year and more, but it was as if I was listening in on a crossed line. Everything seemed garbled, and I was only able to pick up the occasional phrase like "paranoid schizophrenia", and then one chilling passage with alarming clarity, ". . . has been mentally abnormal for a very considerable time", and soon afterwards, ". . . I thought he was a potential danger if left at large".

What on earth are they talking about, I asked myself. My head was now pounding like a trip hammer, and I switched off, as effectively as if I had pressed a remote control button and blacked out a television screen. I knew that what I was hearing was all part of the major plan. I had to be publicly disgraced before I could be sent on the clandestine mission for which I had so long been preparing. The voices droned on, like wasps in an apple orchard. I was sitting behind the steering wheel of my old jeep on the edge of a forest far behind the enemy lines in German-occupied France. The spare wheel on the front of the vehicle bore the legend "Little Tanky". Tanky was the nickname I had been given when I joined the SAS and I had bequeathed the name to my jeep, which was my proudest possession, for it was no ordinary run of the mill jeep; it was so powerfully armed that it was like a battleship on wheels. Mounted above the steering wheel in front of me was a single Vickers machine gun. Sitting beside me was Lieutenant Gurney peering through the sights of a twin-Vickers, and in the back was the third member of the crew with another twin-Vickers. Carefully stowed in special containers were enough grenades and explosives to wage a full-scale battle.

No one spoke and the hum of the insects in the nearby forest was clearly audible. Suddenly the pastoral silence was shattered by the throaty rumble of a vehicle, and seconds later a German staff car with a pennant fluttering on the bonnet came into view. Lieutenant

6

Gurney whispered, "There must be a high-ranking officer in it. We'll have it."

The staff car was only a hundred yards away when we hosed it with a mixture of armour-piercing, tracer and incendiary bullets. I saw the windscreen shatter into thousands of marble-sized fragments, and before it crashed into a ditch I saw a uniformed officer feebly waving a gloved hand from the window. I fired a short burst to finish him off. Then the car blew up. I felt no remorse, only a great sense of elation. I was only doing what I had been trained to do. It was just one more Kraut to my personal tally.

I don't know why that particular incident should have come to mind for it was just one of many similar episodes during my cloak-and-dagger days with the SAS. What I did know was that for months I had been preparing myself for a return to those wartime days because for a considerable time an inner voice had been telling me that I was being recalled for duty and should stand by for a highly dangerous and secret assignment which would require all my old wartime skills – how to carry out acts of demolition after being parachuted from a low-flying aircraft, how to kill silently with my bare hands, with a piece of wire, or a razor sharp dagger, how to withstand the most brutal interrogation without breaking down and revealing anything important to the enemy.

I felt a sharp nudge in the ribs and I was brought back to the present and the realization that no one believed that I had been selected for a secret mission that could alter the course of history. Then I heard the dispassionate voice of Mr. Justice Lawton asking a witness if he was satisfied that I was not feigning illness (a view that was held by a considerable number of people at the time), and the witness stating that I was not pretending but had for some time been violent and aggressive, and periodically been in an excited and deluded state and subject to telepathic influences and hidden voices.

For a fleeting moment my eyes caught those of Doris my wife who had never missed a day to visit me in the mental hospital where I had been for almost a year. Rain, snow, fog or ice, she had made the thirty-mile journey by public transport to comfort and encourage me. My mind went back to the night I decided to end it all.

I was being detained in a locked ward at Netherne Mental Hospital in Surrey where I was being treated with drugs and electric shock treatment. Life was a series of peaks and troughs, and during one period of relative normality another patient told me of some of the allegations made against me, and showed me some newspaper cuttings. It was totally against the rules, for the doctors had stressed that newspapers chronicling my alleged misdeeds should be kept well out of my sight in case their revelations made me worse.

I listened, and read, and felt sick.

When I had finished I thought: not only am I crazy, but I am dangerous. I might even hurt Doris who is now saddled with a nut case for the rest of her life. It's possible I might never recover.

With me the thought is often the spur to immediate action. I lay on my bed waiting for a convenient moment to escape from the ward, and when it came I slipped out and made my way to the railway line, but my intentions were thwarted by a high wire fence running parallel to the line, so I headed for the main road. In the distance I could see the Star public house, and I said to myself: "better to go out near the beer. When I get to where I'm going I can say I came from a licensed star." (I really thought and talked like that.)

The road was very busy, but I waited at the kerb for a heavy lorry travelling at high speed. At last one came along, and as it drew near I stepped off the pavement and walked into it. I felt a tremendous blow on my hip and lost consciousness. Fortunately, although I did not think so at the time, the vehicle passed clean over me, the wheels missing me completely.

I sustained a cracked pelvis, head injuries, and concussion which did nothing to improve my memory. When I regained consciousness in Redhill Hospital, Doris was at my bedside holding my hand.

I told her it had not been accident, and she pressed my hand and said, "I know, but you can beat anything, including mental illness. Get up off the floor and fight."

Her words strengthened me more than any medicine and I decided: no more suicide attempts. See it through.

To describe or attempt to define my illness is like trying to trap a globule of mercury under a thumb. Experts in the field of mental illness find it difficult, a patient impossible.

Although I knew I had tried to kill myself I also believed that I was indestructible. In some perverse way the incident had become part of the secret operation I had been preparing for, and therefore I would not be allowed to die.

The reader may, with some justification, wonder how and why no one had spotted symptoms of madness much earlier, they seem so obvious. The simple answer is that throughout the onset of my illness, although I was aware that something was wrong, I became extremely adroit at concealing my condition from others. I was a human chameleon. One person might notice something odd about my behaviour and comment on it, and a short time later find me acting perfectly normally. That happened to fellow police officers and medical experts who examined me within a comparatively short period of each other. Furthermore, my police training had made me very adept at concealing the true situation.

I returned to the present to find the jury had needed less than a minute to find I was unfit to plead.

In a voice that seemed to me doom-laden, Mr Justice Lawton ordered that I be detained in strict custody until Her Majesty's pleasure be made known.

I felt a sharp nudge in the arm and I realized it was a prison officer indicating that I should leave the dock. I rose, took one glance at the rapidly emptying court and followed the polished boots down to the cells. Once again it occurred to me that I had to have this public humiliation before I could take part in the hush-hush mission with my old wartime outfit, the SAS.

As I sat in the van that was taking me to Brixton Prison, I repeated like an incantation the three words which had stood me in such good stead during the war: Who Dares Wins.

I asked what was to happen to me and was told that I would be held in Brixton until a decision was reached as to whether I would go to Broadmoor or back to Netherne Mental Hospital.

I hardly remember going through the reception procedure at the prison; it's a blur, a vague dream which I was watching happening to another person. I sat on a bed looking at the cell walls unable to grasp the reality of the situation.

The steady tread of boots echoed like drumbeats along the corridor outside. They shuffled to a halt and I heard the clank of keys as the lock was unbolted.

The door swung open and silhouetted in the corridor were two figures who looked as if they had stepped out of my past.

"Oh, my God," I thought, "another belting."

One of the men moved to my left, and I saw the other was holding something in his hand, and I stiffened myself for the violence about to be administered. But there were no blows. No kicks. No dizzy explosion of pain as the men in black went to work.

Instead, unbelievably, the clenched fist of one man was vigorously shaking a bottle. "The doctor wants you to take a dose; it'll calm you down."

I watched him, confused, as if I had awakened from a troubled dream. His companion standing in the doorway jingling a bunch of keys smiled in a friendly fashion. I swallowed the medicine.

"What time is it?" I asked.

"Four o'clock," said the first officer, who then passed me a plate on which was a solitary kipper. "A bit early for tea, but you missed the lunch break. They thought you might be a bit peckish. With a bit of luck you can have a breath of fresh air in the yard later. All right?"

"Lovely," I said. The cell door clanged and the footsteps receded into the distance.

I tried to puzzle it out. The cell, the barred window, the sense of brooding, unknown terror. It all seemed so terrifyingly familiar and I was overcome by a sense of *déjà vu*. I was back in the POW camp.

I gazed down at the kipper, and thought, well, this is an improvement. I noticed there was no knife or fork. Did they think I was so mad that I would do myself an injury? I shrugged and ate the kipper with my fingers.

Later I was escorted round the exercise yard by a young prison officer and I knew where I was – Brixton Prison. I had been there in an official capacity many times in the past in order to interview prisoners . . . but I had never penetrated this far.

In the yard a couple of standard roses struggled for survival, their leaves coated with prison dust. I worried if Doris could cope with the garden at home. I looked at the soot-grimed walls flanking the prison and wondered if I could break out. I had done it before, in the other place, impelled by the desperation of a possible death sentence.

An aeroplane left a vapour trail in the clear June sky and I watched it until it disappeared behind the gaunt outline of the main block. What wouldn't I give, I asked myself, to be back with the lads on a sky drop behind the enemy lines?

If only I could make a break for it! But the reality of my situation became apparent the more I thought about it. Where would I escape to? There were no friendly lines to strike for, no welcome back like before. Certainly no hero's welcome. I had to take my medicine.

"Let's go back in," I said gruffly.

In the morning a young prisoner was assigned to shave me; it appeared that I could not be trusted with anything sharp. He said, as he lathered my face, "I never thought I'd end up in the nick shaving a detective sergeant."

"That's all right," I said, "just don't make it too close."

The days passed with agonizing slowness, relieved only by the twenty minutes Doris was allowed each day. When I saw her I thought, "What's a flower like you doing in a dung heap like this?"

Alone in my cell I had little to do but think, and some words of my father's kept recurring like a phrase in a record where the needle has stuck, "You're no good son. You'll end up inside one day. Mark my words."

For once he had been right.

His prophesying, which was more akin to wishful thinking, I could shrug off, but one thing did haunt me during most of my waking hours. The "Brick Case" was more or less over for me, but it had not yet begun for three young detectives who had worked under me at West End Central Police Station. They still had to stand trial for conspiring with me to pervert the course of justice, by making unlawful arrests, making false statements and fabricating evidence – namely, planting pieces of brick on demonstrators.

It was alleged to have happened on 11 July, 1963, during a visit to London of the King and Queen of Greece . . .

Chapter Two

On the evening in question, all leave had been cancelled and extra men were drafted into the area of Claridge's Hotel where King Paul and Queen Frederika of Greece were staying during a visit to London. Trouble was anticipated in the form of a vociferous demonstration mainly against Queen Frederika, who some people saw as a kind of Machiavellian figure wielding enormous political influence from behind the scenes in Greek politics, and who encouraged a régime of suppression. The previous night there had been trouble outside the hotel, and the tension was heightened by the knowledge that Her Majesty Queen Elizabeth was going to visit the royal couple in their hotel.

It is the inalienable right of anyone in this country to demonstrate against anyone or anything they find politically distasteful, but it has to be done peaceably, and that is what the police had turned out in depth to ensure.

They had every reason to fear that violence might erupt – the previous evening a police inspector had been struck in the face by a brick which inflicted a wound that required nine stitches.

I had seen him as I was walking out of West End Central Station, standing, white-faced and shaking, with blood streaming down his face, and thinking how awful it was that people could not disagree without resorting to violence. The sight of his injury really upset me.

The next night I remember leaving the station and heading for Claridge's in Mayfair, an area in which it had been tactfully suggested I should not be allowed to work because of my rather extrovert nature. But a demonstration was not likely to bring me in touch with the wealthy denizens of that upper-crust citadel.

I can recall walking down the front steps and nothing more: my mind is a complete blank. I wish I could remember what followed, but I can't. I can only relate what others have said.

Perhaps I should not have been on duty at all because there had been considerable concern over my health and growing deafness and the excessive amount of work I was doing. I had been told by superior officers to take things easy as I had often been working more than a hundred hours a week. Furthermore, reports had reached senior officers that attempts were being made to discredit me and £1,000 was on open offer to anyone without a criminal record to "set me up" – gangland parlance for framing me. It had even been suggested to me that I should be moved to some nice quiet backwater where I could take a desk job and get really fit and well. That did not appeal to me at all because it seemed like conceding defeat to the villains. I wanted to stay at West End Central and see it through, but my pending leave made it unnecessary for my superior officers to make an immediate decision.

As I left the station I apparently turned to a young police officer and said, "We've got to stop them throwing stones at Royalty."

The evening may be a blank to me but I have over the years read everything I could about it, enough in fact to fill several books. The following is by necessity a condensed account, but I have endeavoured to be as objective as possible. It certainly is not an attempt to vindicate myself.

Among the demonstrators outside Claridge's was Donald Rooum, a cartoonist, teacher and typographer, who was a member of the National Council for Civil Liberties. He was a self-admitted anarchist who felt intensely about the situation in Greece and was parading up and down with a banner on which were the words, "Lambrakis RIP", a man whom he believed had been murdered for political reasons. Although he advocated peaceful demonstrations he was in his own words "consciously playing the brinkmanship game with the police". He was not exactly a newcomer to demonstrations because he had been in trouble with the police during a sit-down for the anti-nuclear Committee of One Hundred.

According to him he was approached by me and three other officers whom he asked to return his banner which had previously been taken away. With that he said I struck him a violent blow on the ear and arrested him, saying, "I've got a desperate one here."

I appeared to Mr Rooum as a bullying type of man, similar to some he had met in the army.

He was taken to West End Central Police Station, and on the way to the charge room he said I struck him again and accused him of being prepared to "Boo the Queen", and hit him three more times. I then produced a piece of brick saying, "There you are me old darling. Carrying an offensive weapon can get you two years."

I then went away with the portion of brick, and soon afterwards Rooum heard me repeating details of his arrest and stating that I had found the brick in his pocket.

Whether Mr Rooum had prepared himself for such an eventuality I do not know, but he certainly had his wits about him for his mind went back to a book he had read entitled, *Science in the Detection of Crime*, by a former Scotland Yard officer, and he realized that if he could prevent the brick being placed in his pocket he could prove his innocence because there would be no trace of dust in his pocket and no fingerprints on the piece of brick. That would make nonsense of my evidence.

To achieve this, however, it was essential for him to remain in custody over night in order to prove that he was wearing the same clothing when he was examined by an independent forensic expert. For that reason he did not seek bail, but he refused to sign for his property which included the piece of brick.

The next morning he appeared at Marlborough Street Magistrates Court where he was represented by a solicitor from the National Council of Civil Liberties. He was remanded on bail, and from court he went to his solicitor where he was given a change of clothing while his own were sent to be scientifically examined.

When he again appeared in court an expert stated that he had not found any traces of brick dust in his clothing, and the magistrate acquitted him on the grounds that there was a reasonable doubt.

I was apparently visibly shaken by the decision which prompted Rooum to remark later, "I am sorry to say I was not sorry to see him so shaken."

However, that was not the entire story of The Brick Case. On the same evening that Rooum was arrested, three youths were also detained and accused of possessing pieces of brick. One of the youngsters, who was only 14, said he was arrested by me after he was heard to call out, "Is anyone going to boo her?", and I used the words, "Right me young son, you're nicked."

A 16-year-old youth, a member of the Campaign for Nuclear Disarmament and the Committee of One Hundred who had gone to Claridge's to demonstrate about the fascist rule in Greece, heard the remark about booing and was immediately arrested by one of the young detectives under my supervision. They alleged that at the police station they were assaulted and pieces of brick planted on them by me.

14

A third youth had also been arrested, and I was alleged to have said, like some benevolent Santa dishing out goodies, "This is for you, and this is for you," "A present from Uncle Harold," and "The biggest brick for the biggest boy," and accused them of throwing bricks.

One of the men described my behaviour as being more fitting to a Nazi officer in a friendly moment. Me! A report by a senior officer said, "He was regarded as a man who was kindly and considerate to children and the elderly, and who was abhorrent of the bully."

The youngsters were collected by their parents and allowed to go home; at that time no one made any complaint against me.

I had always had the reputation of being something of a rough diamond, loud-mouthed, prone to gesticulating a lot and raising my voice, but that night my behaviour struck some of my colleagues as being way over the top. Others thought I was just my normal boisterous self.

There is no disputing whatsoever that my conduct did arouse grave misgivings in the minds of some senior officers who were present at West End Central that night.

Superintendent Frederick Burdett, normally stationed at Tottenham Court Road, was at West End Central because of the extra work that was envisaged as a result of the demo. He was known as a strict disciplinarian where police matters were concerned, and an officer who did everything strictly according to the book. At the same time, he was scrupulously fair. I admired him.

He was very concerned at the way I was conducting myself because he could get no sense out of me. I was red-eyed, looking extremely tired and unable to control myself. He thought I was drunk until he realized I was perfectly sober, and he formed the opinion that I was heading for a mental breakdown. Because of the delay in charging the youngsters he had become very angry and reminded me they were juveniles, but I seemed to resent his intrusion and did not recognise his rank until I saw the insignia on his uniform, then I came rigidly to attention and became a different man. Apparently I explained the delay in charging them by announcing, "No, we'll go out and get some more."

He took me aside and reprimanded me, whereupon he said my behaviour altered dramatically, "like a spring gradually uncoiling, and as he gained his self-control so he relaxed". A short time afterwards my demeanour seemed perfectly normal.

No matter how facile it may seem, I had no idea of the furore I had created. I was in another world. The writing was on the wall but no one could read it.

Superintendent Burdett considered submitting an adverse report, but on hearing about my deafness and my overworking, plus the assurance that when the backlog of work was cleared up I would be made to take things more gently, took no further action.

It was not until the early hours that I was able to go home, and I spent four hours with a detective sergeant friend to whom I appeared most upset because the youngsters "ought not to have mixed up with the crowd they were with".

Shortly afterwards Doris and I went on holiday and I returned seemingly fit and relaxed in the opinion of my colleagues, and ready for work, but what they did not know was that I had packed my halucinations in the luggage when we set off. We had planned to go to Yugoslavia but I suddenly changed our plans and told Doris we could not go via Italy but had to drive through Switzerland because I had received information that someone was waiting to kill me. I spent my time climbing mountains and revelling in tough physical exercise, explaining to Doris that I was preparing for a special job and that I had to be careful as agents were watching my every move. She was plainly disturbed, and I justified my odd behaviour by saying I was being tested, hypnotised and brain-washed in readiness for a special job I had been chosen for. Some time earlier I had told her, "If someone tells you I'm having a breakdown you mustn't worry about it. It's all part of a plan," and she had to trust me and stop worrying. Dear Doris, knowing about my wartime experiences, ignored her better judgement, which was to speak to a senior officer and confide her fears, and swallowed my story.

A lot had happened during my absence from West End Central. Mr Rooum had alleged wrongful arrest and imprisonment and the planting of evidence, and a writ against me was about to be issued and Detective Chief Inspector Harry Pike had been detailed to investigate other complaints of impropriety that had been made against me.

Harry, an extremely good detective and an ardent pursuer of the truth, interviewed me about the complaints and grew increasingly concerned about my health. He attempted to obtain a statement from me about the allegations, but found I tended to stare into space and become extremely tense and uncommunicative.

During a further attempt he found a marked deterioration in my ability to concentrate, and it took him four hours to take a statement that normally would have taken a fraction of the time. I just could not recall events he was questioning me about. Not unnaturally he formed the opinion that I was far from well. But he was confused by his own diagnosis when he attended court the next day and saw me handle an expert witness in a manner which he described as "superb". His situation was made that much more difficult by the information that at an examination by Sir John Richardson, Consultant Physician to the Metropolitan Police, I had been passed as fit for duty.

Mr Pike was so astonished at the decision that he took the precaution of telephoning the Medical Board to make sure I had in fact attended, and when he was assured I had, he had no option but to accept Sir John's diagnosis, but he insisted that I limit my duties to work in hand.

About a fortnight later Mr Pike told me to be available at West End Central Police Station where a writ was going to be served on me on behalf of Mr Rooum, and he counselled me not to say anything when it was.

According to him I became very emotional, clenching and unclenching my fists and muttering that I would find it very difficult to remain silent as there were a lot of things I wanted to say. Then I broke down and said, "I'm a simple man, but I know what I'm paid for, and I'm just not being allowed to do my job," and "I can't go on remaining in the office because I feel I'm getting money by false pretences." Then, in a trembling state, I went on to protest that I was the victim of a conspiracy among thieves and villains in the West End to destroy my character and get me transferred. That was true, but to suggest Mr Rooum was part of it was absurd.

When the solicitor arrived, I attempted to leave the station, but Harry Pike stopped me and took me before Chief Superintendent Starritt to whom I protested, "These villains are doing their best to crucify me." The Superintendent asked me quite firmly if I thought I was fit for duty. "Fit as a fiddle, Sir. All I want to do is go out and get some thieves."

It was not exactly a helpful remark to make when I was about to be accused of a criminal offence myself; soon afterwards I again broke down and wept uncontrollably.

Chief Superintendent Starritt sat me down and had a long heart to heart and told me I should see a doctor as I needed help. He also pointed out that I was due to appear at Chelsea Juvenile Court next morning to give evidence in the case of the youths who had been arrested at the demonstration. He took the view, quite rightly, that, even though a complaint had been made by them, in the interests of justice the evidence should be tested in open court.

Detective Chief Inspector Pike accompanied me to the court where

Mr Rooum was standing in the lobby waiting to give evidence on behalf of the two boys. I did not recognize Rooum and went up and said, "Wotcher, me old darling, what about playing football for us on Sunday?" I had been trying to get together enough players for a soccer match as I was a firm believer in keeping the officers under me fit.

There was not enough time available for the case to be heard, and in the early hours of the next morning when I was walking the 15 miles home, an incident occurred at Clapham where I apparently arrested some youths and took them to the local station where a senior officer refused to charge them.

My behaviour was such that I was again examined by Sir John Richardson who certified me as being unfit for duty and in need of psychiatric advice and treatment, but I ignored his advice and soon afterwards I went on holiday to Swanage.

My own doctor saw me and suggested that I seek psychiatric treatment, but I declined and told him to leave my house. By now my conduct was becoming out of hand and it was inevitable that I would have to agree to being seen by a mental expert. I was examined at home and a certificate was issued for my admisison to Netherne Hospital under Section 29 of the Mental Health Act.

I am sure that there was a strong suspicion in the minds of some of the public who had followed the newspaper reports that there had been a massive cover-up and the police were looking after their own. Nothing could have been further from the truth.

While I was in hospital a parcel addressed to me was intercepted which contained a book entitled *Broadmoor, A History of Criminal Lunacy and its Problems* and was inscribed "From the Chaps and Slags. With love, you nut case," and on a photograph of a cemetery was written, "Poor ol' Harry," and a grave marked, "Reserved for you".

Mr Rooum was awarded £500 for false imprisonment, malicious prosecution and assault. Unknown to me, Dr Calder had written to the Deputy Commissioner saying, "He is quite mentally unfit to defend a civil action brought against him. I consider his judgement much too impaired to do this."

When the charges against two of the youths were due to be heard at Chelsea Juvenile Court, no evidence was offered and one was awarded £250, the other £200 damages.

In March, 1964, I was collected from hospital and driven to Marlborough Street Court to appear with three young detectives on charges of conspiring to pervert the course of justice.

I just could not believe it was happening to me, and I voiced my disbelief to Mr Cessari, an Italian restaurateur, a friend who had introduced me to many hard-working people in Soho who wanted to see crime eradicated in the area they had chosen to live in. I had even visited his family in Italy which was in the area where I had operated with the SAS. He told me sadly that alas it was true, and he had come to the court because he was worried that I might be hungry, and had arranged for a meal to be brought in.

Although the medical experts had decided I was as mad as a hatter, the hearing went ahead and I and the three officers were committed for trial at the Old Bailey.

There I was found unfit to plead, but after a lengthy trial the other three officers were found guilty. Two of them, both aged 26, were jailed for four years, the other, aged 21, for three years.

Mr Justice Lawton told them, "Honest police officers are the buttress of society. But dishonest perjured officers are like an infernal machine ticking away to the destruction of us all."

Mr Victor Durand QC who defended them described me as a tyrant who had imposed his will on them. I emerged in the public eye as some sinister Svengali, a corrupting influence on those who worked under me.

It was a long time before I was allowed to know the result of the case, and when I did it upset me very much. They were the dedicated young men who had read the scrap of paper I kept in my wallet, and I knew it meant as much to them as it did to me. I was known to be a strict disciplinarian, but they still came to me with their professional and domestic problems.

I do not dispute my role in The Brick Case, but never until my dying day will I believe those three young officers were guilty. One was a Scout master, another a devout Christian who had tried, unsuccessfully, to get me interested in religion. Looking back I can't help feeling that it was difficult for them to have got a fair trail because I believe it was virtually impossible to get an unprejudiced jury. Not that the one that tried the case was biased, but the officers had been accused of conspiring with me, and although I had been found insane I had been sent to Brixton Prison to be kept in strict custody, which in the eyes of most people was a verdict of guilty.

Furthermore, I could not see how a jury could be unaffected by the knowledge that the charges against the youths had been withdrawn and they had been paid compensation. What conclusion could the jurors reach other than that there had been a "frame up"?

I am naturally biased in favour of the three officers, but I am not alone in my opinion. At the subsequent Public Inquiry into my conduct, Detective Superintendent Ronald Townsend voiced an opinion I heartily endorse. He made it clear that, although he accepted the jury's verdict of guilty, he was unable to accept the validity of it. They were strong and courageous words from an officer who was known to be a strict disciplinarian and a man who would never tolerate anything that reflected on the honour of the force.

A lot of people thought I had got away with it, but in fact I paid a far higher price than anyone else; twenty-five years in a twilight world of fantasy and make-believe, interspersed with periods of reality. And there is a pile of medical records thicker than a telephone directory to prove it.

Chapter Three

I am not a whole-hearted believer in the theory that home environment moulds the man-to-be; as a solider and later as a policeman I saw too much of human life to accept such a glib solution. Children with everything – doting parents and all the home comforts – can turn out to be bad hats, while others who have known nothing but grinding poverty and brutality develop into perfectly law-abiding citizens.

I came from the latter type of background, and although I did not emerge as someone who wanted to put the world to rights I vowed that I would be the antithesis of my father. He was, not to put too fine a point on it, a bastard – a mean, cruel, sadistic tyrant who terrorised his family, made few friends and left not one endearing memory. There were no flowers and no tears when he died in 1968. My own epitaph was "Gone and not missed". My loathing and contempt were kindled by the memory of what he had done to my mother.

Ironically those flaws which I so totally despised were later to be attributed to me. I find it quite incomprehensible.

Tom Challenor was a Victorian throwback of Dickensian dimensions. In the early days he drank heavily and often, and his temper, unpredictable at the best of times, was likely to erupt into a red haze of brutality, and I was invariably the target.

I was born on 16 March, 1922, in a mean, typical Coronation Street style house in Bradley, near Bilston in Staffordshire. The toilet was in the yard, and the basement was always full of water. A smog seemed to hover over the town like a heavy brown blanket, a constant reminder that the majority of its inhabitants owed their precarious living to the steelworks.

Although I was christened Harry Gordon, my family name was Peter, a name that was bestowed on me as a result of the oft repeated remark of my grandmother, who, whenever she called, would comment, "Holy Peter, is he grizzling again?" Clearly I was not the perfect baby, and a wailing child was not the ideal companion

21

in a small overcrowded house where the shortage of money was a constant worry. It is said that love goes out of the window when poverty knocks on the door, and maybe that is what happened to my father when he lost his job in the Depression of the 1930's. He beat me at the slightest pretext, but from an early age I decided that I would never give him the satisfaction of seeing me weep or hear me ask him to stop. Perhaps I should have done, then he might have eased up once he had established his dominance. I must have sensed that that was what he wanted, and it only made me more stubborn.

It was never just a clip round the ear or a smack on the backside, but a thorough going over in which he used his thick leather belt or clenched fist. His blows were always aimed low in the region of the stomach where they inflicted the most pain, but were not visible to nosey neighbours or school-teachers who might ask questions. Looking back I'm amazed he never inflicted a serious injury because his work in the steelworks had given him massive shoulders and a deep chest like a Staffordshire bull terrier.

Although his brutality was reserved for me he showed the same lack of affection to my mother and my elder sister. As long as he could get his beer, that was all he worried about. It's a terrible thing to say, but that is how it was.

The only good quality I can recall about him was his immense capacity for hard work, but that did not save him from joining the queues of the unemployed during the Depression. But he was too proud to spend his days lounging on the corners of the squalid streets, or maybe he missed his beer, so when he heard that the battalion medical officer of the Staffordshire Regiment, under whom he had served in the First World War and whom he greatly admired, had been appointed Superintendent at Caterham Mental Hospital in Surrey, he decided to ask him for a job.

He stuffed some clothing and a few personal belongings into a rucksack and set off to walk to Surrey. The long trek was rewarded with a job as a nurse at Caterham.

Before leaving he assured my mother that he would send for her and the family as soon as he was settled, but the weeks became months and nothing was heard of him. My mother, left with a young family – Doris, two years older than me, Tommy six years younger, Hazel, and the baby of the family, Richard – was forced to go out charring to keep the wolf from the door. She was a small slightly built woman who was totally subdued by her domineering husband, but when she heard that he had taken up with another woman she borrowed some money from her mother, and with me and Doris in tow, caught the next train south. No matter what his shortcomings, he was her man.

There was a short sharp altercation between husband and outraged wife in which my mother assumed the ferocity of a wild beast whose offspring are threatened. The upshot was that the interloper was sent packing and mother and her brood moved in. For good or bad we were a family again.

Although my father continued to single me out for regular chastisement, life was relatively harmonious. Then one evening a few years after arriving in Caterham, my father went on a monumental booze-up in a public house in Merstham. Not relishing the thought of the long walk home, he stole a cycle and on the way got a puncture. He decided to keep the cycle and next day while he was repairing the puncture, the police arrived and took him away. He appeared in court and was fined, but as a result of his brush with the law he was transferred to Leavesden Mental Hospital in Hertfordshire.

My father was a belligerent Micawber who was constantly in debt and this necessitated many a moonlight flit from one house to another in order to escape irate creditors. Such sudden departures became an accepted part of family life and we made eight nocturnal moves in less than three years. What to most families would have been a major upheaval was minimal discomfort to us. We possessed so little in the way of furniture and other belongings that we could fit everything into a borrowed van. We became so adept that our neighbours and creditors never learned of our departure until it was too late. Like a storm-tossed ship we finally came to harbour in Garston, a suburb of North Watford.

Despite the turmoil of our unorthodox family life and the interruptions to my education brought about by the constant changes of address and schools, I proved a promising pupil at Leavesden village school, and one of my earlier reports noted that I had a receptive mind, learned quickly, and had an aptitude for English.

It was the first time I had enjoyed a long spell of uninterrupted education, and I worked hard and happily. I can still recall my excitement when I ran home tell my parents that I had won a scholarship to Watford Grammar School.

"You can forget any bloody fancy ideas about grammar school," said my father. "At 14 you're going out to work, sharp as you like. I've supported you long enough. You're going out to earn your living, like all the other lads. Grammar school . . . you?"

I will never forget that blow to my academic hopes. It still rankles when I think of the years I spent during my adulthood trying to catch up on my education.

At the time it would have been useless to argue; my father's word was law, and so I settled down at school waiting for my fourteenth birthday when I would become a man capable of earning his own keep. One of my last tasks was to submit an essay I had written for a competition sponsored by the RSPCA. As I did not entertain any thoughts of winning, I promptly forgot all about it. By then I had discovered something much more captivating and exciting than essays – girls. One pretty little girl in particular attracted my adoring gaze across the playground. But it was adoration from a distance.

Then the headmaster asked me to attend school one evening and stoke up the fires for a parents' whist evening, and what had seemed a chore became near bliss as the young girl was there helping to make coffee. Later in the darkened cloakroom we kissed.

The next morning the school assembled as usual in the main hall. When the headmaster appeared he looked solemn and extremely grim. I felt a tightening in my stomach when he called us to attention and summoned me to the front. My crime had been discovered, and I wondered how many strokes of the cane it merited.

Then the headmaster's face broke into a beaming smile and he said, "Well done Challenor. You have won the essay competition, your class will be given the afternoon off." I was stunned and relieved, and as I stumbled back to my place I saw my pretty little friend, white as a sheet and visibly shaken. If only such innocence would last.

That was a mere infatuation compared to my real love – sport. I was a strong sturdy boy with a natural aptitude for it.

I was school captain at games and physical training and had what is called a good eye for a ball. I was particularly promising at football, and had already played for Watford Schools XI and scored a goal; no mean achievement considering the competition.

I was selected again and my horizon was limited by the dream of one day playing league football for Watford FC. Two days before I was due to play for Watford Schools team I was in the kitchen busily dubbining my boots – bought at a jumble sale and two sizes too big – when my father came in. "You can put those things away," he said, "and start earning some money for a change. I've got you a part-time job."

It was as the lather boy in the local barber's shop. I would start work as soon as I finished school at 4 p.m. and lather stubbled chins and make sure the steam-heated container was well stocked with hot after-shave towels, until 6 p.m. On Saturdays I would start at nine and finish at six. The wages were 2/6d. I did not mind working but the harshest blow of all was the announcement that I was to start on the day I was due to turn out for Watford Schools. I pleaded with him to postpone it, but he would not. "The money will come in useful."

I could not dispute that every extra shilling would be welcomed in our house, but I knew my mother would not see any of it; the local publican would be the beneficiary.

When I left school I also left the barber's shop, still ignorant of the meaning of the words my boss whispered to everyone after a shave or haircut, "Anything else you require, sir?" I was acutely aware that the future did not look at all promising. My educational aspirations had been brusquely stifled, and my ambition to be a professional footballer had been killed in the kitchen. Now my sole ambition was to put as much distance as possible between me and my father, and in the quickest possible time. But it was 1936, the year of the Jarrow hunger marchers, and if you were lucky enough to land a job the wage envelope was too slim to make for independence.

I was fortunate to find a job as a trainee mechanic in a nearby garage, and more on the strength of my prowess on the soccer field than my skills with the internal combustion engine I was then offered a job with Scammell Lorries as a machine shop apprentice. They were short of a good winger for the works eleven. I also had the added advantage of being a talented boxer, and Scammell's were short of a man for their team.

By then I was a powerfully built teenager, strong enough for my father to keep his distance. Although no believer in the Queensberry Rules, he was astute enough to know I would take no more beatings, and a mutually sullen truce was called.

I was happy at Scammell's, combining hard work with plenty of sports, but after six months I left to join the nursing staff at Leavesden Mental Hospital. Not to be near my father, but in order to keep away from him: single men lived in.

Although my motives were far from altruistic, I soon developed a genuine sympathy for the unfortunate inmates. I worked in the terminal ward where a lot of people were dying of tuberculosis or just old age, and I spent many hours telling them stories which might have lacked literary merit, but brought a small glimmer of sunlight into their grey and hope-lacking days.

When they died I cleaned and washed down their corpses and laid them out in readiness for burial. I was also called upon to help deal with the more violent patients, and I learned that gentle persuasion is far more effective than brute force.

My own future was as bleak as the patients' I tended, and I was aware that I was leading an extremely rudderless existence. My routine developed into an almost unalterable pattern; at the end of a hard and often disturbing day I gravitated to the Crown public house where I set out to quench a thirst that was as prodigious as my father's. My drinking was only matched by the number of girl friends I had.

I had no illusions as to where this dead end existence was leading and I realized I would have to do something drastic about it. After one of our numerous rows my father had warned me, "You're no good, son. You'll end up inside one of these days. That's how you'll end up. Mark my words."

Although my father from his greenhouse position was the last person to proffer such a warning, I had an awful feeling he could be right. I had frequently been invited to take part in some criminal enterprise, but had rejected it. I wanted excitement, it was true, but not that kind. My fear was that I might succumb out of sheer boredom.

My reprieve from the dark and seemingly unending tunnel came the day when the dry as parchment tones of Neville Chamberlain announced on the BBC that we were at war with Germany. I can't profess to have followed the Munich toings and froings of the Prime Minister with his umbrella and a moustache which would have sent my erstwhile employer ordering me off to fetch the trimming scissors, but there was a genuine sense of relief when he arrived back at Croydon clutching a piece of paper and announcing peace in our time. The euphoria was short-lived, and like so many young men I was filled with a patriotic fervour. The streets of London emptied of children as if some unseen pied piper had entranced them away. Sandbag emplacements sprung up at the entrances to office blocks and the big stores in Watford, and the milkman and dustman appeared in the blue overalls of Air Raid Wardens. Windows were blacked out and covered with strips of brown paper to minimize the effects of flying glass. The sirens wailed and nothing happened. The total annihilation we had been led to expect would come tumbling from the skies did not arrive.

I had not made a close study of the political scene, but I knew that Hitler represented something evil and my country was doing the right and honourable thing in going to the aid of a country which was no more than a small space on the map of Europe, but to which we had pledged support. That may sound naive to the more sophisticated and politically conscious youngsters of today, but the mood of the country was one of buoyant confidence exemplified by songs like "We're Going to Hang out the Washing on the Siegfried Line". The fact that we had not got the means to do it worried no one.

I was 17½ in September, 1939, and I was determined to join up and do my bit. There would be no more aimless drifting from job to job; I now had a purpose in life. The adventure I craved was mine for the asking, and I could find it without breaking the law.

As soon as I was 18 I volunteered for the Royal Navy, but the Senior Service was more concerned with my minor hernia (later rectified at a military hospital) than my enthusiasm to get into action before it was all over. I tried for Royal Air Force air crew duties but was rejected because of insufficient educational attainments. Frustrated, I decided to soldier on until the arrival of my call-up papers.

I was still anxious to contribute something to the war effort and so I left the hospital and became a dumper driver and general labourer at the site of a new aerodrome which was being built near Leavesden for the De Havilland aircraft company.

The hard work suited me. It was an open air life and manhandling hundredweight sacks of cement, and shovelling tons of sand toughened me to a peak of fitness, which was ideal training for the military service that could be only a few months away. Meanwhile, I continued to frequent the Crown and add to my amatory exploits, often I am ashamed to confess with women who sought to deaden the pain of their husband's absence in the forces in the arms of casual pick-ups.

I eagerly awaited the delivery of the post each morning, but months passed and I had still not received my call-up papers. In 1941 I moved with the firm to the north-west of England to work on an extension to the airfield at Speke near Liverpool. It was my second time away from home and I revelled in my new-found freedom.

The need to complete the extension in a short time meant that everyone had to work very long hours, including Saturdays and Sundays, but that meant much overtime and thick pay packets at the end of the week.

Liverpool was packed with shipping from all parts of the world, most of it from America with Cash and Carry war materials and later Lend-Lease. The streets were crowded with Commonwealth troops and British soldiers departing for the various battlefronts which had sprung up. Food was scarce but beer plentiful, and the pubs were crammed to suffocation. Digs were almost impossible to obtain. I was fortunate to find accommodation in a dingy lodging house sharing a bed with three Irish labourers. We slept head to toe with two people at each end of the cramped bed. I found it no great hardship because I had never experienced much in the way of home comforts. With me it was really a case of what you've never had you'll never miss. Because of the nature of the work I was doing it was not until April, 1942, that I received the familiar buff-coloured envelope containing my call-up papers, and by then I feared the powers-to-be had left it too late. Although the British people had not lost their optimism, the early euphoria had given way to a steely determination and the war was now viewed as a battle for survival.

Dunkirk was a distant memory, large areas of London had been devastated by the Luftwaffe, the Battle of the Atlantic was at its peak, and although, following Pearl Harbor, America was now our ally, there was little indication that the victorious advances of the Germans and Japanese would be stemmed.

My joy at being called up was short-lived. Instead of posting me to a fighting unit, the Army decided to utilize my medical experience and I was assigned to the Royal Army Medical Corps.

Not only was I bitterly disappointed, I was furious. I was hard, muscular and itching for action, and all I was fit for was handling bed pans and handing out the Number Nines, the army's cure-all. That, I knew, was arrant nonsense because I was well aware that the Medical Corps carried out extremely brave and hazardous work in the front line, but it was not for me. I had set my heart on being a fighting soldier. My imagination had been fired by the exploits of the RAF pilots and the Desert Rats, not by the unsung deeds of the stretcher-bearers and ward orderlies.

When the time came for me to leave for the training depot, I felt too ashamed to tell my friends at the Crown that was going to be a non-combatant.

Within a week of arriving at Crookham for my initial training, I requested an interview with the Adjutant at which I asked to be transferred to the infantry.

He was sympathetic but adamant. "I'm sorry Challenor, but we need you as much as anyone else. Chaps with your sort of nursing experience are in short supply. That's the way it is, I'm afraid."

I returned disconsolately to my training, learning how to transport a badly wounded man to safety, the treatment of battle casualties, and the rudiments of how to set up a field hospital.

I did not know it, but only thirty miles away at Burskedon a young Commando officer, Captain Pinckney, was laying the foundation stone of a hush-hush mission codenamed Operation Airthief. He and a friend, Jeffrey Quill, were planning to hi-jack a Focke-Wulf 190 fighter from enemy-occupied France. Just the kind of work I was dying to get involved in. I was later to get my wish, for I became part of the team Pinckney led on a dangerous mission in Italy.

The plane he aimed to steal was an advanced fighter that was proving to be a thorn in the side of the Allied air forces, but if one could be handed over intact to our boffins they would be able to find the answer to its lethal qualities. But the operation was scrapped following one of those bizarre wartime mix-ups which even the most fertile-minded novelist could not have envisaged.

Oberleutnant Arnim Faber took the wrong turning whilst piloting one of the planes on a patrol over the Channel. He became engaged in a hectic dogfight with a Polish Spitfire squadron and, having escaped unscathed, he headed for Wales instead of his own airstrip near Caen. Over RAF Pembrey he performed a victory roll before making an impeccable landing in front of a delighted welcoming committee.

Faber, who had an English grandmother, proved a model of co-operation, thoughtfully pointing out many of the aircraft's secret refinements, including one for self-destruction should it land in enemy territory. It was that secret. The RAF, delighted to have a perfect specimen of the three-month's-old fighter handed to them on a plate, wined and dined wrong-way Faber before packing him off to a POW camp.

While that was happening, I was posted to a holding unit and soon afterwards we were ordered to Algiers.

We sailed in convoy, and during a very rough passage the ship I was in lost seven lifeboats, and another carrying nurses was torpedoed. Life aboard the ship had been awful, cooped up below decks for most of the time and crowded together like battery birds. The air was impregnated with the smell of vomit, urine and excreta, and the little time we were allowed on deck to exercise was never long enough to allow fresh air to fumigate the mess decks and toilets. So it was with a sense of immense relief that we passed through the Straits of Gibraltar and headed for Algiers which to me then meant no more than a film starring Charles Boyer and Hedy Lamarr.

On arrival my unit was attached to the First Army, the Anglo-American force which had landed in North-West Africa to sandwich Rommel as Montgomery broke out of El Alamein. But again I found myself standing on the sidelines. We were held in reserve.

Booze was dirt cheap and the only action I saw was in the bars where frequent fights broke out between us and the Yanks. The only bright spot of news was the assassination of Laval in Algiers.

Hardly had we time to get to know our bearings than we were moved to another reserve base some distance outside Algiers.

War, someone had said, is ninety per cent boredom and ten per cent action. With me it was total boredom until one morning two rakish looking officers – one of them was Randolph Churchill, son of Winston – drove into camp on a recruiting mission. They were from No. 62 Commando and were looking for likely candidates. I was among the first to volunteer, but there was a catch – I was to remain a medical orderly. I protested, but it did me no good; once the Army has classified a man it is almost impossible to break out of the rigid convention and get a transfer.

When we arrived at the Commando base camp near Philippeville, the new outfit was still in its formation stage, with men drawn from 3 and 4 Commando and other infantry units. Somewhere along the line I lost my cap, and as supplies of the coveted Commando green beret had not yet arrived, I was issued with an old Tank Corps beret and was promptly christened 'Tanky' – a name which stuck with me throughout the war.

Although officially a medical orderly, I wheedled my way into all the activities of the camp, explosives training, shooting with all types of weapons – our own as well as those captured from the enemy – unarmed combat, boat work, endurance tests, and every sphere of guerrilla work. The endurance tests were aimed to separate the men from the boys – 100-mile marches through the most rugged terrain, with a full pack and running up a near-vertical mountain of bare rock as sharp as a razor's edge and dotted with dense patches of prickly thorn, and reporting to an officer with a stop watch at the top, all before breakfast. Anyone who failed the strenuous muscle-torturing exercise had his papers marked RTU – returned to unit.

I took to the life like a duck to water and my proficiency was very high in every category. There was no doubt that I was the most aggressive medical orderly the Commandos ever had.

It is said that if you want something badly enough you'll get it. Well, that certainly applied in my case. One morning I was marched into the Old Man's office where I was told to hand over my medical duties to another orderly. I was going to join a fighting unit.

The system I had been told you could not buck had capitulated. No paperwork was involved. Just a verbal order.

If we worked hard we certainly played hard on those all too rare occasions when we were allowed a brief respite in the nearby town of Philippeville. As I was an experienced driver I was given the job of driving the liberty truck, a three-ton Bedford lorry. When we arrived in the town we set out to get monumentally drunk, a difficult task for young men as fit as we were. But we managed.

I drove the truck back like a demented stock-car driver with the wheels perilously close to the edge of the dirt road which had a precipitous drop into the sea below, the lads hanging on like grim death with one hand and pummelling on the cab shouting, "Slow down, you crazy bastard."

Back at camp a self-enforced emetic in the form of fingers down the throat brought up the beer before tumbling into a tent in readiness for the dawn call which would herald the race up the mountain.

After a minor raid on a small island near Tabraka – we found three Germans only too willing to surrender – we settled down to more extensive training. I was determined to attain a high degree of efficiency in every sphere of Commando work because I wanted to be among the first selected for any forthcoming operation. Only a young man who has served in a top-class fighting outfit will understand my feelings. But I had no fear of death, and if I was unfortunate enough to be killed I would take as many of the enemy with me as possible.

Then buzzes began to hum along the grapevine: something special was being planned for us. We had heard such rumours before, but this time there was a strange sense of expectancy, there was talk that the group was to be expanded, strengthened and developed into something much more potent than a normal commando unit. We were to be an extremely elite outfit.

Chapter Four

Then came a period of frenetic activity while 62 Commando was transferred into part of the 2nd Special Air Service Regiment. I had heard many stories of the incredible exploits of the 1st SAS in the desert under the command of the legendary Colonel David Stirling, and I felt a surge of pride at becoming a member of that cloak and dagger organization which had introduced a new kind of battle technique by harrassing the enemy behind his own lines.

Before I had time to get over my sense of elation, I was ordered to attend a briefing for a submarine operation called Marigold. Colonel Stirling must have had an odd sense of humour because he liked to name his sorties after flowers.

By May, 1943, there was more than a glimmer of light at the end of the tunnel and the scent of victory was in the air. The invincible Afrika Corps, one of Hitler's favourite armies, had been systematically ground to pieces between the advancing 8th and 1st Armies in North Africa, and attention was now being focused on the next phase of the war in the Middle East – the conquest of Sicily and the invasion of Italy, "the soft underbelly of the Axis". But as a prelude there were to be many feints and probes in strength before the real thing. Marigold – or the Sardinia Job, as we called it – was to be one of them.

Parts 1 and 2 of the operation were under the command of Captain Courtney of the Special Boat Section with three members of the SBS, and Captain Dudgeon and seven other ranks of the SAS.

With other members of the team I slipped out of Philippeville and went to Algiers to board HMS *Maidstone*, the mother ship to a flotilla of submarines. As it was to be my first taste of action I was comforted to find I was in the same section as Sergeant Fitzpatrick, a tough professional soldier whose air of coolness impressed me considerably. (Sadly, he was brutally murdered in a later operation in France.)

After a night's sleep in a hammock abord HMS *Maidstone*, during which I spent more time on the deck than in the canvas cot, we were told to prepare to board the submarine *Safari* which had the reputation of being one of the crack subs in the Mediterranean; no mean compliment considering the headlines the others had made.

Part 1 of the operation was to land Captain Courtney and Sergeant Thompson by fol-boat – a canoe-like vessel – on a specified point on the Sardinia coast where the Captain was to leave a notebook at a marked spot. Presumably to be picked up by an agent.

Part 2, to be carried out on another part of the coast, involved us all. The object, we were told, was to take a prisoner from a poorly manned guardhouse for the purpose of interrogation in order to gain information about the German strength in Sardinia prior to the launching of Operation Husky, the invasion of Sicily in July, 1943. The rest of the garrison were to be wiped out.

Safari, under the command of Lieutenant R.B. Lakin, slipped away from *Maidstone* under cover of darkness and headed for the open sea. A submarine under wartime conditions is unbelievably cramped; with extra personnel plus their kit it was sheer hell. The dosshouse bed I had shared with three Irishmen in Liverpool was four-star comfort in comparison. The daylight hours were very long at the time, and this meant the submarine had to remain submerged. In a short time the air became fetid and the bulkheads dripped with condensation. The SAS men, unused to living in such a confined area, found it uncomfortably claustrophic. It was a voyage I have no wish to repeat. I imagine the conditions were only marginally better than those on the old slave traders.

Despite being unable to move without tripping over someone's legs or equipment, there was a surprising degree of comradeship between the submariners and their enforced guests. We idled the interminably long hours away lying in our hammocks swung between the reserve torpedoes, idly conjecturing on how much explosive was contained in the sinister-looking "tin fish". Five days after leaving harbour, *Safari* reached the area of Part 1 of Marigold, and a periscope reconnaissance of the zone revealed movement at a house, a pill box surrounded with barbed wire, another with a camouflaged canopy, and a third sited on the beach, but no defences, at least as far as could be observed, for half a mile southward.

When night came the submarine surfaced in a blanket of comforting darkness and Captain Courtney and Sergeant Thompson clambered into a fol-boat and paddled for the beach, reaching the shore approximately 500 yards north of their intended landing point. They left the boat under a small sandy bluff and headed inland over a firm sandy beach to a line of bushes. While the Sergeant remained concealed in the bushes keeping an eye on the canoe, Captain Courtney went further ahead. He saw a light coming from a house and heard voices and dogs barking, but no one came out and when he had left the notebook at the appointed place he and the Sergeant returned to the submarine.

Part 1 of Marigold had gone strictly according to plan.

The next day *Safari* reached the area of Part 2 and an agonizing periscope recce was carried out which lasted from 0800 hours to 1530 hours, during which time we had to rely on terse comments from the commanding officer to know what was going on. Four men were seen moving in and out of the guardhouse, but no movement was observed at the other defensive positions. The period of inactive waiting is more tense than the actual combat which follows; one does not dwell on thoughts of death but on disfigurement or some disabling injury which will leave you crippled and impotent, and chews the nerve ends ragged. When the time for action comes and the adrenalin is pumping, there is no time for morbid introspection; survival is all that matters and killing the enemy the prime objective.

Captain Courtney decided that the route from the proposed landing area to the objective would take too long owing to a very steep incline, and, as speed was so important, he decided to land at a point where there appeared to be some rocks about ten feet high which would provide ideal cover for the boats and conceal them from the guns covering the area. In fact, the rocks were partly submerged, making it far from the ideal spot it appeared to be.

Because there were enemy surface craft patrolling the area, the submarine Commander's orders had been specific; the safety of the craft was not to be jeopardized by any undue delay or any prolonged activity which might alert the Germans to the possibility that the landing parties had arrived by submarine.

At midnight *Safari* surfaced and, as the waves lapped over the upper deck, we inflated the four-man dinghies by foot pump. The compressed-air bottles which would have done the job in half the time were for emergencies only. As the dinghies were extremely slow, even with four men paddling, it was decided that the fol-boats, which carried only a two-man crew and were much faster, should do the towing. We stood on the deck gulping down deep lungfuls of fresh air to clear them of the foul air we had been breathing during our long submersion.

As soon as we started for the beach things began to go wrong. There was a north-west current of about half a knot which lengthened our journey from an estimated half-hour to one and a half hours, and when we attempted to land at the proposed point we were forced to abandon it because of the underrated rocks, and we had to pull off and land elsewhere. Thankfully there was no sound or movement from the shore.

As we were so behind schedule it was decided that we would not deflate the dinghies but have them ready when the time came to pull out, which meant taking the risk of them being detected, although it turned out to be a decision that saved our lives.

The going was hard as we carefully made our way up the bluff, and our boots made a heck of a din on the loose shale – so loud that we felt sure someone would hear us. Then it happened. Private Hughes dropped his gun and there was a clatter of steel on stone. I can still hear the clatter now; it seemed to echo along the beach like an avalanche. Seconds later machine guns and small arms fire opened up from all directions. Then the enemy lit a ground flare and suddenly from pitch darkness we were standing fully exposed in incandescent brightness like actors spotlighted on a stage. We were only about a third of the way up the slope and exposed like ducks in a shooting gallery. The sound of the gunfire was deafening and we instinctively put our heads down, although we kept moving. Despite our exposed position, it was obvious that the Germans high above us could not see us clearly, for most of their bullets went safely over our heads. It was my baptism of fire, and I was relieved to find I wasn't scared stiff; instead I eagerly waited to hear the order to charge the enemy. To my disappointment, Captain Courtney had the experience, plus a clear head and cool blood, to know better, and he ordered us to withhold our fire, as it would pinpoint our position, and to disperse and make our way back to the boats.

I found myself alongside Sergeant Fitzpatrick and together we got down to the dinghies where we were joined by two others, one of whose name eludes me, but I shall call Butch. Although still under intense fire we managed to launch one of the dinghies and clamber aboard.

We began paddling like mad but did not seem to be making any headway and the bullets were ricochetting off the water like angry hornets. Then when I turned my head I saw that Butch had got in facing the wrong direction and was paddling against us.

I bellowed, "For God's sake stop paddling and turn round. Are you with us or against us?" But he was too numbed to take any notice.

We then started to move round in our seats as if playing some crazy version of musical chairs. Then, just when we had succeeded, we noticed that Butch had done the same, so we were back to square one. It was sheer pantomime and, despite the grave danger we were in, I burst out laughing. Sergeant Fitzpatrick did not see the humour of the situation and pulled rank and told us to bend our backs and get busy with the paddles. Gradually we began to pull away with the enemy's bullets putting up little spouts of water all round our very vulnerable dinghy. Gradually as we merged into the darkness the firing became sporadic and we were able to compose ourselves enough to take a compass bearing on the rendezvous spot with *Safari*. I thought to myself, "No way is it still going to be there." Then I noticed that I was having to plunge deeper and deeper with my paddle to reach the water. I looked over the side and realised that in the mad exodus from the beach someone had knocked the emergency air bottle full on and the dinghy was being inflated to near bursting point. I yelled at the top of my voice, "The bloody thing's still blowing up," and again I was convulsed with laughter. I leaned over and adjusted the release valve on the dinghy which set up a high-pitched wailing noise which promptly alerted the enemy to our position and they opened up again.

The bullets skittering over the surface of the water reminded me of the game of ducks and drakes, but they were well off target, presumably because the sound had become distorted and the Germans had no real idea of our whereabouts.

By this time we knew that we were well behind our ETA (estimated time of arrival) and the submarine would have departed long ago. I began to wonder how long it would take us to paddle back to Algiers. In my mind's eye I was trying, in the dense darkness, to picture our exact position in relation to North Africa and what emerged was far from encouraging. "How long do you think it'll take us?" I asked Sergeant Fitzpatrick. "No idea, but we'll make it," he said confidently.

We remained silent, saving our breath for the long voyage ahead, and all that could be heard was the sound of our paddles biting deep into the water and our breaths heavy with exertion. Then a large shape like a surfaced whale loomed darkly to port and I rested my paddle and exclaimed, "What a beautiful sight!"

The Royal Navy had turned a Nelson's blind eye on their orders not to jeopardize the ship by remaining in the area longer than the agreed time of departure. We were long overdue, and the rumpus on the beach must have alerted the Germans to the fact that there was a ship of some considerable size in the vicinity because we could not have paddled all the way from Africa. Yet they had waited. It was so moving I felt tears springing to my eyes. My admiration for the Navy had always been high, but it soared to the heavens that night, and that's where it has remained.

As we bumped against the hull a sailor stretched down to give me a hand and said jocularly, "Well! Where's your prisoner?" I replied with a grin, "Still sitting behind a bloody great machine gun."

We were glad to learn that the others had made it also, and as we clambered down the conning tower, there were members of the ship's company standing by to hand us tots of Nelson's blood – thick dark rum that set our insides on fire. Captain Dudgeon was the last to return and he broke the sad news that the other member of his fol-boat, Sergeant Loasby, was missing. (Later we learned he had been taken prisoner.) In such a closely knit outfit as ours the loss of even one man tempered our relief at having survived, but it could have been far worse, considering what a cock-up it had been.

I said to one of the ratings, "What were you silly bastards doing waiting for us?" and he replied, "We thought you must have hit trouble, and the skipper was making arrangements to put a landing party ashore to help you out." Time and time again during the war the Navy had helped the army out – at Dunkirk, Norway, Greece, and Crete. Then the whole future of the war had been at stake, but this time they had done it for a mere handful of pongoes whose absence wouldn't have been missed by anyone.

Safari dived and headed for the open sea, but after a short time nestled on the sea bed where she remained for several hours in total silence; we were forbidden even to speak. High above us we imagined the German ships sweeping the sea with their detector equipment, trying to pick up the slightest noise that would reveal our position. The hours passed with agonizing slowness as we sat huddled together, afraid to ease our cramped limbs in case we made a noise.

Then the order was given to start engines and we resumed normal sailing, arriving at Bône harbour at 0830 hours on 3 June – we had been away a whole week. Apart from leaving a message and discovering that the enemy were very much on the alert, we had achieved very little.

We said farewell to our submariner friends, then piled aboard lorries which were standing by to take us back to base.

The raid may have been a failure, but it had given me great personal satisfaction; I had faced the enemy for the first time and felt no fear.

In fact my only regret was that I had not had a chance to kill any of them.

No sooner had we arrived back at Philippeville than we were tossing our kit into another lorry. We were going to Mascarrah on the Moroccan border for parachute training. Clearly those invisible beings who controlled our destiny had not lost all confidence in us.

It was explained that we would do three practice jumps – any more would be pointless as the sole purpose of parachuting was to get us from one place to another in the shortest possible time.

I thought to myself that it was proving to be a strange war for me. I had been turned down by the Royal Navy, yet been in a submarine. The Royal Air Force hadn't wanted me either, now I was going to work with them.

Mascarrah was as hot as Hades. The sun hung in the sky like a copper salver, and everything seemed to be shimmering in the heat haze. This meant we had to train in the early hours immediately after dawn; the rest of the day we just sweated it out in the one-man pup tents which were like tandoori ovens. The salt tablets we took to combat the deficiency caused by dehydration gave us a tremendous thirst which the lukewarm water did little to slake. Sometimes in the evening we were allowed into Mascarrah where there was a little French cafe which miraculously sold ice-cold beer. There we would sit downing glass after glass and sweating it out almost immediately. It was surprising that everyone remained so incredibly cheerful; everyone that is except Butch. Although he was a close friend, I did not realize that he had been badly shaken by the intense fire we had come under during the abortive raid. I tried to make him snap out of his moody silences with somewhat heavy-handed jokes and hearty Service humour. It was well intentioned, but my brash exuberance had the opposite effect to that which I wanted to achieve. Butch became more and more withdrawn and intense.

Before our first jump I began teasing him, trying to jerk him out of his morose silence. On the aircraft as we checked each other's equipment before dropping he asked me, "How's mine, Tanky?" "Hmmm," I replied as I checked the static line on his parachute with exaggerated care, "I don't know." This note of uncertainty nearly drove him frantic and I regretted being such a fool. He completed the jump without incident, but shortly afterwards he requested a meeting with the troop commander and asked to be returned to his parent unit. I did not see him again. What I did may have been callous and insensitive, but I'm glad I did it. At least he learned before it was too late that he was not cut out for the SAS.

A parachutist's first drop is like a first love: an experience that can never be repeated.

It was particularly so in my case because I hate heights. Even standing on a high building makes my stomach churn, and the thought of jumping terrified me. Maybe that is why I adopted such a casual attitude to Butch; subconsciously I was cloaking my own fear, but I knew I had to go through with it if I wanted to remain in the unit.

I trudged across the tarmac to the waiting Dakota, fumbling with my harness and paying particular attention to the static line (which opens the chute), to make sure it was not tangled. My heart was pounding like an old crock whose big ends had gone as I took my seat alongside the other members of the team. The engines revved into life and the Dakota trundled across the tarmac in a cloud of thick red dust. Then we were airborne and there was no time for further misgivings. The stand-by light flashed and the voice of the instructor bellowing, "No 1!" (the first man out) echoed along the fuselage. I heard the roar of the slipstream before I stepped into nothing. There was a terrific whoosh as the chute opened and the harness jerked under my armpits and my hurtling fall earthwards was reduced to a slow gentle descent. I was floating on air. I did not even feel the bump when I hit the ground and tumbled over as I had been taught to do. I felt exhilarated. A man who knows no fear has nothing to conquer, but I had dreaded the thought of jumping out of the plane; now I had done it and would happily do it again. Two more jumps and I was a parachutist entitled to wear my wings and claim two shillings a day extra pay.

It was during this training that I met Major Roy Farran, a stocky man with a very strong face, cold penetrating eyes, and a row of medal ribbons on his tunic that were evidence of why he had become a legend among fighting soldiers. He had fought in several campaigns as a tank commander, been wounded a number of times, and escaped from Greece after being taken prisoner in the bloody defence of Crete. I was "Tanky" to him from the start, and we became close friends – a situation only possible in a freebooter outfit such as ours – and we have remained so ever since.

Then it was back to Philippeville once more, and the training we had previously undergone turned out to be child's play. Day and night the base hummed with activity and rattled to the sound of small arms fire and the ear-numbing crump of explosives. Clearly sabotage was going to play a prominent part in our future activities, for we spent a tremendous amount of time learning how to destroy everything from bridges and railway lines to vital installations, and experimenting with just how much explosive was needed for each kind of target. We also rehearsed with all kinds of fancy devices.

The small arms drill would have driven a conventional instructor crazy. It was nearly all close-quarter stuff and what was called instinctive firing. Our weapons consisted of .45 automatic pistols, Thompson sub-machine guns, American carbines and captured enemy guns. I became skilled in the use of all of them, but I favoured the .45 which I fired cowboy fashion from the hip, knowing that the heavy-calibre bullet would stop anyone, no matter where it struck.

There was no break in the process of making extremely fit young men even fitter; what would have been considered the peak in any other outfit was not good enough for the SAS. We learned how to handle every type of portable craft, and were even taught how to wrestle with unwieldy 12-man West African dories in the turbulent Mediterranean surf. It was a miracle that none of us were drowned.

In addition, we had to undertake long route marches with 60 lb packs on our backs into the most inhospitable areas of the surrounding desert. The average "scheme", as these vigorous exercises in self-reliance were called, would last several days, during which we existed on a brew of tea, biscuits, and tins of compressed meat. They taxed us to the limits of physical and mental endurance, but I revelled in them. Nothing seemed to blunt my seemingly inexhaustible appetite for more, and although some tempers got a little frayed around the edges, I never lost my boyish sense of devilry. In any other outfit I would have ended up in the glasshouse.

During one scheme about twenty of us were holed up in the underbrush on the side of a hill waiting for the remainder of the group to catch us up. I spotted Sergeant Laurie Brownlee's men trudging wearily down the road in single file, heading for the rendezvous point, and I could not resist the impulse to make a joke of it. They had been eaten alive by mosquitoes and sand flies and it was as hot as a griddle; everyone was looking forward to dropping flat on their backs and tossing off their pack which now seemed to weigh a ton.

I picked up my carbine, aimed and dropped a couple of bullets in the dust a few inches away from the sergeant. The reaction was not quite what I expected because his men dropped flat and returned the fire, clipping the branches of the shrubs where we were concealed. So we retaliated and things began to get a little dodgy. Bullets were flying everywhere until one man stopped one in the arm and everyone came to their senses.

We managed to explain away the wound as an accident, and there was no inquiry or Court Martial, but a general order was posted telling us to cut out that kind of bloody nonsense.

Apart from our own over-exuberance, Philippeville had other dangers. There were vicious scorpions which bit like gin traps, and in the morning you always shook your boots because they were a favourite sleeping spot. A transport sergeant became seriously ill after being bitten by one which crawled into his sleeping bag. But worst of all were the mosquitoes which thrived in a nearby malarial swamp, and before the source was discovered most of the Regiment was down with malaria. It was a particularly virulent form of recurrent malaria that was to affect us in later campaigns in Italy and France.

I had never taken my anti-malaria tablets, convinced that sheer will-power could defeat the attentions of the mossies, but one day playing cards during a midday break I was convulsed by a bout of uncontrollable shivering. Although it was midsummer I put on a thick coat and swaddled myself in a blanket, but the shivering continued. "You've got it," said one of my mates knowingly, while others pointed out that it was the price for not having taken my tablets. That was rubbish, because many who took them regularly still went down with it. I was taken to the Military Hospital, and after about ten days the attack was quelled, but it was only a temporary respite. It was to return later, with devastating after-effects and certainly contributed to the sad events which took place many years later.

Chapter Five

The fortunes of war were at last swinging in favour of the Allies, and although a lot of fighting still lay ahead there was a confident feeling that it was no longer a question of *if* but *when* we won the war.

In January, 1943, the defeat of the German Army in North Africa was imminent when President Roosevelt and Winston Churchill met in Casablanca to discuss future strategy. Surprisingly, Roosevelt stressed that victory in Europe was more important than the defeat of Japan which was America's closest and more immediate danger, and this could only be achieved by a full-scale invasion of Normandy. The normally belligerent Churchill, possibly still haunted by the spectre of the wholesale slaughter of the 1914–18 war, favoured the invasion of Italy as a prelude to Overlord. Before this could be achieved, however, Sicily, which lay like a football on the toe of Italy, had to be occupied.

Almost six months after that historic meeting, the American and British 8th Armies landed on the south-eastern end of the island in the middle of a fierce storm. It was the largest amphibious operation ever mounted in military history, with nearly 3,000 ships and landing-craft taking part. The unpredicted storm, far from wrecking the plan, proved to be an unexpected bonus to the seaborne forces, for the Germans, lulled into a sense of false security, did not maintain their customary vigilance. It was a totally different story for the airborne invaders. More than a third of the gliders landed in the sea, and American paratroopers were widely scattered over southern Sicily. The 2nd SAS experienced similar misfortunes; one group from Kairouan, who were to have prepared a dropping zone near Mount Etna for three plane-loads of parachutists, were dropped into a Prisoner-of-War camp instead.

My own contribution to the invasion was minimal. I did not even land. The day after the initial assault my outfit took off in an Albemarle from Kairouan, an air-strip in North-East Tunisia, but for some unexplained reason we were not allowed to fire any identifying Verey lights, and over the coastline of Sicily it seemed as if every anti-aircraft gun in the Allied fleet opened fire. They threw everything at us including the proverbial kitchen sink, and as I sat in the buffetted aircraft I thought to myself: those poor sods in Bomber Command have to put up with this night after night. But that was little consolation as we climbed, dived, and weaved to avoid the red and green tracers which seemed to be looping towards us with deceptive slowness.

We circled round and round the dropping zone, but received no landing signal and the pilot was forced to turn back. Over the coast we ran into another ferocious barrage, but we emerged relatively unscathed. Over the Med, heading for base, we heaved a collective sigh of relief until the pilot's voice came over the intercom to tell us to prepare the dinghies for ditching . . . the aircraft was running out of fuel. Our evasive action to avoid the ack-ack fire, followed by the prolonged search for our dropping signal, had meant we had been airborne far longer than had been anticipated.

Thankfully we did not need the dinghies because the aircraft managed to reach an American bomber base on the tip of Tunis. The pilot informed us on landing that he had flown the last few miles on empty tanks.

That was the end of my role in the Sicily invasion.

Back at base I heard of even more alarming cock-ups, and I seriously doubted if the invasion would succeed. One of our lads who did land was Trooper Stanley Jones, nicknamed "Dead Pan" because of his impassive manner. His expression never altered no matter how tall a story I told him, and I told him quite a few. He even swallowed the yarn that a Russian Princess was writing to the Colonel using the code name "Randy Olga".

His expression did register the minimum of surprise, however, when he was told he would be taking part in an airborne drop, because he had never undergone parachute training. But he quickly suppressed his misgivings, and aboard the Albemarle he was soon his dead-pan self. The other paras comforted him by saying that the training course was a waste of time and he hadn't missed anything, and there was nothing to jumping – it was a piece of cake.

Over the dropping zone Stan was bundled out in a rush to maintain a "tight" stick and he felt a sense of relief followed by a surge of elation when his 'chute opened and he found himself descending at what seemed an almost gentle speed. Then he glanced up and his jubilation turned to near panic – there was a hole in his 'chute. The nearest member of the "stick" heard him bellow, "You bastards have given me one with a hole in it."

He was in no danger at all . . . no one had deemed it necessary to explain that the hole was essential for the proper control of the parachute and to prevent the canopy collapsing.

Deservedly Stan survived the operation and the remainder of the war.

Meanwhile, I remained a frustrated soldier. Here I was, a highly trained fighting man who had served in the Commandos and joined the SAS for the action I craved, but consistently denied it by a conspiring fate. I was not even given an explanation why Stanley, who had never jumped before, had been selected for the operation while I had to remain at base.

My warhorse enthusiasm for battle had now been replaced by a cold yet intense hatred of Germans, fostered by the chilling stories I had heard about the Gestapo, concentration camps, and the wholesale destruction of entire towns and their innocent populations. I vowed that any Germans who came my way, hands up or not, would be killed.

For several months we continued to play soldiers, trying to improve on what we considered was already perfect. The only thing that kept us on our toes were the repeated rumours that something big was in the offing, but invariably the buzzes turned out to be ill-founded.

Then one day the atmosphere changed. When the next buzz started going the rounds there was an indefinable feeling that this time it was the real thing. Thirteen of us – four officers and nine other ranks – were selected for a period of intense specialized training.

Tracking and map-reading were stepped up, and we were introduced to even more sophisticated explosives drill than had figured in our previous courses. When we began to concentrate on pinpointing targets on railways and the cutting of lines, we guessed we had been earmarked for a sabotage operation.

We worked hard on the methods of eliminating sentries by taking them from behind with a minimum of noise. I spent a lot of my free time stalking through the bushes with my stabbing knife in my hand. I also became very accurate at throwing it.

On 5 September Captain Pinckney, whose plan to high-jack a German fighter had been thwarted by the faulty navigation of a pilot, took us aside and gave us the first inkling of what it was all about. In the shade of an olive grove, out of the blazing Mediterranean sun and beyond the hearing of inquisitive ears, he outlined "Operation Speedwell", or what I called, and still do, the Italian Job. Take-off was in two days' time.

We were to be dropped into Northern Italy to derail trains in tunnels by explosives, the purpose being to reduce the flow of enemy troops and materials to the front.

Captain Pinckney was a highly respected officer with an impressive record, a big man in every sense of the word, six foot plus yet never needing to raise his voice. Quietly, in a matter-of-fact tone, he outlined our various tasks particularly warning of the likelihood of encountering sentries guarding the tunnels. "You'll know how to handle that problem," he said, and we all laughed. He made it sound like a picnic jaunt to Hampstead Heath, although we knew it would be anything but that.

In a small outfit such as ours little remained secret for long, and it was soon common knowledge that Colonel Bill Stirling (David's brother) thought that not enough aircraft and men had been allocated for what he considered a vital operation. The whole Allied advance could be affected by the success or failure of our mission. If his advice had been heeded, German reinforcements to the Salerno bridgehead by rail would have been negligible and lines of communication totally disrupted.

We were split into two groups, one under Captain Pinckney, the other under Captain Dudgeon, and we would be landed in two separate night drops.

I felt distinctly uneasy; I had only made three jumps and none of them had been at night. What's more, we would be deep behind the enemy's lines in hostile mountain country. A further danger was that we were going into an unprepared dropping zone, and no one had the vaguest idea of the conditions we were likely to encounter.

The purpose of the operation – the destruction of trains in tunnels buried deep in the Appennines – seemed a piece of cake compared to what was to follow. Somehow, by guess and by God, we had to make our way back to friendly lines.

Today technological advances have removed most of the hazards which faced us. If the Op had been mounted in Vietnam or the Falkland Islands the raiders would have gone in and out by helicopter the same night, but more than forty years ago we were totally dependent on Shanks's Pony and a hard footslog through enemy-held territory towards the Allied armies which had landed at Reggio on the toe of Italy, three days before the launch of Speedwell. That was some five hundred miles away, the distance from London to Aberdeen.

It was optimistically estimated that the Allies would be advancing so quickly that contact would be made in a week. In wartime things seldom go according to plan, and that was certainly true of Speedwell.

Although the Italians surrendered on 8 September, the Germans reacted swiftly and skilfully, almost as if they were glad to be shot of the Eyties. They made full use of the inhospitable terrain which was more helpful to the defenders than the attackers, and the well-organized resistance kept the Allied advance to a snail's pace.

That made the success of our operation much more imperative. By cutting the jugular vein of supplies, the Americans and British would be able to regain their momentum.

Captain Pinckney and his seven-man group were to attack the Bologna–Florence and Borretta–Pistoia railway lines while Captain Dudgeon's group of six men, of which I was a member, was to be split into three parties. Captain Dudgeon and parachutists Brunt, Sergeant Foster and Corporal Shortall were to attack sections of the line between Genoa and La Spezia, while Lieutenant Wedderburn and I were assigned the line between La Spezia and Bologna.

Captain Dudgeon was only 23 but a splendid commander. He stood over six feet tall and was viewed as something of a Captain Bligh character. Oddly enough it did not diminish the affection we held him in. He was a strict disciplinarian who could raise a laugh where other men would have brought scowls of discontent. Charisma was not a word that was in common use then, but it certainly applied to him.

At Philippeville, while orderly officer, he strode into the marquee where lunch was being served. A special treat on the menu that day was lemonade. He marched up to the first table and put the time-honoured question: "Any complaints?" "Yes, sir," ventured a bold voice, "Not much powder in the lemonade, sir."

He rapped his swagger stick on the table like someone quelling a mutinous rabble. "Give the men WATER." We all responded with a rousing cheer.

Captain Dudgeon, out of earshot, was somewhat incongruously called Toomai, after the elephant boy in one of Kipling's stories, though he was, in fact, built on the massive scale of the elephant itself and would charge through the thickest undergrowth like an enraged bull. We loved him and would have given our lives for him if necessary.

After the initial briefing, the next forty-eight hours sped by in a whirlwind of activity which left us with little time to brood on what lay ahead. We checked and rechecked maps and all the other paraphernalia of an operation, loaded the tube-like panniers with ammunition, explosives and foodstuffs, and cleaned and recleaned our weapons.

I was armed with a first-class and most lethal Schmeisser machine pistol, drawn from the SAS armoury of captured weapons. It had a 9 mm. calibre 32-cartridge magazine and was capable of firing five hundred rounds per minute effectively up to a range of 150 yards.

Over our uniforms we wore US blue-grey overalls which at a distance made us resemble Germans.

I also carried a .32 pistol, and strapped to my leg was a combat knife honed to a razor sharpness for close-quarter work on sentries. Apart from them we had been told not to attack any other troops if it could be avoided. We were to be as silent and as secretive as possible; the destruction of vital supplies was our main object. If any explosives were left after we had completed our line blowing, it was to be used in nuisance attacks on electric pylons and telephone lines.

Our food was very basic: bully beef and sardines, raisins and cheese, plenty of char and tins of fifty Players cigarettes.

Each man was also issued with thousands of lira with which to pay Italian peasants who might help us with food and shelter, and every officer was given several gold coins, worth about £10 each, as a reserve currency to be used only as a last resort. It was the only time I had found the army to be generous with money.

A cloak and dagger touch was added to the operation by our Intelligence Officer, Major Eric Barkworth. His inventive mind produced a stream of intriguing emergency devices. Being a pipe smoker, I was issued with a pipe with a minute compass secreted in the stem, and inside the lining of the pouch was a silk map of Italy. In view of what was to happen to me I would have preferred an extra change of boots and underwear.

Although we were dropping into an unknown future, we were afforded no special privileges on the morning of D-day. Reveille was at 7.30 a.m. and we had our usual breakfast. There was no marked tension, just an air of general excitement and anticipation. We were impatient to get cracking.

In the afternoon we had a final briefing at which Captain Dudgeon warned us that if we were forced to drop from a height we should be careful to check our drift so that on landing we could link up with the others. Shop talk over, he produced a bottle of whisky which we drank among the olive trees. At 5 p.m. we boarded a truck and drove out to the Albemarle standing on the edge of the air strip where mechanics crawled ant-like over the wings and engines making a final check.

I made myself comfortable by the open doorway of the aircraft, having a last minute chat with my friend Sergeant Fitzpatrick who had come along to wish us good luck. He sniffed deeply, then said, "You know, Tanky, I can't stand the smell of these planes any more. I don't want to drop any more."

It must have been one of those premonitions that men sometimes have. A year later he was dropped into France where he was cornered by Germans and killed along with all the others in his party.

Such misgivings struck no responding chord with me. Normally I experienced a tightening of the stomach which was invariably a sign of trouble ahead, but I felt nothing. I was completely at ease, just as if I was embarking on a training exercise.

The engines fired into life and we taxied along the dusty runway before lifting off like an overfed pelican straining to become airborne. Ahead lay an uncomfortable $5\frac{1}{2}$-hour flight before we reached our objective in Northern Italy – the high ground near Bergo val di Taro, north of La Spezia.

The Albemarle, which carried a crew of two pilots, radio operator and navigator, was only equipped to take ten paratroopers, so we were very cramped indeed in the space forward of the large dropping hole in the floor at the rear of the fuselage. It meant we had little leg room, and if we wanted to ease our cramp-stiffened limbs we had to be careful not to bang our heads.

Soon after crossing the coast we were in complete darkness, unable to read or smoke in the blacked-out plane, and there was little to do but lean back on our parachute packs and doze or talk. I couldn't snooze so I joined in the aimless chatter and we talked without any real knowledge or conviction about the respective merits of Italian women and Arab women, and whether the booze where we were going would be an improvement. The general consensus was that there had to be an improvement in both on what we were leaving behind.

Ever practical, Captain Dudgeon said that unlike the desert the mountains would have a plentiful supply of clear mountain water, which prompted me to remark, "Blimey, sir, in that case we should have stowed some lemonade powder in one of the containers."

My rather juvenile crack convulsed everyone and the plane echoed to our laughter. A none too well developed sense of humour was a prerequisite of SAS life. But the carefree guise could not be maintained indefinitely and sometimes we lapsed into silence, staring unseeingly into the murky darkness of the aircraft, seeing nothing but the white teeth in our blackened faces. I knew we were all pondering on what kind of reception was waiting for us in the Italian mountains.

There was no heating in the Albemarle but we were packed in so close to each other that we became hot and sticky under our denims, and the urge to add to the smog by smoking became almost unbearable. The engines drummed a monotonous accompaniment to our chatter, and after five hours our enthusiasm to plunge into the unknown was greater than ever. Like the women and wine we had been debating, anything had to be an improvement on the conditions in the aircraft.

Shortly before midnight the pilot passed word that we were crossing the Italian coast. We would never have guessed it, but for a short burst of flak which ceased abruptly as we flew inland.

"Ten minutes to go," warned the Despatcher, opening the hatch in the fuselage floor. Immediately the slipstream roared in, chilling the sweat on our bodies. We rose unsteadily and began to go through the familiar stages preceding a drop. We got into jumping order, checked our equipment by the shaded light which had been switched on and glowed like a bloodshot eye, made sure our static lines were correctly attached to the strong points, and examined the ties on each others' 'chutes. We were now ready for the Despatcher's orders.

Captain Dudgeon had almost to shout to make himself heard above the inrush of air and the roar of the engines. "Remember to watch your drift going down. The stick is to stay as tight as possible. I will remain where I land and you are to walk to me, number six walking on to number five and so on, until we pick each other up."

The light flashed. "Number one," yelled the Despatcher, slapping Captain Dudgeon on the shoulder. He disappeared out of the hole and we followed in quick succession. We knew there was no danger of being too close in a multi-paratroop drop. As soon as you leave the aircraft the slipstream whisks you away, but if there is too long an interval between jumps the stick becomes spread out and separated by ever-increasing gaps, which get even bigger on landing.

I was Number six in the dropping order and therefore last out. I remember gasping for air as the icy slipstream caught me. This was followed by the stomach-wrenching feeling of falling free. Then there was a hard jerk on my shoulders as the canopy billowed open above me.

I looked up to make sure my rigging lines were not twisted, and I saw the Albemarle disappear to the right. Then I checked the position of the rest of the stick; they were dead ahead, swinging gently in a straight line and strung out in perfect formation about 100 yards from each other. We could have conducted a conversation in the still night air; in that rarified atmosphere sound is magnified and travels quickly.

To the left, in the direction of La Spezia, an air raid siren wailed mournfully. "A bit bloody late with the alarm clock," I said to myself with more than a hint of relief. But it wasn't a serious threat to us because it was soon silent. Clearly it hadn't been meant to warn of our arrival.

It was a perfect night, cloudless and moonlit, and down below the Appennines looked like gentle hillocks. It had been a high drop, 7,000 feet, the highest I had ever made. My three previous ones had been in the region of 300 feet, aimed at hitting the deck as quickly as possible. This time we were in no great hurry.

The earth came rushing up to meet me and I plunged into a small tree which cushioned my twenty feet per second fall. I released my harness and spent a frustrating time ripping the 'chute from the branches. As soon as I had got it clear I scraped a hole with my knife and buried it. An abandoned 'chute was tantamount to announcing our arrival.

I looked around and saw I had landed in a small copse on a scrub-filled mountainside. I began to walk on my line bearing to link up with Lieutenant Wedderburn, using a low whistling sound which was our pre-arranged recognition signal. An hour later I had linked up with him.

Captain Dudgeon had a rapid roll call and was gratified to learn that there had been no injuries or hitches; it had gone as smoothly as a practice run. He then satisfied himself that no immediate alarm had been sounded and that our location was far enough from any large mountain track for us to be able to relax for a few hours before searching for the supply containers at first light. A sentry was posted and we stretched out on the ground and lit our first cigarettes since leaving base. Our wads were charless: the tea was in the containers with the rest of the provisions and our sleeping bags. But it was a warm night and we could happily do without either.

At dawn we were awakened by birds and the impressive spectacle

50

of a red sun climbing up over the rim of the Appennines. I shinned up a tree and located the containers through my binoculars. The distinctive red and blue 'chutes were directly ahead and only 200 yards away. They stood out like a sixpence on a sweep's backside, and we hastened towards them before anyone else spotted them. Everything was intact and when we carried them to the scene of our bivouac Captain Dudgeon gave us the go-ahead to light a fire. We opened tins of bully and brewed up tea, the first drink and food we had had for several hours.

For the rest of the day we did little but check and recheck our bearings on salient landmarks, climbing trees to confirm our position, and poring over maps. Then we worked out our compass bearings for the next move at nightfall – the route to our individual targets. Then we buried the containers and waited for dusk.

A rendezvous was arranged for seven nights ahead, at a point on a stream between Pontremoli and Villafranca.

Our partings were low key, in typical unemotional SAS style, just a cheery wave and a call of "Good luck". The other four marched off in single file along a wooded mountain track. That was the last I saw of them.

It was much later that I heard of their fate. Captain Dudgeon and parachutist Brunt ambushed a German truck and killed the occupants, then used the vehicle to make faster progress towards their objective, but after a short time they were captured at an enemy road block. The following morning, without a trial, they were executed by firing squad. A German doctor who was present wrote to Captain Dudgeon's father at the end of the war and said they both died bravely and with dignity.*

Sergeant Foster and Corporal Shorthall were never seen or heard of again, and to this day nothing is known of their fate. The exploits of Captain Pinckney I'll recount later.

Left alone on the side of a mountain, Lieutenant Wedderburn and I checked our compass bearings once more, then set off towards our own objective. The mountain air was cold, clean and invigorating,

* This book had been completed when I read a letter from John Baxendale in the SAS magazine *Mars and Minerva*. Towards the end of the war in Italy he was attached to 78 Section, War Crimes, SIB, and during his investigations was led to two well concealed graves, one of which contained the uniformed body of Captain Dudgeon. In the grave alongside was a skeleton without any positive means of identification, although it was clearly a British soldier. He told me later that he was led to the graves by a 12-year-old boy. The Italians had placed small wooden crosses at the foot of each grave. The bodies were reburied in the military cemetery in Florence.

and as we moved with purposeful strides we could hear a guard dog barking noisily in a distant village, and down below we could see and hear a rushing mountain stream.

I felt the adrenalin pumping through my veins and thought: "With any luck I'll soon be killing my first Jerry sentry."

Chapter Six

As I looked at the stocky figure of Lieutenant Wedderburn trudging ahead of me, back bent under the weight of his pack, legs thrusting him forward like a skilled climber, I reflected that only in an SAS unit on a hush-hush behind-the-lines job could two such contrasting men have been tossed together. In peacetime we would never have met, having little in common and coming from such different social backgrounds. But in the weeks and months that followed, linked by the common bond of danger and hunger, we became as close as brothers.

In small party raids such as the one we were engaged on, where each was dependent on the other, the formality and aloofness that existed between officers and men in a normal regiment was replaced by mutual respect. When you eat together, sleep together and perform bodily functions in sight of each other, you can't always be returning salutes. Having said that, although I was "Tanky" to him, he was always "Sir" to me, and when he made a decision I did not debate it with him.

We were chalk and cheese in nearly every respect. I was strongly built, deep chested, over 5 ft. 10 ins. tall and from a not too happy working-class home where, from my elementary school, I had been tossed into the deep end of life to make my own way from one dead-end job to another. I was stubborn, defiant, a trifle wild, but totally loyal to anyone who commanded my respect. And Lieutenant Wedderburn had that.

Thomas MacLeggan Wedderburn, on the other hand, was an upper-middle-class Scot from Edinburgh whose law studies had been interrupted by the war. Pushing thirty, he was fairly old for an SAS officer, but he was tremendously strong and his mountaineering experience, gained from peacetime climbing in the Highlands and the Swiss Alps, made him an indispensable member of the Speedwell team. He was stockily built and on the short side; the top of

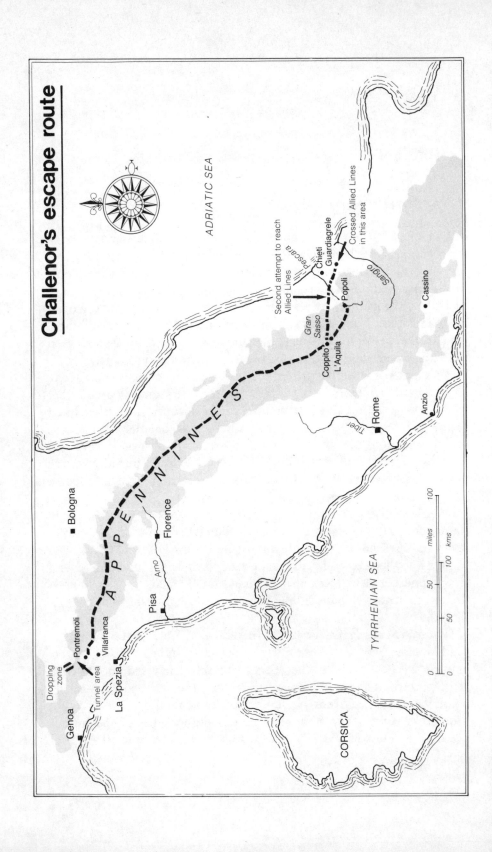

Challenor's escape route

his head was on a level with my chest, and he peered owlishly through thick heavy-framed glasses. It was inevitable that he was nicknamed "Tojo".

We climbed steadily through the night up steep slopes studded with rocks and scrub, stopping every now and then for Lieutenant Wedderburn to make compass checks. Although it was a clear moonlit night, taking accurate bearings was difficult and our progress was slow.

It was 3 a.m. and visibility had considerably improved when we nudged each other and pointed to the bottom of a mountain opposite; snaking around the foot was a railway line with a bridge spanning a wide stream. We cautiously clambered down, careful not to dislodge any loose stones, to examine the bridge, but after close scrutiny agreed that we would have needed a truckload of explosives to blow such a massive structure. Slightly disappointed, we consoled ourselves by reminding each other that our objective was to blow trains in tunnels, and so we decided to follow the lines throughout the remainder of the day in the hope of coming across a tunnel.

We slogged on night after night, sleeping as best we could during the day under any bush that offered reasonable concealment. We were seven days into our mission before we found a tunnel. The lines disappeared into a mountain, and we were in no doubt that it had to be a long one, a comforting thought because it meant we could lay charges a considerable distance from each other on the "Up" and "Down" lines. Once placed in position we would have plenty of time to leg it to safety.

We kept observation from a nearby vantage point and noticed that there seemed to be lengthy intervals between trains entering and emerging from the tunnel, and that most of the traffic consisted of goods trains.

We checked our charges and transferred them to smaller packs. To blow a line we would need 3 lbs of plastic 808, which looked as harmless as sticks of plasticine. The sticks would be taped to the rails and connected by instantaneous cortex fuse to an ordinary fog signal detonator inserted into a gun cotton primer.

It was crude but effective. When the wheels ran over the fog signal it detonated the whole lot and blew out a section of the line. The train was derailed and as the trucks ploughed into each other the tunnel would be completely blocked from roof to floor. Clearing it would be a long and laborious task. At least, that was the theory. In practice we had yet to see it work.

Just before midnight we crept down to the mouth of the tunnel leaving our larger packs behind in our hide-out. It was dark and the moon had deserted the sky, so Lieutenant Wedderburn had the bright idea of attaching strips of the tape, used for binding up the explosives, on the occasional rock or bush to assist us in making our getaway.

We assumed that the tunnel would have sentries posted – it was after all a vital supply line – so I slipped ahead with my knife at the ready to pierce from behind the heart of any sentry. I volunteered for the job as I considered myself something of a dab hand as a silent killer. To reach the entrance I had to splash through a small stream running alongside the line. The gurgling and splashing of the water over stones helped to deaden any sound I made; even so I paused every few seconds to listen for a challenge from the mouth of the tunnel, but none came. I took no chances because sentries are renowned for slipping off to have a quick drag at a cigarette, but after a stealthy inspection I realised one had not been posted. I felt quite deflated and I thought, "Easy drop, now no bloody sentries."

I returned to Lieutenant Wedderburn and whispered, "All clear. Now let's go and get a train or two."

Inside the tunnel it was as dark as a cellar and as cold as charity, and we stumbled along like blind men, tapping on the line which was a substitute for a white stick. Gradually our eyes became adjusted to the dark and 100 yards into the tunnel we attached our first charges on the outside rail of the "Down" line from Pontremoli, a job which took only five minutes but seemed like years.

Then we stumbled on for a considerable distance and planted more charges on the "Up" line. Despite the chilling cold, we were both sweating and I needed no urging when Lieutenant Wedderburn whispered, "Well done, Tanky. Let's get out of here."

We were walking out as fast as the conditions would allow when suddenly I heard it. I straightened up, craned my head, and said, "Listen! There's a bloody train coming."

We stood immobile in the darkness as "Tojo" listened intently. There was no doubt about it, a train was approaching fast, making the line hum. And it was travelling on the "Down" line where we had placed the first set of charges.

"Good God," said Wedderburn. "Move man. Run like hell."

I needed no prompting. I ran like an Olympic sprinter with "Tojo" prepared to settle for Silver. Neither of us had any wish to be buried at the scene of our triumph. The train seemed to be getting closer as we headed for the small circle of light ahead. Our boots caught against

1. The author in 1945.

2. Captain Pinckney:
   "a highly respected officer
   with an impressive record" (p.45).

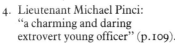

3. Lieutenant Hugh Gurney:
   "a quietly spoken, tough-as-
   teak veteran" (p.90).

4. Lieutenant Michael Pinci:
   "a charming and daring
   extrovert young officer" (p.109).

5. Lord John Manners:
   "he slotted in perfectly,
   without sacrificing an ounce of
   respect" (p.114).

the line and sleepers, and our lungs were near to bursting, sheer desperation propelling us at a speed we would never again match.

As we broke clear of the entrance we hurled ourselves into the stream just in time to see the train thundering into the tunnel. Seconds later there was a rumbling boom magnified by the confined space of the tunnel. This was followed by the screeching and rending of metal being torn apart and piling up against the roof. Dense smoke billowed out of the cavernous entrance. We stuck up our thumbs in a gesture of triumph – without doubt the train had been well and truly derailed.

We clambered out of the stream wringing wet but smiling. Then we heard the rumble of a train on the "Up" line. We listened in awe for the inevitable boom. When it came it was even louder than the first. Again it was followed by the awful rending of steel and splintering of wood. Then an eerie silence descended.

The two T's – Tanky and Tojo – had claimed two trains at one go and completely blocked the La Spezia–Bologna line as ordered.

We soon found the first of the tape markers, and followed the trail that led us back to our big packs, and, without pausing to take a look at the devastation we had wreaked, we headed up into the mountains, anxious to put as much distance as possible between us and our handiwork. Within minutes the place would be crawling with Germans.

We also had to keep our rendezvous with Captain Dudgeon and his men, and, elated by our own success, were anxious to share it with them, at the same time hoping to hear they had fared as well.

We kept marching, higher and higher, heading south for Pontremoli. The weather was still extremely mild, and soon we were sweating from the exertion and the weight of the equipment we were carrying. Our knees and arms were bleeding from the numerous cuts and grazes we had received from frequent falls on the jagged rocks, and we were terribly thirsty; fortunately the mountain streams were plentiful and the water pure. After four hours hard marching, during which I gratefully recalled those pre-dawn clambers up the Jebel, Lieutenant Wedderburn called a halt and we rolled into our sleeping bags, hid in the undergrowth and slept like men satisfied with the knowledge of a good day's work completed.

Our rendezvous was by a small church near a stream below Villafranca, betrween Pontremoli and La Spezia and to reach it we had to leave the cover of the mountains and make for the lower ground where the Germans were likely to be found in strength.

When we reached our map reference, a point on the bank of the stream, we were surprised to find that Captain Dudgeon was not there. He had issued strict orders that no one was to wait more than three nights, and time was not in our favour.

The period of waiting was one of tense and mounting anxiety. We climbed up into the mountains during the day and descended at night to see if the others had turned up. It was a nerve-testing ordeal, because the rendezvous was less isolated than we had been led to believe, and the nearby road was frequently used by German lorries. There were also a number of Italians in the area.

By now, unshaven, hungry and exhausted, we were feeling the strain of the continuous game of hide and seek, and one day, instead of heading for higher ground, we decided to sleep in a ditch not very far up. We rolled into our sleeping bags and immediately fell asleep.

I awoke to the sun shining in my eyes and a heavy boot prodding me in the ribs. I grabbed my Schmeisser, expecting any second to feel the butt end of a German rifle and determined to make a fight of it. But when I looked up I saw the smiling face of a middle-aged Italian peasant farmer.

"Inglesi?" he asked. I thought: so much for the uniforms which are supposed to make us look like Germans. I nodded. He then began speaking in French which Mr Wedderburn understood and which he translated for me. "He's inviting us to follow him to his farmhouse." We followed him to a rambling square-brick house surrounded by primitive barns, and he led us into a big flag-stoned kitchen with beams festooned with hams. Outside we could hear the constant tinkling of cattle bells.

It was the first time for more than a week we had had a roof over our heads, and the smell of cooking made our stomachs rumble. The farmer must have heard the audible signs of hunger for he told his wife to feed us, and she served up great mounds of steaming spaghetti which we washed down with glasses of wine, before mopping our plates with great chunks of still warm bread.

The grizzled farmer watched us, smiling sympathetically at our hunger. Were we parachutists? he asked, and "Tojo", knowing the Italians had surrendered, felt he could trust him and confirmed that we were and that we were looking for our comrades. The old man said he would try and make some enquiries in the village, adding that he would have to be extremely careful as the place was crawling with Germans and he did not want to risk giving us away.

That night we rested in comfort on the straw in one of the barns. After the flinty beds we had become accustomed to it was sheer luxury, and for the first time since we had landed we woke up warm and refreshed, and for a change not chilled to the bone. We spent the next day at the farm, but when there was still no sign of Dudgeon and the others and the farmer had not been able to learn anything in the village, Wedderburn decided we would have to leave.

It was a decision I was glad I had not had to make, although I agreed with the order. They were well-armed, self-reliant and just as able as we were to make their way back. it was not as if we were leaving them in the lurch. Even so, I had a nagging feeling of guilt.

Before heading for the Allied lines we agreed that we should use the remaining explosives on a last train-wrecking expedition. Below the farmhouse we could see the Pontremoli–La Spezia line, and the farmer told us that some trains were still running below the area where we had blocked the tunnel. We decided to leave at midnight, and Wedderburn offered him some of the lira in payment for our food and shelter, but he refused. "Tojo" insisted that he take one of the gold coins, and although it represented a considerable sum to the old man, he said he would never spend it but would keep it as a memento of our stay.

It was our first experience of Italian hospitality and we were to enjoy it time and time again in the future. Homes were opened to us although our hosts were aware of the great risks they ran. If they were caught sheltering Allied troops, particularly paras, they faced execution and the wholesale destruction of their homes, crops and livestock.

Like many British soldiers I had been slightly contemptuous of the Eyties, but my opinion was to undergo a radical transformation. I will never forget their kindness and the fact that I owe my survival to them. I found them incredibly brave and I can only assume that the poor performance of the Italian army was due to the fact that their hearts were not in the cause of Fascism.

It was on 18 September, eleven days after we landed, that we placed our second charges. When we had completed the task we crossed the rails and headed for high ground in readiness for the long haul back to safety, but we had only reached the foothills when we heard the whistle of a train. We paused and listened, waiting for the inevitable.

As an ear-drum-shattering explosion echoed round the hills we burst out laughing, shook hands, and headed south, making for what we believed to be the Allied lines.

We decided to travel by day, confident that we would be safe as long as we kept to the Appennines – the rugged mountain spine of Italy – skirting any towns that might harbour enemy garrisons. It was going to be a cake walk, I told myself. Just a question of heading south by the sun and using the high ground as a friend. We had dared and won, and it was time to go home. But our success did call for some kind of celebration, and I suggested to "Tojo" that we might spend some of our operational money on a few bottles of wine and have a good booze up. He was not very receptive to the idea, reminding me that we should remain fully alert at all times, and that it was our duty to get back as soon as possible. When I suggested that we might try and find "a bit of the other", that was also shot down in flames.

"I don't want any moves in that direction, Tanky. It would be highly dangerous," he admonished.

I consoled myself by thinking it wouldn't be too long before I would be able to let my hair down without any danger of waking and finding myself peering down the barrel of a rifle.

An Autumn sun was blazing from a cloudless sky as we set off south. Buoyed by the success of having knocked out three trains, we became so over-confident with our run of good fortune that we overlooked what had been drummed into us during the survival lessons: never relax. We were abruptly reminded of our flagging vigilance when we stopped for food by the side of a mountain track, ate our corned beef, raisins and cheese with a cuppa, packed our gear and walked straight into the path of two German soldiers. They were only twenty yards away, flanking an Italian who was labouring under the weight of a huge bundle of laundry. It was too late for us to retreat, so we had no alternative but to move forward, bluff our way through and hope our uniforms would pass as German issue.

We got closer and closer and I could sense that our appearance was causing considerable unease among the Germans. Then I saw their faces and knew damned well that my fears weren't groundless. I could see they knew exactly who we were. My finger curled round the trigger of the Schmeisser looped over my shoulder, as I worked out my next move: if they try to stop us I'll cut them down, but I can't hose the bullets or I'll kill the Italian. I'll have to do it in two bursts. I was a highly trained professional killer, and was not in the least perturbed at what I had to do. Members of the SAS are not encouraged to be morbidly introspective over leaving a trail of widows and orphans. We had to be as detached in our killing as a bomber pilot raining death on an unseen target. In fact, our training was concentrated on making us not only efficient but enthusiastic.

The two Jerries looked like base troops, soft and flabby from a life well behind the lines, and it was obvious too that they hadn't the least desire to tangle with two heavily armed, bearded and swarthy men who were walking purposefully and menacingly towards them.

We came abreast of each other and I nodded cheerily as if to assure them that there would be no trouble unless they wanted it. Then we had passed them. I stopped and looked back, and saw they were doing the same. At that point we reached a bend in the track and made off like greyhounds out of their traps, only our hare was the high ground.

There was no doubt in my mind that if there had been a shoot-out we would have emerged unscathed. The two Germans would never have unslung their rifles before we cut them down. They had not been trained for instinctive shooting as we had, but the sound of gunfire and the discovery of two dead men would have resulted in patrols scouring the area, and we would have been forced to revert to the slow torture of night marches.

As we slumped behind the nearest cover Mr Wedderburn said, "Those Germans daren't report us. If they do, what are they going to say? That they let us stroll past without even challenging us?"

We moved slowly but steadily southwards until time became a meaningless blur. Days became weeks and weeks turned into months. There were long periods of discomfort and boredom interspersed with brief hectic moments of excitement. Danger dogged our footsteps and there was an ever-present threat of betrayal. We seldom ventured from the high ground, and we became resourceful travellers, acquiring a tramp's instinct for hospitable stopping places.

When we started we could hardly speak a word of Italian, but during our enforced halts we worked hard on the Italian-English phrase books which we had been supplied with, and as time passed we became fluent in the use of key sentences. When we encountered Italian farmers they were invariably helpful and kind, and at great risk to themselves and their families would provide food and shelter for the night. The only time we encountered hostility was at the house of a priest who could not get rid of us quickly enough. When we were out of luck we ate chestnuts from the trees, and washed them down with pure mountain water, then slept in the scrub cradling each other to keep warm.

As we had no calendar I'm unable to put an exact date to it, but one day as we were approaching a solitary farm outside a small village we were confronted by a huge dog baring lethal-looking yellow teeth, and snarling from deep within its throat. We froze, and as I slipped the catch on my Schmeisser in case he made a leap for my throat, a broad-hipped woman of about thirty emerged from the house, flanked by two farmhands. *"Tedesci?"* (German) she asked. Wedderburn replied, "No, *Inglesi.*" To our immense relief she called the dog off, and came towards us. She had the most beautiful eyes, and I have always had a weakness for eyes.

In a long and faltering conversation we learned that her husband, an officer in the Italian Army, had been killed in the Western Desert and she now ran the farm with her brother and two hired hands. Her brother was now at the bedside of their mother who was seriously ill, and she would have to join him later. As she spoke I kept rummaging through my limited vocabulary for the words I wanted. When I found them I whispered, *"Belle occhi"*, (beautiful eyes), and I could see the compliment pleased her. She smiled and led us to a shed piled high with bales of straw and told us to make ourselves comfortable while she prepared some food. We had had a pretty gruelling day, and after the meal which was washed down with copious glasses of rich red wine, "Tojo" retired to the shed where he stretched himself out and drifted into a deep, snore-punctuated sleep.

I sat by the open door cleaning my guns, which did not need it. It was all a pretence, and I knew it; I was simply waiting for her to make an appearance. I could not forget the look in her eyes. Just before dusk she came out of the house and began to walk towards the village, the dog following closely at her heels. I called out, *"Lupo"*, his name, and he came running towards me. She waited, and when I joined her she smiled and asked me my name. *"Pietro,"* I said – Italian for my family name.

She said hers was Maria, and she pinched my cheek and said, *"Cattivo Pietro,"* (naughty Pietro), and I responded with *"Cattiva Maria,"* and we both started laughing. I pulled her hair, and then we were wrestling in a none-too violent manner, and laughing we tumbled to the ground.

The inevitable happened. It was bound to with a beautiful young woman who had long ago lost her husband, and a red-blooded young man who had been deprived of female company far too long.

Lying on my back, smoking a cigarette and stroking her hair, I thought: what a life for a soldier! A bellyful of grub, some glasses of wine, and a beautiful woman. What more could a man ask for? It had been more poetically expressed by Omar Khayyam centuries earlier, but at the time he was a poet unknown to me. I walked her to the outskirts of the village then made my way back to the shed.

Lieutenant Wedderburn was sitting up in the straw. "Where the hell have you been, Tanky?"

"I went out for a slash, Sir, and I thought I heard voices down the track towards the village so went to investigate."

He relaxed and asked, "Everything all right?"

"Couldn't be better, Sir," I said with feeling, and we settled down for the night. I felt no sense of guilt, and I know Maria didn't.

We were awakened next morning by the sounds of the farm animals. Outside the sun shone in a glorious blue sky, the birds sang, and I felt at peace with the world. Maria called us to come in for breakfast which consisted of hot milk, bread and figs. Her brother came in, and after introductions had been made he informed us that the route we intended to take was clear of Germans. We bade them an affectionate farewell and resumed our trek southwards.

One evening, after a particularly punishing day, we came across a little shanty hut in the mountains on the outskirts of a small village. There were one or two goats foraging for grass, and an old man emerged as we approached. He made us most welcome and pointed to a pile of some kind of weed grass which was lying on the crude table, and said, "Share my food". He spoke a combination of Italian and Brooklyn, explaining that he had spent his formative years in America.

He divided the grass into three portions and poured olive oil over it. If you are hungry enough most things are delicious, and we were ravenous. When our rations were issued no one at base had envisaged us being on the run for so long. I looked upon this grass as one of the survival foods which had been overlooked in the lessons back at base. There was no wine, and the old man, apologising profusely, explained that he could only afford one bottle a week.

Lieutenant Wedderburn pulled out a thick bundle of lira and peeled off several notes and handed them to the old man, and I knew he had decided that the time had come when we should relax over a good drink. The previous night like scores of others we had slept in some bushes cuddled in each others arms to repel the cold, and the strain of such physical discomfort, coupled with the fear of being betrayed or captured, was beginning to show and he clearly thought we were safe enough with the old man to take a risk. I tossed in some more notes, saying, "You had better take a barrow."

When our host returned from the village we settled down to some solid drinking. I remember well into the night trying to sing a dirty song, but failing to get an audience. The old man was fast asleep with his head on the table, and Mr Wedderburn was gravely trying to explain to him the finer points of mountaineering.

In the morning our heads felt like massive weights on our shoulders, but after a solid breakfast of goat's milk and chestnut bread, we felt fit enough to face a long day's haul. We thanked the old boy, who seemed sorry to see us go. He obviously did not have many callers. The survival courses had not included anything about the therapeutic value of getting "stoned", but as we trudged off we both agreed that it should. We felt better than we had done for weeks.

Time began to have little meaning and we walked like automata, indifferent to the weather. Often it poured with rain, and we just kept going, letting our clothes dry on us. As we were always travelling high in the mountains we could keep observation on any enemy movements, and when we saw any Germans near a farm or village we gave them a wide berth. That meant we had to eat what was at hand, and often that was no more than raw chestnuts washed down with water.

One morning we came across some Italian women doing their laundry in a stream outside the village, and as we could not see any Germans we slipped down and asked them if it was safe for us to venture into the village. Before the women had time to answer a German car halted on the road nearby and a young woman pushed us down and quickly covered us with a pile of washing. We could hear German voices and realized two of them had come over to chat with the women, and from the tone of their voices it was obvious they were trying to flirt with them. The laughter of the women was transparently false, and I moved my Schmeisser in readiness to jump up and open fire, but I felt "Tojo's" hand physically restraining me. We lay perfectly still until we heard the car drive off, and the women whispered that it was now safe for us to come out. Mr Wedderburn gave me a mild ticking off and explained that if I had shot the Germans the women would certainly have been hanged. As usual he was right. But I had developed such an intense hatred for them that I often let emotions overrun my common sense. Later in the war I was to kill many Germans in France and Germany. I never took a prisoner – something I'm not too proud of, but they were inhuman bastards who seemed to take a perverse pleasure in killing innocent people as a reprisal for some trivial offence.

Instant death would certainly have been meted out to the old man who gave us a lift in his cart. We were approaching a village when he stopped his cart which was loaded with sheep to warn us that the Germans were there in substantial numbers. I groaned aloud because it meant a wide detour. The old boy must have understood, for he motioned to us to get into the cart and lie down among the sheep. We did so, but the beasts panicked and stamped and trod on us as we trundled through the village. One of them crapped all over my head, and "Tojo" burst out laughing and told me it was lucky.

The next village was completely clear of enemy troops and the locals made a great fuss of us. The village schoolmaster casually remarked that but for our beards he would have taken us for Germans, and that made me think: I had never seen one with a beard, and it was obvious that while we continued to sport them our slate-grey American overalls were no protection at all. The problem was discussed over a bottle of wine, and a barber was promptly summoned. For the first time since we had dropped we enjoyed the luxury of a shave from a barber who really knew his job. I did not know it then but the next time I was to be shaved by someone else was in Brixton Prison.

We had lost all track of time, not knowing which month it was, but each day brought a fresh adventure or a near brush with the enemy. Some days we had food and shelter, others we did not. We had travelled a considerable distance, but our target still seemed a long way away. For the first time we began to have serious doubts about making it.

Mr Wedderburn's feet were very swollen and he was having difficulty in walking. I was feeling far from fit myself, suffering from what was very much like the preliminary symptoms of a severe bout of influenza, but I knew it was not that. I was about to suffer from a recurrence of malaria. Wedderburn was experiencing great pain whenever his feet touched the ground, and I was aching in every limb and shivering so much my teeth rattled like castanets.

When we reached the next village I collapsed against a wall and an Italian came up, warning us that we should move off as the place was crawling with Germans. I turned to "Tojo" and said there was no point in us both being captured and he should carry on alone. He refused even to consider it. We were in it together. The SAS knew no other code.

A group of excited Italians gathered round us and engaged in animated conversation, and the next thing we knew we were smuggled into a big house where we were told we could remain until we were fit again. In the room where I lay on a bed I could hear some Germans talking in the street below, and I was overcome with an urgent need to pass water. I knew I was running a great risk, but I just had to get up and find a toilet. Fortunately, there was a chamber pot under the bed, and as I relieved myself I saw I was passing thick, rust-coloured urine. That's all I bloody well need, I thought. An attack of jaundice as well. I knew the two illnesses often went together.

The village doctor was summoned and I was given a series of injections, and in a short time I was fit enough to get up and peep out of the window. One morning I saw the same doctor who had treated me perform an operation on a sow. After an injection the animal was rolled on her side in readiness for having her ovaries removed. This apparently encouraged the pig to put on weight. The doctor made an incision in her side, then put his hands in and pulled out her entrails. When he found what he was looking for he snipped them off, pushed the entrails back and stitched her up with string before dabbing the wound with some tar. He then slapped her and she trotted off to her trough and started eating. "You've been in good hands, Tanky," I said to myself.

In the evenings we played cards with the family in whose house we were staying, and sometimes a young lad came in to play his guitar and sing. The family would not take a penny from us, and although everyone in the village knew we were there, no one ever thought of betrayal.

I spent hours studying my Italian-English books and was building up a good vocabulary of words and a lot of useful phrases. I did not worry too much about tenses or grammar, relying on gestures and acting to make up for any shortcomings. The family got as much pleasure out of it as I did, for the Italian is flattered when someone takes the trouble to speak his language.

We knew that the villagers were running the same risks as we were, for Hitler had issued a directive that captured SAS men were to be shot and the same punishment would apply to anyone harbouring them. So after three weeks we decided the time had come for us to move on.

The weather changed for the worse and the first snow fell on the mountain peaks and the wind pierced us like a stiletto. We trudged head-down against the buffeting wind and the blinding snowflakes which seemed as big as saucers. By the time we reached Coppito, a small village near L'Aquila, we were in pretty poor shape. Wedderburn's feet had swollen again and now resembled a couple of pumpkins, and my malaria had returned. It was obvious, with the deteriorating weather and our physical condition, that we would have to halt for a while.

Near L'Aquila was a prisoner-of-war camp, and when the Italians surrendered hundreds of Allied POWs had made a break for freedom. The Germans had rounded up most of them, but a considerable number were still at large in the mountains living off the hospitality of the peasant farmers. Among these was Mama Eliseio who had never closed her door to any soldier in need of food and shelter.

We were directed to her home and at our first meeting with the redoubtable Mama Demenica Eliseio the weather changed for the better. It seemed, and turned out to be, a happy portent, for this remarkable woman, a Mother Earth figure, was to play an indispensable part in our lives over the following weeks.

Mama was about fifty, small, plump and swathed from head to toe in heavy black. From her face, wrinkled by unremitting toil and the harsh way of life, beamed dark brown, birdlike eyes. She radiated motherly concern for us. Even now, forty-five years later, I feel a lump in my throat when I think of her.

Her husband had gone to Australia before the war to start a new life for the family, but before they could join him hostilities started and they were stranded in Italy. Mama now ran the farm, three miles from L'Aquila, with the help of Mimino, her 21-year-old son and her lovely daughter Anita, who was one year younger.

When we entered Mama's life she and her family were sharing their meal with three British POWs at an open-air fiesta. It was a Sunday, a feast day, and they were celebrating in the traditional fashion. The soldiers were alarmed at our approach, thinking we were Germans, dressed as we were, and with weapons slung over our shoulders. "Take it easy," said Wedderburn. "We are British Paras on our way to the lines, and we're just about all in." The relieved men shook our hands and one said, "You'll be safe here, this is a good area. The people have been very kind to us. Meet Mama Eliseio."

Her first words were, *"Fame?"* (hungry?)

"Si, molto fame," I replied. *"Stanco e male"* (tired and ill).

She smiled and gestured to us to sit down and eat. We wolfed down the food and wine while Mama and her family nodded approvingly. While we ate the POWs gave us the first up-to-date news we had heard for several weeks. It was not good. The Allied advance had been halted at the River Sangro, and at Cassino about 80 miles away, and it looked as if the stalemate might continue throughout the winter. As the lines were static it would be very difficult to cross them, whereas if they had been fluid we would have been able to get through with comparative ease. The bad news was lessened by the fact that we would have to hole up anyway because we were in no fit state to carry on.

That was all very well, but where would we stay?

Mama did not hesitate: "You must stay with us."

Chapter Seven

Lieutenant Wedderburn and I shared a small hut in the fields which was normally used as a store for hay and firewood, and visited the farmhouse for meals. To reach it we had to make our way through the vineyard, past the two cows, a horse, and squawking chickens, keeping a vigilant eye on the billigerent pig that acted as a watchdog. In the kitchen a huge fire glowed and the spaghetti seemed constantly on the boil.

We realized we were putting the family at grave risk because the farm looked down on the village which was stiff with Germans, but although Mr Wedderburn's feet improved with each day and my malaria was receding, neither of us was fit enough to leave. We thought the risk could be reduced if we could get hold of some civilian clothes and Mimino recommended the local tailor who arrived at the hut and measured us for suits which we paid for with operational money. We had so much money we could afford the best, and when the tailor arrived with the finished product they were very good indeed. They were typical Italian suits, dark pin stripes, and we looked very smart. But more important we looked like locals.

Apart from our binge it was the only money I had used. When I offered any to Mama she waved it aside. "No, no. You may need it later."

Anita complimented us on our appearance, saying, "You look very handsome." I replied, "I will wear it when I marry you." Mama shrewdly intervened, "No, you must wait until the war is over." No doubt every soldier passing through had said the same thing.

The weeks went by and "Tojo" and I became immersed in the lives of the Eliseio family. We helped as best we could around the farm; nobody went short and the war seemed a long way off. I continued to work hard at my Italian and practiced on anyone who was prepared to listen.

Despite the fact that Mimino was only 21 he was nevertheless padrone (head of the house) by virtue of his father's absence, although he had not passed the traditional test which in normal times marked a man's entitlement to be called padrone. He had yet to kill a pig in the time-honoured manner; the swift insertion of a sharp knife behind the ear ensuring a quick and painless death. Mama suddenly decided the time had come for him to perform the ritual, and I felt sorry for him. The pig was the savage brute which kept intruders at bay with his fearful grunts and tusk-like teeth.

I might have had no qualms about killing Germans, but the primitive method of slaughter appalled me and I said, "Let me put a bullet between its eyes." The family were horrified that I should make such a suggestion. "No, no," they chorused. "This is the way it has always been done."

The beast, which weighed a couple of hundredweight, was not going to be led like a lamb to its slaughter, and it needed Mimino, two helpers and myself to get it into the yard. It squealed, snorted and snapped and lashed out with its big trotters. But eventually we got it onto its side and suspended it over two raised planks, its head hanging over a bucket. Now it was the moment of truth for young Mimino, and all eyes were on him as he stood over the pig like a matador about to perform the coup de grace. He placed one hand on one of the ears, eyed the spot carefully, then plunged the long-bladed knife right in up to the hilt. The pig grunted, heaved, and then was quiet. Blood gushed into the bucket. The pig died quickly. Mimino had done his job well and the applause that followed meant he was now a fully fledged padrone. I nodded approvingly; an SAS man could not have killed a German sentry more efficiently.

Mimino was a fine young man, strongly built and very good looking, and he took his initiation with great gravity. He was by nature a quiet man, with no girl friend, and quite abstemious as far as the wine went. In the same unemotional way he accepted the risks he was running in helping us. If we tried to express our gratitude he turned away.

Nothing was wasted from the pig, emphasizing the frugality of their life. The body was shaved and the bristles used in brushes. The blood was used for making a delicious black sausage, and the nails and bones were boiled down to make soap. The intestines were utilized for sausage skins.

That night there were pork chops grilled over an open fire and served with the best wine. Then more pork, and more wine, until late into the night. The women seemed to eat little, hovering over the plates to replenish them when they were empty. They got as much pleasure from that as we did from eating.

By Christmas Eve it had grown bitterly cold and the snow was thick on the ground and falling in penny-sized flakes. But nothing, the war nor the weather, could halt the traditional celebrations. The villagers called on their neighbours, brandishing their best wine and drinking their way through the village, very much in the style of our own first footing at New Year. Quite bold in my civilian suit, I joined the revelry and by midnight I was monumentally drunk and found myself being propelled into the church for Midnight Mass, where blearily I tried to make sense of the book I had been handed. I glanced across the aisle, blinked, then looked again and bitterly regretted my over-indulgence. Just a few feet away were rows of field grey uniforms, stiffly chorusing the Christmas hymns. It had an instantly sobering effect. To leave would have invited discovery so I stayed put, hoping they would not suspect me in my civvy suit and joined in the seasonal devotions as best I could.

When we left the church it was apparent to me that the Germans had also been celebrating for they started to pelt each other with snowballs. A few villagers joined in and I groped in the snow hoping to find a heavy stone I could encase with snow. Fortunately I was unlucky. Then I was violently sick, and as I staggered away I shouted, "God didn't hear you bastards." Either they were too drunk, or my remarks incoherent, for they continued with their snowball fight.

On Christmas Day we noticed a marked increase in German activity in the mountains, and learned that a number of escaped prisoners had been rounded up. Wedderburn and I had a council of war and decided it was better if we split up, and he went to stay at the house of a woman called Philomena on the outskirts of the village while I made off to one of the many grottoes which honeycombed the mountains near the farm.

I arrived there feeling lonely and dispirited, and my mood was not improved when I tumbled onto a pile of straw and dislodged a very fat rat. I stayed there just dozing and trying to study my phrase book in the semi-darkness and hoping it would not be too long before the Germans stopped their manhunt.

About 3 a.m. on the morning of 27 December I was aroused by the sound of rapid firing and the rumble of engines, but I dared not leave the cave to find out what was happening, and it was some time later that Anita told me what had happened. The Germans had raided Philomena's house and captured her and Mr Wedderburn. Philomena was executed for harbouring him. I did not know what had led them to the house, but I did know the time had come for me to leave. I knew that the Germans would find his hand gun and silk map and deduce he was an SAS officer, and that there was a likelihood of other men being in the area. This would certainly lead to a thorough search and I would not risk endangering the Eliseios. Worried as I was about Wedderburn's fate, I knew there was nothing I could do to help him. I had to move and move fast, but my damned malaria was making one of its infuriating appearances; I felt groggy and shivered continuously in my light suit. I knew the British lines were somewhere south of Chieti and they were static, which would make the crossing hellishly difficult, but I had the silk map in my tobacco pouch and the compass in my pipe. I told Mama of my decision and she said, "Stay here. We can hide you. The weather is too bad and you are sick."

I told her my mind was made up, and she said, "All right, but Anita will take you through L'Aquila to where the road leads to Popoli." I embraced Mama and walked arm in arm with Anita through the village like a courting couple, until we reached the Popoli road. I kissed her and she burst into tears and begged me to take care. I trudged along working out in my mind the route I had to take. Once through Popoli I had to turn left towards the Adriatic and Chieti. I walked all day, and as I neared Popoli the skies above were filled with the throaty rumble of aircraft. When I heard the bombs shrieking down I knew it was an RAF raid. A German car skidded to a halt just ahead of me and the occupants – a German and an Italian – jumped out and dived for cover. From the side of the road the German beckoned me to join him, but fuddled by the malaria I replied in English, "Don't worry, they're mine." The German was too preoccupied by the explosions that were tearing the town apart to notice my strange reply, but the Italian did, and when the raid was over he crossed over to where I had taken shelter. Fortunately the German was too busy trying to start the car to pay attention. The Italian asked, "Are you English?" and I was too cold and weary to deny it. "I'll see you here at midnight. Wait for me. I can help," he whispered.

I hung around for the Italian, but as time passed without him appearing I became so cold I feared I would freeze to death unless I kept on the move, so I continued on through the town until I came across a derelict and deserted house by the railway. The windows were boarded up so I knew no one could see inside. I went up the rickety stairs, and in one of the first floor rooms I found a fireplace. I broke up an old chair, ripped up parts of the skirting board, and lit a fire. I was not only shivering from the bitter cold, I was also shaking from malaria. I moved as close to the flames as possible to try and get warm and, desperately tired after my long walk, fell into a deep sleep. I woke with a start. A pain like red hot needles was stabbing my back and there was a smell of burning cloth. My coat was on fire. I ripped it off and beat out the flames, but the damage had been done; there was a large hole in the back. I looked at my wristwatch and saw it was nearly midnight. There was no more wood to burn and if I stayed I would either die of frostbite or malaria. I had no option but to try and make it to Chieti.

The road was bustling with German vehicles and every time one rumbled into view I dived into the ice-covered ditch by the roadside. It was so exhausting that I did not notice I was approaching a village. Jogging along, head down and utterly exhausted, I was stopped in my tracks by a sentry's challenge. A torch was shone into my face blinding me and making it impossible for me to pull my gun out of my pocket. He thrust his rifle at me and asked for my papers. In my crude Italian, assisted by numerous gestures, I spun him a yarn about my cow escaping in the RAF raid on Popoli and I was looking for her. He grunted and motioned me to a nearby hut. Inside was a sergeant and a group of soldiers warming themselves round a glowing fire. I stood beside them and repeated my story about the lost cow, and I thought the sergeant had swallowed it. He may have done, but he was not taking any chances for he sent a soldier off to find a pro-German Italian. As soon as he spoke I knew I had had it; he spoke far too quickly for me to respond. I shrugged my shoulders and said, "*Englander, Englander*," and I found myself staring down the barrels of half-a-dozen rifles. Then I was searched and my pistol and the silk map I had been using were found. There was a marked change in the behaviour of the sergeant. I was a dangerous man disguised as a civilian. The sergeant asked me if I was a parachutist and I gave him my name, rank and number.

The sergeant was a decent man; he let me remain by the fire and later gave me some soup and a cigarette.

Next morning, escorted by an armed guard, I was marched through the village to army headquarters where I was taken before a fairly high-ranking officer. He seemed a pleasant enough old fellow and he sounded quite sympathetic when he said, "You are armed, equipped with a map and dressed in civilian clothes. This is a serious matter. I am required to hand you over to other people." He did not say who the "other people" were, but I had a shrewd idea. I was then taken to an outer office to await their arrival, and about an hour later I heard the sound of a car stopping outside. In the brief period before they made their entrance I tried to work out what to do next; I knew that name, rank and number would not satisfy them. I had to think of something that would result in them treating me as an ordinary prisoner of war. Apart from that, I had to buy time. It had been instilled in me that as a member of the SAS it was my duty if captured to escape. I had no time for further thoughts because the door burst open and two SS men strode in. One wore the death's head insignia of an officer, the other twin lightning flashes on his collar. Neither spoke a word. The leading soldier walked up, raised his right hand and hit me with a pulverising backhander that sent me spinning across the room. Another blow knocked me to the floor, and the officer delivered a brutal kick to my stomach. Then I was dragged to my feet and bundled into the car and driven to the SS headquarters in Popoli. There I was frogmarched through the building into a courtyard and shown a wall pockmarked with bullet holes and stained with blood. There were more stains on the cobbles below. Presumably they wanted to put me in a receptive frame of mind. Then I was marched back to the building and put before another officer who spoke fluent English. "Search him," he snapped. I was stripped naked and forced to undergo a thorough and humiliating examination. They peered into my mouth, tugged at my teeth, peered under my armpits and into every orifice, including my rectum.

"You are not a soldier," said the officer icily. "You are a spy and will be shot if you do not help us. We want to know what you have been doing and where you have been."

Although I was still groggy from the beating I wondered what I could safely tell him without endangering any of my comrades. "I am in the Special Air Service Regiment. I have been on an operation. I went down with malaria and an Italian stole my uniform."

The officer leaned forward and said, "Tell me more about the operation."

I thought I could safely tell him about the trains because he would have heard about it in any case. "It was a train-blowing job north of La Spezia."

He pressed me to tell him more: how many men had been involved, where we had come from and so on. I replied, "I have already given you more information than I am required to do as a prisoner of war," and he said, "So far you have given me no details to prove you are a soldier and not a spy. I say you are a spy. And you will be shot as one."

He gestured with his head for me to be removed, and once again I was hoisted under the armpits and dragged out of the office. I was taken to a part of the building where civilian prisoners were kept and thrown into a cell with nothing but a filthy mattress on the floor. My escort then removed my clothes and shoes and took it in turns to give me a beating. The pain was intense and all I could do was protect the most vulnerable parts of my anatomy and curl up like a foetus. They seemed to be experiencing considerable pleasure from it because they showed no sign of wanting to stop. But eventually they did, and they went out leaving me face downwards on the mattress with split and swollen lips, and a body that was one vast ache. It was then that I vowed I would never take a prisoner.

The beatings were repeated during the next few days, invariably followed by a period of interrogation. Often I was denied any food.

While I was in the cell the RAF decided to pay another call on Popoli. When I heard the drone of engines I dragged myself to the window and through the bars saw the Germans running pell mell for the air raid shelters. Beaten, bruised and bloody, I roared my satisfaction and burst out laughing at the spectacle of the Master Race running like scared kittens.

Unfortunately, a sergeant happened to look up and see me. He stopped, his face contorted with fury, drew his Luger and fired several shots at me. I fell flat on the floor, thinking, "You're a bloody fool, Tanky. You won't get away with this. You shouldn't have laughed."

When the All Clear was sounded, several of them came into the cell and gave me a fearful hiding.

Soon afterwards I had to undergo another interrogation. "Ah," said the English-speaking officer, "the SAS gentleman. You have had plenty of time to consider your plight and realize the serious position you are in."

I nodded.

"It would be of considerable assistance to you if you decided to co-operate. Be sensible. Help us and you help yourself. What we would particularly like to know are details concerning the organization of the SAS."

I stood as much to attention as I was capable of doing. "I'm sorry, but I have nothing further to add."

"Very well," he said. "I do not intend to waste any more time. You will be taken to Aquila camp where the necessary documents will be prepared for your execution."

That night I was handed back my clothes. The pouch and pipe were still in one of the jacket pockets, and although they had found the map, they had not discovered the compass concealed in the stem of the pipe.

Although I faced imminent execution I was quite relieved to be moving to the camp. Not only would the beatings cease, but I would also be in the company of British POWs and while there was life there was hope. Some of my countrymen might be prepared to help me escape.

On arrival at the camp I was put in a dormitory occupied by a considerable number of prisoners. As time was running out for me I immediately started to examine the dormitory looking for a possible escape point.

The dormitory was on the first floor of a building near the gates. Below it were the quarters for captured officers – British, Commonwealth and a few Italian – some offices and ration stores. At the rear was an exercise yard circled by a double barricade of barbed-wire fencing and look-out towers, and the prisoners' cookhouse. The black bread, cabbage and watery soup which formed the prisoners' monotonous diet was fed through the hatch by a guard. It looked very escape-proof, but I spent some time studying the hatch and felt a faint glimmer of hope. It was a desperate plan, but I could not afford to hang around devising a more elaborate escape. I also noticed that a number of Italian women entered and left the camp, possibly washerwomen for the Germans, who were never stopped or hindered in any way.

That evening I told my fellow prisoners how I intended to escape. It caused a certain amount of scornful laughter, but knowing I had nothing to lose they readily agreed to help. I explained that there was a slim chance of getting out dressed as a woman.

One of the lads had a pair of knee-length black woollen socks, picked up while on the run after escaping when Italy surrendered and the guards became very lax, but he had been recaptured by the Germans who feared a guerrilla army would be formed in the mountains. Another chap produced a large square of material in which he kept all his belongings. It made a perfect shawl. We then gathered together all the needles and thread we could find and spent hours sewing up one of the lice-ridden blankets from a bed. When I put it on it made a passable skirt, the hem coming down below my knees. I then rolled up my long johns and put on the black woollen socks. The lads then gave me a shave with the best blade available, and rubbed white plaster from the walls onto my face. They all thought I was mad, but I solemnly pronounced "Who Dares Wins". But when I got into bed in order to snatch some sleep in case an opportunity arose in the morning, I felt far from confident; it seemed so hare-brained.

The next morning one of the chaps reported that the German who collected the rations had gone and the hatch was open. I donned my female attire and one of the boys wrapped his greatcoat around me and when we reached the exercise yard the lads milled around me in a collective wall to obstruct the view of the machine gunners in the look-out towers. We shuffled slowly in the direction of the hatch, and when we reached it I peered through and saw that the store and corridor leading to the offices were empty. "Okay, lads," I muttered, "off we go." Three men in the protective circle lifted me up and heaved me through the hatch, feet first, into the ration store.

Someone called, "Best of luck, Tanky," and once again I was on my own.

The average German is an arrogant sod and I was banking on not being given a second glance if I bumped into one. Not many elderly Italian women retain their beauty, they work too hard for that, but they were Cinderella compared to me. I shuffled down what seemed an endless corridor resisting an overwhelming urge to hurry. The door of an office opened and an orderly clutching a folder of documents nearly bumped into me, but he hurried past without a word or a glance.

I reached the end of the corridor without further incident, pushed open the door and found myself standing outside the main building. Only one more obstacle remained – the perimeter fence gate, some thirty yards away, guarded by two soldiers.

I had walked 300 miles since the tunnel-blowing job, but the distance between me and the gate seemed far longer. I could feel the beads of sweat on my forehead, and I tightened the shawl around my shoulders. I deliberately took my eyes off the rifles slung over their shoulders and focused them on the handle of the gate. I reached the gate with an inner voice whispering: This is too good to last. I waited for the order to halt, but it did not come. I reached out for the handle and characteristically the sentries made no effort to help an old peasant woman. I stepped through and shuffled up the road. I heaved a deep sigh of relief, then the totally unexpected happened, adding a touch of pure farce to what had been a stupid venture. As I was passing some Germans who were waiting for transport, I was conscious of my long johns slowly slipping down below my skirt. The soldiers stared at me with mounting curiosity as I carried on walking while at the same time

76

trying to tug up the wayward underpants. It would be ludicrous, I told myself, having got this far to be caught with my pants down. But the Germans made no attempt to stop me, presumably thinking it was the kind of thing to be expected of a peasant woman. I felt like Old Mother Riley in one of those old pre-war comedy films.

As soon as possible I moved off the road into the fields, moving fast and most unladylike in the direction of Coppito. I was reminded of Christmas Eve when I had joined the Germans in prayers and carols when I caught up with an ancient-looking man with a donkey-drawn cart who invited me to clamber into the back. I could not resist stretching my arms heavenwards and shouting, "He didn't hear you, you bastards." I turned and saw the old man was crossing himself and muttering, "*Povera donna*" (poor woman). He thought I was mad. At a junction in the road I got off, waved him goodbye, and although weakened by hunger and the repeated beatings, I covered the ground to the Eliseio farm in an amazingly short time.

Never able to resist a practical joke, I adjusted my skirt and shawl and hammered on the door. Mimino opened it and looked most concerned at the old woman crouched in front of him. I said in a voice to match my appearance, "*Sono molto vechior fame*" (I am very old and hungry).

I relented when I saw the worried look on the young man's face, and said, "*Sono Pietro in vestita la donna.*" (I am Pietro in a woman's dress.) He called out over his shoulder, "Mamam, Pietro is here, he is still alive." I was pulled inside and deluged with affection from the Eliseios. Soon I was scoffing eggs and drinking glass after glass of wine while I brought them up to date with my adventures. While they looked for some clothing for me I puffed contentedly at a cigarette and relaxed. They pressed me to stay, but I would not hear of it. They had taken too many risks already and I would return to my old hiding place in the grotto.

I made my way up the mountainside and flopped down on the bed of straw. It was like returning home after a long absence.

Chapter Eight

I woke in the night feeling terribly ill. I knew from past experience that I was in for another dose of malaria, but what I did not know was that I was also suffering from pneumonia brought on by exposure and my prison experience. I was a physical wreck, as weak as a kitten and covered with lice. When I did not turn up at the farm Mama was so worried she came up to find out what was wrong. She did what she could for me, but over the next couple of days my condition worsened. My temperature soared, and I became delirious, tossing and turning on the straw-covered floor and groaning incoherently. Mama got hold of a hypodermic syringe and went into Aquila where she managed to buy a quantity of quinine. Not knowing the correct dosage required she erred on the generous side and administered a syringeful, Anita holding me still while she injected my buttocks. She did this repeatedly over the next few days. They fed me with spoonfuls of warm milk with bread in it, but when there was no sign of improvement Mama became seriously alarmed, and a family meeting was called at which it was decided I would have to be moved to a more suitable place than the cave.

Enquiries were made and the engineer of L'Aquila expressed his willingness to take me in. His house was outside the village, but near a road which was being increasingly used by German army vehicles. Somehow or other they managed to get me there without being detected. There I was put to bed and Mama, Anita and the engineer's wife took turns to nurse me and dig the lice out of my back. Gradually I began to recover, and as I got stronger I could see from the window that German troop activity had stepped up considerably. Apparently the village was agog with stories of my escape dressed as a woman, and much as I appreciated their pride in my achievement I knew it could result in my being discovered and the engineer and his family executed. I felt I had to move on again. The engineer and his wife urged me to stay, but I was adamant, and as soon as it was dark I headed for a hut where I had been told a group of escaped POWs were hiding. It was a struggle to reach it high up in the mountains, and by the time I did my chest felt as if it was on fire and sweat was pouring out of me.

When I swung the door open the hut was empty; the POWs had moved on. I started shivering uncontrollably and knew I would never survive the intense cold without food and no means of warming the place. Reluctantly I made my way down again and returned to the engineer's house. I managed to knock before collapsing. The next morning I was moved back to the grotto where once again I became very ill and Mama resumed her injections, still using full doses. Soon I had a continuous ringing in my ears which I thought was the after-effect of the savage beatings, but it was only many years later that I learned it was brought about by the massive doses of quinine.

As my condition worsened I began to think I was going to die; I was an incurable invalid. Mama clearly felt the same way, for one night she came and lit a candle. I told her the Germans might see it and she replied with what sounded like *"Dio e qui"* (God is here). Then she knelt on the hard stony floor and prayed aloud for me. I fell asleep, not a great believer in the force of prayer, and in the morning the fever had abated and as the first fitful rays of sunshine filtered into the cave I knew my cynical disbelief had been badly dented.

The care and kindness continued for several weeks, and by April 1st I felt I had recovered enough strength to resume my hike towards the Allied lines. The invading forces, I learned, were still stalemated in the Chieti area on the Adriatic coast, and that was the way I planned to go. I left to tears, handshakes and cries of *"Buona fortuna"* (good luck), and it did not occur to me that "April Fool's Day" was not a very propitious day to start out.

There were heavy troop concentrations around Popoli and I knew I would have to take the mountain route over the Gran Sasso range. I would have preferred the lower ground where it was warmer, but I was not in a position to choose. In the mountains the snow still lay thick and the going was hard. I trudged on, often knee-deep in the snow and permanently wet. Sometimes, below, I caught a glimpse of Germans digging in and setting up gun emplacements. I had no clear idea of how the war in Italy was progressing, for the last hard news I had been given was that the Germans were holding on to Cassino and Anzio was still a bridgehead.

Still suffering from the after-effects of malaria and pneumonia and often in a semi-delirious state, I was surprised to find I had a companion walking beside me. To this day I do not know whether he existed in the flesh or was merely an hallucination. Whatever the truth, his presence comforted me. He was dressed as I was in a civilian suit and he wore a trilby hat. "*Italiano?*" he asked, and I replied, "*Inglesi*". Falling into step beside me, he said, "Me too."

As we moved higher into the mountains he told me he was a prisoner on the run. I was too ill to indulge in lengthy conversation while my thin suit could not fend off the biting wind and my shoes were leaking and falling apart. Occasionally I heard his voice. "Keep going. Not long now. We'll rest soon."

Without his encouragement I doubt if I could have made it to the village of Rocco where we stumbled across a farm and managed to obtain some food and spend the night sleeping between the oxen who were extremely dirty but warm as hot water bottles. I slept like a child.

When I woke in the morning the stranger had gone. I assumed he had gone on alone thinking he had a better chance of surviving without me. I was still not sure he existed and I dare not ask the family who had sheltered us if he did in case they said I had arrived alone.

The next day, fortified by a breakfast of warm milk and bread, I made good progress and gained the high ground overlooking the Pescara River. The weather seemed milder and for the first time I heard the rumble of British guns pounding the German positions around Chieti. I stopped to take stock of the situation. The only way across the river was over a low dam, and that was guarded by a solitary sentry. I had two choices – I could stay in the mountains and wait for the British, or try to bluff my way across. I chose the latter. I walked down and said, "*Buon Giorno*" to the soldier, but he ignored me completely. Once across I abandoned the main road and made my way through deep country towards the British lines. The only person I encountered was an Italian who offered his services as a guide. He earned money, he said, by smuggling POWs through the German positions. I explained that I had lost all my money, and he shrugged and said it did not matter as he was paid by the British. He took me to a house where four South African pilots were hiding until the Italian decided it was an opportune time to leave. He left me with them saying he would be returning shortly with information about the latest Allied position.

He returned an hour later, a shaken man. "I have just seen the bodies of two men; one a friend who was also a guide, the other a British soldier. They have been shot through the head by the Germans." He then apologized and said he could not help us any more.

The five of us put our heads together and discussed what we should do without a guide. The South Africans decided to return to the mountains and wait for the Allied breakthrough. I had not got this far in order to turn back, and I said I would press on alone.

By now I had lost my compass, but in the dark I could see the muzzle flashes of the British guns and I knew I only had to walk in that direction. As I made my way cautiously through the night, I often heard the sound of German voices and the growl of transport and was forced to make detours. I came to Guardiagrele, which had changed hands several times during the fighting, and decided it was too risky to go through the town, but before I had a chance to skirt it two Germans suddenly emerged from the shadows. Some distance back I had seen several notices in Italian warning that civilians found in a military zone would be shot without warning, so I threw my hands in the air and called out "Englander". I was sick at heart at having to give myself up when the British lines were so close.

The two soldiers escorted me to a front-line position where the Germans were dug in on the side of a steep hill. They looked all in, and every now and again a British shell would smash down sending everyone diving for cover. The captain in charge listened attentively and seemed to accept my story that I was a POW on the run and that an Italian had stolen my uniform when I was ill with malaria. I remained there most of the day under an intense artillery barrage.

In the evening the officer gave orders for me to be taken to a hut some distance off where I would be safer from the British shells which were raining down with devastating regularity. Arrangements would be made to move me back when the situation eased.

The hut was occupied by three Germans who were detailed to keep an eye on me. They were grey-faced and red-eyed and suffering from the effects of having been too long under fire. In the corner of the hut was a large barrel of wine from which they frequently filled their mugs. They invited me to join them and I needed no further persuading. Some hours later I was quite drunk, and fell asleep on the floor. When I awoke the sun's first rays were brightening the sky. I was still half-drunk when a crazy idea came to me. The Germans were sitting round the table half asleep and clearly not fully recovered from the night's carousing. I took off my shoes, leaving one in the middle of the floor where my guards could see it, then I moved to the door and started cleaning the mud off the other one. Obviously I was not going to make a run for it in my bare feet. I took a bearing: slightly south of the sun would be the British lines, only a few kilometres away. Behind me all was quiet. I carefully put down the shoe, then I was off like a hare. I was stumbling, running, falling and scraping my bare feet on the rocky surface. I reached a deep gully and dived into a clump of bushes. I was quite alone. It had to be the middle of no-man's-land. Just then the after-effects of the wine coupled with my weakened state took effect; between the opposing armies I had to attend to what can only be described as a gigantic call of nature. My feet were bleeding and so painful I took off my long johns, split them in two, wrapped them round my feet and struck out for the British lines. Once I had to dive for cover to avoid a German patrol returning from a reconnaissance, but as soon as they had passed I plodded on. Then I was pulled up by a staccato shout of "Halt!". It did not sound like a German command, but neither was it English. "Take it easy, chum," I called out. "I'm English." An enormous Indian soldier emerged from behind a wall and searched me for weapons. I told him I was SAS and returning from an operation. He was convinced and took me to a forward post.

It was the greatest moment in my life. In a short time I was sitting on an ammo box with my back against a tree soaking up the sunshine, a cigarette in one hand and a mug of tea in the other, and all I could say over and over again was, "I've done it, you bastards."

Operation Speedwell was over for me. I had been behind the enemy lines for seven months and emerged a trifle battered but still in one piece.

I was given an air mail letter to write home to my family who must have long since given me up for dead. I even found it in my heart to forgive my father.

"Dear Mum and Dad," I wrote, "With all the luck in the world I got through the enemy lines this morning. I hope you haven't worried too much these last seven months but I have been stuck in the north of Italy. The Jerry took me prisoner in January, but I managed to escape dressed as a woman. He nabbed me again half-way through his lines two nights ago, but I fooled them again and made a run for it without my boots. I shall remember the last three kilometres of my journey for the rest of my life. Well, I can't say much now, so cheerio, your old pal Pete."

As a graphic account of my experiences it was not up to much, but at least the family knew why I hadn't written sooner.

After I handed in the letter for posting I was closely questioned by an officer to make sure I was who I said I was and not a deserter shooting a line. He was a shrewd interrogator and he questioned me about my background and interests. When I mentioned I was keen on soccer and came from Watford he asked, "Where's their ground?"

"Vicarage Road," I replied, "and I bet they're still in the bloody Third Division."

That was good enough for him.

I was given a bath and accorded the honour of sitting down to dinner with the headquarters staff. At SAS headquarters in Prestwick, Scotland, a special order was posted announcing that "Tanky" had made it.

This is an appropriate place to write finis to Speedwell and give an account of what happened to some of the others who took part in it.

Mr Wedderburn escaped from the train which was taking him to a POW camp in Germany but he was recaptured and terribly ill-treated. He later made another unsuccessful attempt to escape and was again badly treated. Much later, in civvy street, forgetful of his asthma, he took an incautious overdose of barbiturates and died. He was a brave determined officer whom I was proud and privileged to have served under.

The Eliseio family went to Australia after the war and Mimino is a successful farmer owning three farms.

It was a considerable time later before I learned from Sergeant Robinson what had happened to the group under Captain Pinckney. Tragically Captain Pinckney was never seen again after they parachuted into Italy. An extensive search was made of the dropping area but there was no trace of him.

Lieutenant Greville Bell was badly injured on landing but when he had recovered he, Sergeant Daniels and Corporal Tomasso succeeded in derailing two trains in tunnels and two more on open lines before making their way back to safety.

Sergeant Robinson, Lance-Sergeant Stokes and Para Curtis also blew a train in a tunnel, and like me were trapped behind enemy lines for a long period. They also experienced great hardships, frequent brushes with Germans, and owed their survival to the hospitality and friendship of numerous Italian familes. They even had the audacity to travel on trains packed with enemy soldiers. They reached the Allied lines on 31 October.

Lance-Sergeant Stokes, whom they had been forced to leave behind with an Italian family because he was too sick to travel, made his way to Rome by cycle when he had recovered. There he worked with a British-organized underground movement before he was captured and sent to Germany where he spent the remainder of the war as a prisoner.

Chapter Nine

When I was sufficiently fit I was moved from Chieti to Bari, and from there I was taken by car to Naples where the Americans flew me to Casablanca, by which time I discovered that the 2nd SAS Regiment had returned to the UK and were based near Prestwick in Scotland and preparing for behind-the-scenes action in France. I was impatient to join them and, apart from having a few old scores to settle with the Germans, I was worried it might all be over before I managed to get away. At Casablanca I just sat around kicking my heels doing nothing and waiting to get to the head of the long queue waiting for transport to Britain. But being a lowly Lance-Corporal I was way down the list. Everyone seemed to have a far more important reason for returning than me.

The motto of the SAS is a constant reminder that its members are meant to employ a marked degree of initiative when the odds are staked against them, so I promoted myself, skilfully altering the flight papers I had been handed, and overnight I became a Lieutenant-Colonel. I went up to the flight shed the next day and had a word with the Master Sergeant in charge of passenger flights, and he gave me the first cancellation on a Liberator heading for a base in Cornwall. He did not question the fact that I was not displaying the rank of a Lieutenant-Colonel, neither did he seem surprised that one so young should have reached such a dizzy height. The SAS were known to be a rum lot.

When I landed on a remote airstrip in Cornwall I was driven to a base nearby where I was medically examined, handed a railway warrant and sent on leave. But I barely had time to become acquainted with old friends in the Black Boy before I received a telegram instructing me to report to the regiment in Scotland – forthwith. After being thoroughly grilled by Major Barkworth, the Intelligence Officer, I was issued with a new uniform and told to resume my leave.

I settled down to enjoy a hero's return, but I was only half way through my leave when I was laid low with malaria and rushed to Hatfield House, the home of the Marquess of Salisbury, which had been converted into a military hospital. There I gazed out of the ward window at the beautiful grounds and the famous oak tree under which the young Elizabeth Tudor was said to have been sitting when she received the news that she was Queen of England.

When I returned home after the Italian Job, the local newspaper carried a story about my escape which, unknown to me, had been picked up by the *Daily Herald* and given a prominent display. The story was read by a young lady, Doris Broome, who wrote to my mother saying how glad she was that there had been a happy ending to my adventures. Mum had received a lot of similar letters but none had impressed her so much as Doris's, so she wrote to her inviting her to visit Garston.

I was out of hospital and happily esconced in my favourite corner in the Black Boy by the time Doris managed to find the time to call at my home. My sister telephoned the pub and said there was a young lady at home who wished to meet me. I sank my pint and hurried home. As soon as I saw her I knew she was the girl for me; not only was she very beautiful, she had such a kind and gentle nature, qualities which nearly five years of war had not managed to blunt. I played the ardent suitor with a vengeance and surprised myself by taking Doris to Cassiobury Park where we sat and listened to the band. Then I took her to a big store in Watford where we had tea to the music of a Palm Court Orchestra, and that night we went to the Black Boy and I vividly recall seeing some RAF lads who had been terribly disfigured, and I thought how lucky I was to have survived my own adventure unscathed. Many, many years were to pass before I realized that not all war wounds are visible.

As my leave drew to an end I told her that I would like to get married next time I was home, and to my delight she readily agreed.

When I arrived at Prestwick I was surprised to see so many fresh faces in the unit, but delighted to be greeted by several old hands.

The following morning I was seen by the Commanding Officer, Lieutenant-Colonel Bill Stirling, brother of the founder of the SAS, who wanted to hear in detail about my adventures in Italy. Throughout my narration I was coughing like a terminal consumptive, and I realized I was still far from being one hundred per cent fit. I dreaded being classified as unfit for duty and I apologized for what I assured him was no more than a heavy cold. He said he hadn't noticed a thing. He was obviously as happy to have me back as I was to be there. In any other outfit my absence would not have been noticed let alone missed, but the SAS was as closely knit and interdependent as the men in a submarine.

I had not long been back when I gained some idea of the cloak and dagger work we would be carrying out well behind enemy lines in France, and I knew it would be some time before the wedding bells would be ringing for Doris and me – the war could well be over before my next leave. I wasn't prepared to wait that long so I requested permission to see Major Farran who listened most sympathetically when I asked for a forty-eight hour pass on compassionate grounds. Doris, I explained, was pregnant and I did not like the idea of the child being fatherless in the event of my being killed in action. The warrant was issued immediately, and I found to my chagrin that I had missed the train to London. Lieutenant Greville Bell promptly requisitioned a motor cycle and drove like a TT rider to beat the train, and I was able to board it some way down the line. (Major Farran always looked bewildered when he saw my son after the war; there was an obvious discrepancy between his age and the story I had spun.)

My unexpected return threw the house into chaos, but I managed to get a special licence and catch a No. 408 bus to Epsom where Doris and I were married the same day in the local Registrar's Office on 1 August, 1944. There were no bells; we were serenaded during the short ceremony by doodle-bugs, and the raid was so intense that Doris's aunt loudly proclaimed that she had had enough and promptly walked out and went home. The Registrar said to me, "You ought to feel honoured," and I replied, "I am, sir," but I should have heard him out before interrupting because he went on to say, "Your name follows that of Lord Brabazon."

The *Watford Observer* reported our wedding under a banner headline: Escape to Happiness.

I got back to Scotland just in time to pack my gear for a move to Salisbury Plain where we lived under canvas. There we underwent extensive training and were briefed on what lay ahead in France. The nature of the operation was so hush-hush that we were confined to base where we became increasingly bored.

For light relief I wrote a skit called "A Night in Sadie's Joint", but when the censor read it he ruled that it was unfit for the gentle ears of the NAAFI girls and the ATS working on the base, and they were forbidden to see it.

Everyone entered into the spirit of the occasion and Major Farran even allowed me and another para to leave the camp and go into Salisbury in the hope of scrounging some costumes from the ENSA unit – dubbed by us Every Night Something Awful – and there we met Googie Withers busy at rehearsals, and she generously let us have everything we wanted.

The show was voted a major success and the evening an unforgettable experience, though the members of ENSA would have been appalled if they had seen us.

The play was about the rivalry between two gangsters who competed for the love of Sadie. I played the guy who gets the girl in the final scene. I had to embrace Sadie, played by a hefty SAS man. Carried away by my debut as playwright and actor I indulged in some unrehearsed burlesque and slipped my hand down Sadie's dress. I promptly collected a haymaking right-hander which sent me sprawling across the stage. The audience roared for more and the curtain came down on a free-for-all between members of the rival gangs which had the audience standing in the aisles shouting encouragement. One soldier was nursing a broken jaw and several others were showing the first traces of black eyes. Some of the ladies from Sadie's establishment looked a trifle battle weary and their costumes were in shreds, but everyone agreed it was better than a night at the opera and audience and players adjourned to the wet canteen which they methodically proceeded to drink dry.

On 9 November, 1944, the *London Gazette* announced that I had been awarded the Military Medal for my exploits in Italy. The citation said: "Throughout the seven months spent behind the enemy lines this NCO displayed the highest courage and determination."

Doris was very proud of me, and I think my father started openly admitting that I was his son.

6. Mimino, Mama and Anita Eliseio (p.66–71).

7.   Major Roy Farran: "a legend among fighting soldiers" (p.39).

Chapter Ten

Operation Wallace, for which we had been selected to take part, was by far the most ambitious task undertaken by the SAS. It was certainly the most imaginative and hazardous. We were to be dropped deep inside the heavily wooded terrain of Central France where we were to carry out mobile guerrilla warfare in which our powerfully armed jeeps were to cause as much chaos and damage as possible to German transport and troops. It was a job I looked forward to with relish. I liked the swashbuckling conception of the operation; ambush the enemy, hit him hard, then disappear at high speed. A sophisticated form of licensed "mugging".

The SAS had operated behind the enemy lines before but never quite on this scale. David Stirling had carried out several successful sorties in the desert and our sabotage work in Italy had piloted a new form of warfare, but they had been strictly one-off pin-prick operations as there was no re-supply from the air, and as soon as our explosives were expended we had to escape to our own lines. As Major Farran put it, "They could be compared to the behaviour of a naughty boy who knocks on perhaps two doors in a street then runs away." This time we were to be supported by the whole weight of Transport Command, and in theory could stay and fight as long as the war lasted and we survived.

On the surface Wallace appeared to the sceptics and military conformists to be a rather haphazard enterprise with more than a flavour of Robin Hood and the Wild West; in fact it was planned with micrometer precision. From D-Day onwards parties had been dropped in to reconnoitre previously selected areas to ascertain if they were suitable as bases where stores could be stockpiled. In this the local Maquis, with their intimate knowledge of the various areas, were of great assistance. By the time the Allied forces had broken clear of the beachhead areas, numerous bases had been established in Brittany, the Forest of Orleans, the Grand Massif, the Forest of Chatillon, and the areas around the Vosges.

Major Farran's squadron, to which I was attached, had its proposed base in the Forest of Chatillon, north of Dijon.

The timing was perfect for Wallace. General Patton's Third Army had broken clear from the Cherbourg Peninsula while Montgomery, acting as the pivot at Caen, was poised to deliver a long-range right hook at the enemy lines. The Germans were falling back presenting us with an essential ingredient for the success of the venture – a fluid front through which our small fast jeeps could infiltrate and cause havoc. Every man was fully aware of the risks and dangers involved, but we were as eager to go as kids embarking on a school outing.

On 19 August our twenty jeeps were driven to an airfield where Dakotas piloted by the British 46th Group were waiting to transport us to France. They were no ordinary jeeps; the upper structure had been removed and each had been specially modified for work in the roughest and toughest conditions. Extra fuel tanks were attached to the side to give them greater range, and there was a larder of tinned food in case anyone was separated from the main group. In addition there were mines, explosives, grenades and a lot of reserve ammunition. Each member of the three-man crew had a colt .45 and a carbine, but the major difference was in our jeeps' awesome fire power. On the driver's side was a single Vickers-K machine gun capable of firing 1300 rounds a minute; a twin Vickers was mounted on the front passenger's side, and another twin Vickers, or a .5 Browning at the rear. The ammunition was a mixture of high explosive, tracer, armour piercing and incendiary. When they all opened fire the effect over a hundred yards was devastating.

I was driver-gunner in the lead jeep of our section. The front passenger seat was occupied by Lieutenant Hugh Gurney, a quietly spoken, tough-as-teak veteran from Cromer, Norfolk; Parachutist Bob Fyffe – nicknamed "Will" after the comedian – was rear gunner and wireless operator.

We landed on the only serviceable strip at Rennes airfield which had just been liberated by the Americans and was pock-marked with bomb craters. Within twenty-four hours of landing the column of jeeps was winding its way along the barely discernible tracks in the forests north of Orleans and heading for our prepared base near Chatillon some 150 miles away. The roads were often deep in mud, and at times we had to skirt round pockets of Germans when we were forced to drive across open country. We passed the occasional village where the excited Maquis greeted us as liberators, the first Allied troops they had seen, and naturally they wanted to celebrate, a temptation that was difficult to resist. They also warned Major Farran in which villages there were German troops.

As long as we kept to the maze of narrow country lanes we were reasonably safe, for the Germans tended to keep to metalled roads. Our first mishap occurred when we were crossing a large road near Montargis and one of the jeeps became separated from the column. Our normal tactic was to choose a point where the main road was crossed by a track, send a patrol jeep ahead and when the all clear was given the column roared across at top speed. The patrol jeep then became tail-end Charlie when the column was safely across. On this occasion, however, the patrol car driven by Sergeant Forster carried straight on and lost contact with the rest of us. Sergeant Forster, realizing his mistake, decided to return to the base in the Forest of Chatillon. On the way he had many exciting adventures, including a collision with a German staff car during which he and his crew killed four high-ranking officers.

We spent the first night concealed in the Forest of Dracy. Although our mission was in its infancy we had already learned that it was best to travel by day as the Germans preferred to move at night because of the continuous straffing and bombing by Allied planes. We made excellent progress and were fifty miles behind the enemy lines and still undetected.

The next morning was largely spent gathering information about enemy movements, and in this respect Captain Ramon Lee, a French officer, proved invaluable. The villagers seemed to sniff us out like dogs scenting a truffle and Ramon was very adept at sifting the genuine from the misleading information.

For the next stage of our journey, Major Farran decided to split the squadron into three sections – eight under him, five under Captain Lee, and the remainder under Lieutenant David Leigh, an officer who had gained considerable experience of jeep operations in the desert. My jeep came under Lieutenant Leigh's command. No one could have a better man in a tight corner, tough, enterprising and totally unflappable.

Major Farran gave orders that each party was to set off at half-hour intervals and follow the same route, although this need not be adhered to if they hit trouble. He emphasised that at this early stage it was preferable to avoid colliding with the enemy. Captain Lee, whose volatile Latin temperament unfortunately overrode the need for caution, accepted some local misinformation that the road ahead was clear and went forward with all the abandon of an old-time cavalry charge, slap into some Germans. He managed to break through, but not before one of his jeeps was knocked out.

Major Farran, not overjoyed at the Frenchman's impetuosity, had no option but to press on and find out what had happened to his unit. An extremely voluble and over-excited local, who saw his role as the spearhead of the newly arrived liberators, jumped on the bonnet of the Major's car and urged him forward. It needed Farran's pistol in his ribs to subdue him, and when he had quietened down he led the unit to a road which wound below a steep cliff. There he jumped down and expressed a desire to go home. Farran also got out, and when he walked round the corner was greeted with a burst of Spandau fire. He dived headfirst into a ditch, and when he peered out he saw about a hundred Germans with horse-drawn vehicles lying in ambush under the trees. It was patently obvious that, though Captain Lee had been able to crash through, there was no chance of his doing so. He had no choice but to withdraw, but not before his men had loosed off a few rounds and set one cart on fire. Retracing his tracks, he left a message with a Frenchman to be passed on to Lieutenant Leigh's unit when it caught up, instructing him to head for a bridge which crossed a river at Merry-sur-Yonne.

We received the message and linked up that night in the Forest of St Jean, over a hundred miles behind the front. There we leaguered for the night near a Priory which had been converted into a farm. In the morning some locals from the village of Château Gerard brought us gifts of flowers, wine, butter and eggs.

Farran expressed his anger with a subdued Ramon by reducing his command to two jeeps, although he still allowed him to lead the column, because of his command of French. Unfortunately a Frenchman of dubious loyalty told Captain Lee that the village of Villaines was clear of the enemy and he ran straight into a group of seasoned Afrika Korps troops. The two jeeps were trapped in a cul-de-sac under heavy fire, and a barrage of grenades. Lieutenant Dodds who was injured when his jeep crashed was taken prisoner along with Corporal Walsh who had remained to give covering fire for Captain Lee and Lieutenant Lord John Manners who managed to break clear.

Major Farran, some distance behind and with no idea what had happened, drove straight into an ambush. As he turned a corner he found himself looking down the muzzle of a seventy-five millimetre gun. He shouted to his driver, Corporal Clarke, to swing into a ditch, but before he could do so two Germans fired the gun at less than ten yards range. They were lucky they were so close for the shell whistled harmlessly over the jeep and exploded on the road behind them. The two leading jeeps careered into a ditch, and as the crews scrambled out they were greeted with long bursts of machine-gun fire. Farran peeped over the top of the ditch and saw the detached spare wheel from one of the jeeps rolling down the road pursued by yelling Germans firing automatic weapons. As they were crawling away from Farran's wrecked jeep, Lieutenant Carpendale, the Signals Officer, remembered he had left his operational maps and codes behind and he went back with Corporal Clarke to retrieve them. When they reached a convenient gully they set up the Bren they had managed to retain and opened fire while Farran ran back through a gauntlet of fire to warn the rest of us who were following up. The Germans were belting down the road firing as they advanced, and one particularly big and blond soldier with a Schmeisser called upon the Major to surrender. Farran fired his carbine and saw him drop. When he reached the two jeeps led by Lieutenant Jim Mackie, he guided him to a convenient lane from where their guns could fire at short range into the German flank. Sergeant-Major Mitchell, with ten men with carbines and four Brens, was posted to the left while Farran held the centre with two more jeeps. Ahead of them, Corporal Clarke was still banging away with his Bren. By now it had developed into a pitched battle with the Germans, who were able to call up mortar and artillery fire. Unwisely the Germans decided to make a charge along both sides of the road, giving the Paras a golden opportunity to open fire at less than fifty yards' range. The Jerries were knocked down like skittles in an alley, with Mackie's troops accounting for a whole platoon which tried to advance across an open field. Despite the heavy casualties, the Germans pressed on with their foolhardy attack and were cut down from all three sides. By now Clarke's Bren had ceased firing and Farran feared he had been captured or killed. Clarkie *had* been captured, but not for long. The German who was leading him to captivity at the muzzle end of his Schmeisser slipped on the river bank and fell into a deep pool, dropping his gun. Clarke made off at full speed and managed to link up with Captain Lee some days later.

Meanwhile, after an hour's hectic fighting, the SAS men were in a desperate situation: the Germans had managed to infiltrate their rear and set up a mortar and machine gun attack. Farran realized that unless

Lieutenant Leigh turned up soon he had no alternative but to withdraw or be wiped out. He also feared that we had been so slow in turning up because we had heard the intense firing and veered off in another direction. So under cover of Lieutenant Mackie's guns he withdrew down a small lane which unfortunately turned out to be a dead-end leading to a mill. The trailer containing the vital wireless equipment was destroyed in the withdrawal, making their plight even worse. But he and his men with the assistance of two locals, M and Mme Defour, managed to make their way over a stream and across country to link up with a narrow rutted lane near the village of Jeux. There a farm labourer warned him that the entire area was crawling with Germans including a Panzer division, fortunately without its armour. Making a wide detour he set off in the direction of the SAS base commanded by Captain Grant Hibbert, but a blaze of headlights which indicated a large enemy convoy forced him to slip into the forest, switch off all lights and wait until the last vehicle had passed. There he wondered what in the name of God had happened to my unit led by Lieutenant Leigh.

We had not, as he imagined, veered off and sought a safer route. When the fighting broke out in Villaines we were more than two miles astern and did not hear a thing. What did arouse my concern was a terrible smell which prompted me to remark to Lieutenant Gurney, "Blimey, there's a broken sewer around here somewhere." He replied with what was almost a dismissive sneer at my gastronomic ignorance, "Tanky, you don't know a good cheese when it's under your nose." I had forgotten he was something of a connoisseur, and that we were passing through an area renowned for its cheese. "Will" Fyffe piped up from the rear, "I'd trade all the cheese in the world for a dram of decent whisky."

Our conversation was an indication of how relaxed we were and how oblivious to what our comrades ahead were being subjected to. Yet behind the badinage we were extremely alert and looking for the slightest sign of danger. As we approached the village we could see no sign of the enemy, then suddenly from the cover of some trees on the side of the road all hell broke loose. The Germans had been lying in wait for us, informed by a collaborator that the squadron was in three sections. In Italy betrayal was virtually unknown, whereas in France it was far from uncommon – for too many the Occupation was more welcomed than resistance, and frequently the Resistance was penetrated by pro-German elements whose role was to betray them and the Allied forces working behind the lines. They were as despised by loyal Frenchmen as they were by us, and when they were caught their countrymen showed no mercy. You had a better chance of survival if you were a German.

My first impression was that we had run into an entire German Division, but once the initial shock was over we hit back with every gun we had in a desperate attempt to make sure our line of withdrawal was not cut. Almost immediately Lieutenant Leigh was shot in the head and dragged clear of the jeep by two of the crew while his driver, Corporal McEachon, continued to fire the Vickers over the steering wheel. At the same time I nipped out of my own jeep to take up position behind a tree to deal with a file of Germans working slowly along our flank. The American carbine I carried was an accurate and lethal weapon and I dropped the three leading Jerries with the same number of rounds. The remainder scampered off, and I pumped more rounds into the bodies of the prostrate Germans just to make sure they would take no further part in the action. When I looked round I saw that McEachon was sprawled across the jeep with blood pumping from a wound in his throat. I waited for a pause in the firing, then sprinted across to his jeep, slung him on my back and carried him to my own vehicle. My tunic was soaked with his blood.

Lieutenant Gurney, who had assumed command now Lieutenant Leigh was wounded, decided there was no hope of forcing our way through the village and he ordered the jeeps to be turned round so that we could escape. We managed to do so but found that one jeep was so badly damaged it would have to be destroyed. This was done with a grenade dropped into the petrol tank.

As we drove off like bats out of hell, "Will" Fyffe leaned across and told me that McEachon was dead. We drove on until we found a ditch by a mill that was one huge blaze of wild flowers, and there we laid him gently on the ground, removed his pay book and dog-tag, hoping the Maquis would find him and give him a decent burial. Although Jerry was in hot pursuit we paused long enough for Lieutenant Gurney to offer up a simple prayer while the rest of us stood heads bowed with our berets in our hands. When we moved off I was too choked to speak, McEachon had been such a close friend.

As we had lost wireless contact with Major Farran, Lieutenant Gurney decided to try and link up with Ramon Lee. By now Lieutenant Leigh was in a very bad way and we decided his only hope of survival was with the Maquis so he was taken at great risk to the home of a well-known member in Eppoise who moved him to a hospital where he died a short time later.

We drove off in the dark and were deluged by a thunderstorm of monsoon dimensions, and soon I was shivering from a bout of malaria. I had suffered an earlier bout for which a French farmer had prescribed a local remedy they called Mirabella, a type of pure spirit made from the fermented juice of small plums. Though it was effective, it had the unfortunate and unwanted effect of making me as tipsy as a sailor on a jaunt ashore, but that was infinitely better than being a burden to my comrades, and in any case a little Dutch courage never did anyone a great deal of harm. Lots of men have distinguished themselves in battle with a mild hangover.

As we entered a village in driving and blinding rain, we were engaged by Germans who were there in some considerable force, and in the pitch darkness and mounting confusion my own jeep and two others got bogged down on the perimeter. One jeep in each unit towed a trailer for additional supplies and equipment, and mine was the unfortunate one. We jumped out and tried to release it in order to facilitate turning the vehicle in the narrow road, but because of the rumble of thunder and the crackle of gunfire we did not hear the order to destroy it and withdraw to the remaining jeeps. It was so dark and the rain so heavy that visibility was down to zero and we decided to hole up outside the village and wait till conditions improved. Unbeknown to us, as the main part of our group pulled out of one end of the village the Germans withdrew from the other and Lieutenant Gurney, Lieutenant Birtwhistle (who had been wounded) and a couple of the lads decided to go back and retrieve two of the abandoned jeeps, leaving behind mine with its trailer.

When dawn broke we managed to contact a civilian, and one Para from Jersey who spoke fluent French was able to discover that the enemy had gone. I thought: What a turn up for the book! We've got to go back and retrieve my jeep which has a wireless we can't work, then set off to find the others who could be anywhere. We managed to get the jeep out without any further trouble and then held a council of war to decide our next move. We devised a simple plan: if we encountered any soft stuff – trucks, staff cars, petrol tankers – we would blast them with every available gun. If we met any armoured units we would drive straight through with our right arms raised in the Nazi salute, and our left crossing ourselves in prayer. It wasn't a counsel of despair, just another example of our almost boyish sense of humour.

The rain stopped and it turned into a beautiful day as we drove at a leisurely pace towards L'Isle-sur-Sereine where we hoped to get a friendly reception and pick up some useful information. It was a largish village, and as we approached it I called to my mates, "Stand by for a ripe load of bleeding trouble." But there was no need for the warning. Men, women and children came streaming towards us waving and cheering and pelting us with flowers. Men tried to greet us with one hand while holding out a bottle with the other. Several of the local Maquis clambered aboard brandishing their guns and clapping us on the back. I was astonished to see people taking photographs. The local leader informed us that a grand meal was being prepared for us; good news that was tempered by the disappointment that he had no information as to the whereabouts of the rest of the column.

As the senior ranker, I had to make a vital decision: press on or remain and enjoy the proffered hospitality. I decided on the latter. Even by peace-time standards the meal was excellent and the wine flowed like tap water. There was more posing for photographs which was followed by long speeches which I could not understand. Not that I cared, for by now I had progressed to the brandy. Glasses were raised in toasts to victory and with the French-speaking Jerseyman acting as interpreter I proposed "Cobblers to the Führer".

Despite having over-indulged in the never-ending supply of wine and brandy, I had enough sense to know that if we overstayed our welcome we would be putting the entire population in jeopardy and I explained that we would have to leave. Our hosts were disappointed but sensible. Whereupon I became quite regimental and insisted that we should leave in style, and in a manner that was a credit to the SAS. I told everyone to stand rigidly to attention by the jeep, and on the order "Mount" to jump smartly in and we would drive off. All went well until the order to "Mount", when I leaped into the jeep and became hopelessly entangled with the twin gear levers and fell into the road on the other side. I tried to regain my composure, but when I remounted I went into reverse, then corrected my mistake and narrowly missed a statue as we sped off at high speed. As we careered out of the village one of the crew remarked, "You made a right fucking mess of that, Tanky."

We pursued an erratic course through the French countryside, and with more luck than judgement managed to contact a 1st SAS officer who directed us to Captain Ramon Lee's position. There we linked up with Lieutenant Gurney and "Will" Fyffe who were overjoyed to see us, although they must have wondered how I managed to drive the jeep in my still half-pissed condition.

When I sobered up Lieutenant Gurney told me he had received orders to take us all back through the lines to Arromanches where we would be shipped to England and dropped back later to rejoin Major Farran. With the aid of an excellent Maquis guide we passed through the enemy lines without mishap, and at Arromanches we boarded a Tank Landing Craft which took us to Southampton from where we were transported to our new headquarters near Watford. Left behind in France was Major Farran and only seven of the twenty jeeps he had started with.

I asked Lieuteant Gurney if there was time for me to visit my mother, and he gave me permission to borrow a jeep and take "Will" with me for a bit of home cooking. But the jeep had to be back by the late afternoon, and we were issued with railway warrants to proceed next morning to our new base. The sight of the heavily armed jeep outside my mother's house caused the whole street to turn out, and "Will" and I were given the VIP treatment. After a brief reunion, we went down to the Black Boy where the landlord, Vic Clapton, refused to let us stand a round. My battledress was still covered with coagulated blood, but surprisingly no one took the slightest notice. When Vic bellowed "Last Orders", a crowd of regulars followed us out to the jeep and started asking questions about the fire power of the Vickers. Instead of a verbal explanation we decided to give them a practical demonstration, and we drove to a piece of waste ground and fired a few bursts. There were loud cheers as we drove off, and "Will" and I agreed that we had been very lucky there wasn't a policeman within earshot. He might have thought the Jerries had landed.

I handed the jeep over to Lieutenant Gurney and borrowed a despatch rider's motor bike to go to Cheam and tell Doris to get the next train to Watford. In the evening we went to the Black Boy where a gypsy woman was telling fortunes. I held out my hand and said, "Tell mine," and as she studied my palm she said, "I can see blood, and there will be more. You will live long, but you will suffer. There is something strange. I cannot tell you any more." I thanked her and offered the customary piece of silver, but she declined. "The blood on your hand is the blood of people who would like to exterminate us. You will always be welcome round my fire."

I was no great believer in the predictions of those who claim to be able to see in the future, and I forgot the gypsy's words and joined "Will" in a rendering of Nellie Dean. We sang all the way home, and that night we enjoyed a really marvellous meal made possible by the neighbours chipping in with some of their rations. I lay staring into the darkness with Doris fast asleep by my side, when suddenly a feeling of apprehension flooded through me. I realized I was looking forward to returning to France and killing more Germans.

Next morning we travelled to Tidworth where we were issued with new uniforms and told we would be taking off for France that night.

At 2 a.m. on 6 September we jumped out of a low-flying Halifax to rejoin Major Farran. Another Halifax had already dropped our jeep. It was a year, almost to the day, since I had parachuted into Italy.

Not only was it freezing cold but it was extremely windy and Fyffe and I drifted into the topmost branches of some very high trees; it took our comrades more than an hour to disentangle us, and then they only managed it with the aid of some ladders borrowed from a nearby farm. Once I was on terra firma I was surprised to see that there were a lot of young boys working in the dropping zone and I was told they were Boy Scouts from Granrupt-les-Bains who had joined the local Maquis. They were living in tents near a mountain stream in a camp that resembled those they set up in peacetime for their annual holiday. I thought to myself: Christ, they're too young to be involved in this kind of thing.

The strong wind had dispersed the containers all over the ground and up in trees, and although everyone worked like fury to collect everything there was still a lot of equipment unrecovered when dawn came. The drop had obviously been heard by the Germans, for at 6.30 a.m. an extremely agitated young lad ran up to Major Farran to warn him that 600 SS troops, four armoured cars, six troop-carriers and twenty staff cars, were approaching the dropping zone. They were clearly intent on wiping us out.

The field into which we had parachuted was encircled by woods, and the only way out was by a lane which led to Granrupt which had a heavy garrison. The Maquis and the scouts disappeared into the forest while Major Farran tried to work out how he could get his men and jeeps to safety. Just then heavy small arms fire broke out in the woods on the eastern side of the dropping area which was still well marked by the parachutes suspended from the branches, and the Maquis retreat became a disorderly race for survival.

Major Farran led the jeeps round and round the field, as he put it, "like a string of ponies", in a desperate search for a way out. A deep stream ran through the forest, but even the tough jeeps could not have forded it and Farran put the jeeps in a hull down position behind a small ridge in the middle of the field in what we feared was going to be a mechanised version of Custer's Last Stand. Then he spotted an area of young saplings protected by a heavy wire fence at the south-west corner of the field. He bellowed his intentions and we roared at full speed for the fence where we got out and cut it before crashing through the saplings like elephants on the rampage. Despite the heavy gunfire I found it very exhilarating and I was wrestling with the steering wheel of the jeep which was bouncing like a bucking bronco. I couldn't refrain from roaring out, "Whoah! Welcome back to bloody France."

We drove as fast as we dared without lights through a cotton wool mist, the engines growling and protesting as we crashed through the undergrowth and weaved our way round trees. Gradually the woods thinned out and we crossed a field which led to the main road. Four miles away we could hear the rattle of gunfire as the Germans hunted down the Maquis among whom were the kids I had been so worried about.

Once we were out of danger Major Farran also became very concerned about the fate of the Boy Scouts who had helped us in the dropping zone, and he sent Lieutenant Gurney with our jeep and a second commanded by Sergeant Vickers to attack the enemy's immediate rear in an attempt to halt their pursuit.

Sergeant Vickers put his jeep in an ambush position by the side of the road and I drove our jeep towards a headquarters truck which was surrounded by several officers and a number of soldiers. They were caught completely by surprise and I slewed the jeep round so that Lieutenant Gurney and I could engage them with the two front guns. In sustained bursts we cut them down like ripe corn with tracers and incendiary bullets. I spotted an SS officer crawling towards us, his face contorted with pain and screaming at the top of his voice. He had obviously been hit by an incendiary bullet and was in indescribable agony as it burned inside him. He ceased screaming and I heard him call "Mother, Mother" in German. I trained the Vickers on him, and the force of the bullets moved him backwards. At least I had put him out of his agony. I looked at my hands and said to "Will", "The gypsy was right." We killed several more and knocked out the headquarters truck before pulling back. Incredibly, as soon as we stopped firing the birds began to sing.

Meanwhile Sergeant Vickers had blasted two staff cars killing the Colonel and second-in-command of the attacking force.

When we rejoined Major Farran, he decided it was best to lie low for a while and we found a hideaway in a dense patch of woodland where we had a meal of raw eggs and biscuits, and I promptly fell alseep over the steering wheel. I liked to have my hands near my gun. Shortly afterwards we enjoyed a much better meal which included freshly baked bread and vegetables delivered by the patron of the village of Passavant where to our astonishment Lieutenant Carpendale had an aunt. The patron also managed to get two French mechanics to drive out on a motor cycle to repair a burnt-out clutch. They were convulsed with laughter at the thought of repairing it with German spare parts.

Carpendale unfortunately had missed what to us was a slap-up banquet, for he had been sent on a separate three-day patrol which had reaped a rich dividend. The object of his patrol was to reconnoitre the Epinal area with a view to finding some means of crossing the Moselle; also to shoot up easy targets if the opportunity arose. He reported back with the news that he had destroyed a large lorry, attacked and destroyed German billets west of Remiremont, and killed twenty Germans who were shaving in a farm yard. But his biggest coup was the destruction of an anti-tank gun with small arms fire. Less encouraging was his news that two thousand extra troops had been drafted to the Moselle Line which meant General Patton was in for a considerable shock. Civilians in the area were also being rounded up and forced to build defences in the vicinity of Le Thillot and Rupt-sur-Moselle.

Understandably we were very concerned about the Granrupt Maquis, especially the boys, but it was not until the war was over that we learned that four of the lads had been killed by gunfire and the local priests – Abbé Mathes and Abbé Masson – both members of the Maquis, had been executed. The Germans had forced the majority of the Maquis to give themselves up under threat of killing all the villagers before razing it to the ground. More than two hundred were deported to concentration camps where 116 of the boys perished.

Soon afterwards we were sent out on a mine-laying expedition which accounted for three trucks. It was very hard going and the jeeps, tough as they were, began to suffer. The jeep which towed a trailer containing explosives and mortar bombs had broken down with a burnt-out clutch, but the two mechanics readily came to our assistance again.

Major Farran decided that we should now move to a new base at Claircy, three miles further east and in a denser part of the forest. The move was precipitated by the news that truck-loads of Germans were enquiring at all the villages in the area about the whereabouts of the parachutists, and there was a report that more of the Maquis at Granrupt had been betrayed.

An hour after settling in at our new base we heard women screaming which could only mean one thing: the Germans were beating the forest. A foot patrol was sent out to find out what was happening, and they returned to say that the village of Hennezel was burning and the Germans were in force along the line of the road running through the forest. Major Farran decided to remain where we were on the assumption that they would call a halt to their search when it got dark. Our problem was that we could not remain too long ourselves as Major Farran had arranged for a re-supply drop to be made at 11 o'clock, the last we would get before we moved on to the Belfort Gap. There was no question of abandoning it because we were low on petrol, enough for just thirty miles and there was little chance of another opportunity. It was extremely risky with the enemy only three miles from the dropping zone and within view of the Belfort road, but it was a risk that had to be taken; without fresh supplies we were a spent force.

Lieutenant Mackie's troop was detailed to guard the crossing in the village near the DZ while the rest of us formed the pick-up party. Dead on time, six planes came in low and dropped two jeeps and their crews: Lieutenant Birtwhistle, Corporals Clarke and Scott, and Paras Roche, Knock and Kirkman. (Kirkman was adrift for some days as he landed three miles away on a main road.)

A new clutch was also dropped, but what delighted us most were the "goodies" which arrived in the enormous number of containers. In addition to plenty of food there was a NAAFI container with cigarettes, newspapers, clean clothes, and some whisky. Major Farran said it was just like Christmas Day, for the Quartermaster had also provided a special gift pannier. It was a pretty tight drop because dawn was just breaking by the time we had collected everything, but the supplies were a great boost to our morale. Our greatest satisfaction though was that there had been no casualties. That was always our biggest worry with a drop.

At an earlier one, two additional drivers had been parachuted in – Corporal West and Para Kalkstein, a small Polish Jew who had been on several missions. West landed safely, but there was no sign of the Pole and it was not until daylight that his body was found with an unopened parachute beneath some trees. He looked as if he was asleep. Some acid from the Halifax's batteries had leaked out onto the floor of the aircraft, and some had eaten through the static line of his parachute which had parted when he jumped. We buried him with full military honours in a small churchyard, and everyone hoped that the prayers which were spoken were in keeping with his faith.

We moved off as soon as the supplies had been loaded and drove in column across the Saône towards the south-west. The enemy were everywhere, for we were nearing the point where the lines of the German retreat converged. Whenever we crossed a road we paused just long enough to lay mines. On one occasion the explosion was so quick we feared the layers had blown themselves up and Major Farran sent the Medical Officer back to treat the injured. Happily the only casualties were some German staff officers whose car had detonated one of the mines minutes after it had been laid.

We pressed on slowly but steadily, and we reached the leaguer area before darkness. We estimated we were somewhere between Vesoul and Luxeuil-les-Bains, and it was far from ideal from the point of concealment. The only wood in the area was barely two miles square and the whole place was crawling with Germans. A worried Major Farran strolled over to our jeep and told Lieutenant Gurney to go out on patrol and see what there was to the west. I was not too pleased with the performance of the Lieutenant's twin-Vickers and I asked Sergeant Young if I could borrow one from his jeep. "All right, Tanky, but I've just cleaned and oiled them, so make bloody sure you return them in the same condition." In the SAS, weapons were much prized personal possessions, and borrowing one was akin to sharing the favours of a girl friend.

We set off along a narrow forest track leading to the main road, and we had only travelled half a mile when we saw a large staff car with a pennant fluttering on the bonnet heading straight for us. Although the Major had given Lieutenant Gurney strict instructions not to shoot up anything on the edges of the forest, it was a target too good to miss.

"There must be a very high ranking officer in it. We'll have it," said Mr Gurney.

I slipped out of the driving seat in order to operate the gun over

103

a wider arc and I heard "Will" mutter, "At least it isn't raining," a remark I found so baffling that I retorted, "What's the fucking weather got to do with knocking off a few Krauts?" I realized later that "Will" was only expressing in his own inimitable manner how foolhardy he thought it was.

The staff car was only 100 yards away when we hosed it with our Vickers. I saw the windscreen shatter into thousands of fragments, and the car completed the perfect circle before crashing into a ditch with dark smoke billowing from it. Through the smoke I could see the black-uniformed officer waving his hand at the window as if appealing for help. I fired a short burst at him and the vehicle erupted in a gout of scarlet flame.

Unfortunately, our action stirred up a real hornets' nest and German troops and two half-tracks were despatched from the nearby village to shoot us up. We saw the half-tracks roaring towards us, and as there was neither the time nor the space to turn I had to drive in reverse all the way back to the leaguer.

Major Farran had just ordered the wireless to be set up for the evening call to London when a fusillade of Spandau bullets began cutting through the branches of the trees. He was understandably furious with Lieutenant Gurney for leading the enemy to our hideout, but his anger might have been muted if he had known the importance of the target, for the French later reported that the shot-up car contained a general. For our sins we were ordered to remain and hold off any pursuers while the rest of the squadron beat a hasty retreat.

Major Farran led the column, and the tail end had just managed to make cover when the three leading jeeps got stuck in the soft mud and refused to budge. As some men cut down branches and bushes to cover the vehicles, others got to work with spades covering up the wheel marks.

Looking back, I realize how gentle our punishment had been. If Major Farran had known the full story of our patrol we might not have got off so lightly. What he did not know was this:

Soon after we had been sent on patrol Sergeant Young and his driver, Parachutist Blunston, were sent out to see if they could find some much needed water. As they drove as slowly and as silently as possible, they heard the sound of intensive firing and they were confronted with the spectacle of my reversing jeep being pursued by the two half-tracks. Sergeant Young attempted to make his way back to the squadron but found himself sandwiched between us and the pursuing Germans. In the gathering dusk he caught a momentary glimpse of my jeep which I had just pulled off the track. "Will" Fyffe, expecting a German vehicle and unable to identify Sergeant Young's jeep in the dark, opened fire with the Vickers the Sergeant had loaned us.

Sergeant Young and his driver dived for cover as the bullets whistled and whined over their heads. Blunston shouted, "It's all right, it's one of ours," to which a furious Young retorted, "I know that, but do they know we're one of theirs?"

As soon as our tracers lit up the jeep we realized our error and stopped firing. We felt awful, and "Will" was almost in tears, certain that he had killed two of our own lads.

Mercifully the only injury was to Sergeant Young's hip which was almost paralysed when he landed on the butt of his revolver when baling out of the jeep. Incredibly he restrained his anger and said, "Tanky, you make bloody sure those guns are cleaned and oiled before you hand them back."

Fortunately, the half-tracks decided that discretion was the better part of valour and did not continue their pursuit, fearing that once they entered the forest they would drive straight into an ambush.

When we realized this, we joined up with the rest of the squadron.

We holed up in the forest, hardly daring to breathe as we listened to the rumble of German transport on the road less than a hundred yards away from our new hideout. Then, to add to our discomfort, it started to pour with rain and, as we huddled together in the squelchy mud, we could plainly hear military policemen shouting to the German drivers to keep a sharp look out for "terrorists".

At first light we dug out the stranded jeeps and manhandled them down the track, not daring to start the engines until we were well clear of the woods and able to head for a denser sanctuary north of Luxeuil-les-Bains. With the co-operation of a small band of Maquis we were able to carry out a number of night skirmishes which were too repetitive in their nature to merit individual mention, except for one which was particularly tragic for me and "Will".

Two jeeps under Lieutenant Gurney were detailed to take part in an operation in the vicinity of the village of Velorcey, and when we set off I had a gut feeling that things were not going to turn out right. As I drove I could see the steeple of a village church and I commented that at least there was somewhere for the French to pray for us. "Will", cynical as ever, quipped that there would also be some who were praying for the Germans. It was an indication of his concern, for by now we had learned the hard way that not all Frenchmen were patriots. A dog could be heard barking loudly in the distance and "Will" flippantly asked Hugh Gurney what it was saying as he did not speak French. I suspected that the joke was aimed at stifling his mounting concern. Like me, some inner sense had warned him that danger lay ahead. We cruised round the perimeter of the village which seemed totally deserted, as if everyone had been warned to stay indoors. The sun had set, suffusing the sky with a rose-tinted glow. Hugh Gurney surveyed the area and selected a suitable spot for the two jeeps to ambush anything that approached from either direction. Our nerve ends were frayed and jagged as the minutes ticked away; something was sure to pass but we had no idea what. It could be a vulnerable lorry or an armoured car. It was so quiet we could hear the drone of insects in the nearby fields and the last calls of the birds before they settled down for the night. Suddenly I stiffened as my ears picked up the faint grumble of engines.

"Stand by," whispered Mr Gurney, and I replied in a matching tone, "Let's hope the first one is a petrol tanker." The six still-as-statues men peered over the sights of their guns into the gathering gloom. With what appeared to be slow motion a convoy of vehicles appeared. The lead lorry seemed like some prehistoric monster as it loomed out of the darkness, and it was only ten yards away when we opened up and pounded it with mixed tracer and incendiary bullets. Any moment we expected to see it slither across the road and grind to a halt. Then suddenly there was a deafening whoosh and the vehicle disappeared in an inferno of flame that scorched our faces and lit up the darkened road. The explosion was so violent I was blown out of the jeep.

"Christ, it's full of explosives," I said, and as I spoke I felt a sharp stab of pain in my left eye. Instinctively my hand went up, and when I looked it was covered with blood. Although concussed I managed to haul myself back into the jeep. The Germans, despite the surprise, were remarkably disciplined and as a whistle shrilled we heard the pounding of boots on the road, followed by a furious burst of firing.

"Let's get out – quick," shouted Mr Gurney, and he waved to the other jeep to pull out. Blinded with blood, I struggled with the gear lever and realized our jeep was out of action. Hugh Gurney roared, "Out. Let's make a run for it."

I staggered away, falling and picking myself up until I was overcome with a sudden fit of nausea. My stomach seemed to split in two, I was violently sick and fell face first into my own vomit. Lieutenant Gurney, with no thought for his own safety, ran back to help me, and as he did so was hit by a hail of fire. I looked up, and through my blurred vision saw the Germans steadily advancing and firing automatic weapons as they came. It was obvious to me that Hugh was dead, and "Will" who had run ahead turned back to help me. He dragged me to the other jeep which was reversing and I was hauled inboard. All I could think of was Mr Gurney, a very fine and brave officer who had been more than a friend to me.

The jeep thrashed down the track and I passed out and fell over the side landing in some heavy scrub at the roadside. "Will", hanging on for dear life saw me disappear and shouted, "Stop, Tanky's overboard." The jeep shuddered to a halt and I was yanked back like a sack of potatoes. The jeep then raced in top gear to the forest rendezvous north of Luxeuil-les-Bains.

On the way I drifted dreamlike into a semi-coma in which I found myself playing cards, and for once had a very good hand. As we broke into the covering protection of the forest at the point where the narrow track bisected a wider path which was used to haul timber, I ordered the jeep to stop. Slipping the safety catch on my .45 colt I jumped down and staggered to the intersection where I roared, "You bastards, you've killed my officer, and I'm going to blow your fucking heads off." My comrades led me back to the jeep, and by the time we reached base my head had cleared.

There Dr Pete Milne, our Medical Officer, extracted a sliver of metal from my eye. Another fragment had slammed through the socket and imbedded itself deep in the bone on the side; a fraction of an inch deeper and it would have killed me. It was too deep for the MO with his primitive equipment to attempt to remove, and he left it where it was. (Two years later a painful septic lump developed in the corner of the eye, and one morning while washing the towel snagged on the piece of shrapnel and I pulled it out.)

Despite vehement objections from the Germans, the villagers gave Mr Gurney a decent burial in the churchyard at Velorcey.

At the same time, Lieutenant Birtwhistle led a raid on a horse-drawn column, setting five carts on fire and killing a number of Germans. Jim Mackie had even better fortune in a shoot out near Luxeuil.

By now, enemy activity was so intense we had no option but to retreat deeper into the forest from where in the distance we could hear the drumbeats of the American guns. We carefully camouflaged the jeeps under layers of branches and shrubs and dug deep foxholes for ourselves. At the same time, a German battery of eighty-eight millimetre guns began to dig in less than a hundred yards from our position.

For three nerve-wracking days and nights we sat in our funk holes listening to the voices of the German gunners. We were so jittery the sound of wild pigs rummaging in the undergrowth was enough to make us sweat. Just to make things a little more uncomfortable it began to bucket down, and we were soon drenched to the skin and ankle deep in slime. My heavily bandaged eye was giving me hell, and to add a little gilt to the gingerbread I developed an awful bout of malaria which I fought off with long swigs of Mirabella. It eased the fever but made me extremely light-headed, which was no condition to be in, considering our plight.

Major Farran, realizing how desperate our position was, sent out patrols in the hope of making contact with the Americans, but they returned and reported failure, although they did manage to mine several sections of road. Penned in as we were, the problem of sanitation was acute and the area quickly became one vast latrine. As the Germans were forced to do the same, the stench was over-powering.

There was an almost indiscernible track leading from our camp to the German artillery's position, and, despite the risk, Major Farran insisted on posting a sentry half-way along it in case the enemy came our way. Although badly injured and groggy with fever, I still had to take my turn. In the middle of one stint I heard a loud bang which literally made my hair stand on end. I backed against a tree to protect my back, and with my one good eye I peered into the gloom ahead. When I was relieved my nerves were as taut as an over-stretched violin string, and I asked, "What the hell was that big bang?" My relief grinned in the darkness and said, "Some silly sod was warming up a tin of bacon on the stove and he forgot to pierce it." I was so tensed up I replied, "Someone should bend a carbine over the stupid bastard's head."

I was trying to doze off in the jeep, feeling bloody awful with malaria and my eye and half-pissed on the Mirabella, when Major Farran came up and told me to prepare some derailing charges as a German self-propelled gun had been spotted travelling along a stretch of nearby railway and firing at the approaching Americans. He and I, together with the Para who had scared me stiff with the exploding tin of bacon, were to crawl through the enemy gun position to lay the

108

charges. I did not feel too confident that we should undertake this very dodgy job with a man who could not be entrusted with a tin of bacon. Maybe Major Farran suffering the same misgivings, for he insisted on doing the job himself.

When we got back to our primitive base the American artillery opened up a counter-barrage on the dug-in German guns and several salvoes landed perilously close to our foxholes. Fortunately the Germans decided to withdraw, and fortified by my malaria "medicine" I fell into a deep sleep.

Early next morning a party of Maquis arrived leading an American armoured car. We were so overjoyed to see the Americans we really did dance for joy. The operation was over and not a minute too soon, for we were all suffering tremendous strain from the constant vigil.

To our surprise, we found our rescuers were from the 7th Army and not the 3rd as we had expected, but that in no way diminished the enthusiasm of our welcome. We piled our equipment into the jeeps and set off on a leisurely drive across France towards Paris. Wallace had been an overwhelming success during which we had destroyed ninety-five enemy vehicles, killed and wounded a lot of soldiers and several senior officers. Apart from the brief interlude at home, I had been behind the enemy lines almost a month to the day.

On our way to Paris which had been liberated by the Americans, we had the satisfaction of passing the charred skeletons of many of the vehicles we had destroyed, and when we reached the capital Major Farran allowed us a week's leave, although strictly speaking it was out of bounds to British troops. We stayed in the best hotels and dined in the finest restaurants, as we were loaded with operational money. The jeep containing our funds had been "written off" in action, and as we carried no paymaster there was no way it could be challenged.

After an enjoyable jaunt in Gay Paree, we drove to Arromanches and boarded a landing craft which took us home. We had left behind in France many comrades, and this lessened our sense of joy when we once again set foot on British soil. We missed them all, but the death of Lieutenant Michael Pinci, a charming and daring extrovert young officer, was particularly poignant because he was inadvertently killed by our own side.

His father, Count Pinci, was a most outstanding man and his son followed in his footsteps. The Count joined the Scots Guards at the outbreak of the First War and later transferred to the Royal Flying Corps where he distinguished himself as a fighter pilot until he was discharged at the end of hostilities with the rank of Squadron Leader.

At the outbreak of the Second War he served as a Wing Commander in the RAF. His many decorations included the DSO, MC, the Legion d'Honneur, the Military Medal and the Croix de Guerre.

Michael, who was born at Pangbourne, Berkshire in 1923, was educated at Lambrook Preparatory School and Sherborne School, but he was equally at home in France where he spent much of his youth. He was turned down for the RAF because of his poor eyesight, but was accepted into the Royal Artillery and later joined the SAS.

On D-Day minus one he was a member of Captain Hibbert's group which was dropped behind the enemy lines to pave the way for Major Farran's squadron. His fluent French made him the ideal person to act as the liaison man between the SAS and the Maquis. He also took part in numerous actions alongside us in which he displayed remarkable courage. Somehow or other he managed to acquire his own Lancia from the family home in France which, unfortunately at a distance, resembled a German car. On 11 September, 1944, while driving along the Dijon-Chaumont road, an Allied fighter straffed it, instantly killing Michael. His body was buried in the local cemetery, but later removed to the Paris Military Cemetery.

Chapter Eleven

After a thoroughly enjoyable twenty-eight days leave, the Squadron was brought up to strength and we started another hectic bout of specialized training that soon had us wondering if we would see the war through to its final conclusion. It was so hare-brained in its conception that I for one was convinced there was no chance of adding a third stripe to the two I now sported on my battle-dress. We had been cast in the role of guinea pigs. If we had been in the Royal Navy instead of the SAS the task for which we were preparing would have fitted into the category of being expected to go down with all guns blazing. I wasn't particularly enamoured with the prospect; the bell had sounded for the last round and I wanted to be on my feet when it clanged again, signalling the end of the fight. As it was, it seemed as if some Top Brass had already allocated us plots in a military cemetery.

It was the time of the mid-December counter-attack by the Germans in the Ardennes, ironically spearheaded by the Wehrmacht's equivalent of the SAS and led by the tenacious Otto Skorzeny, the parachutist who rescued Mussolini from his mountain prison, Gran Sasso. To prove it was not a one-off venture he also kidnapped Admiral Horthy, son of the Hungarian regent. He was very adept at doing what the SAS did: he infiltrated specially selected soldiers behind the Allied lines, and recruited a Germanic version of Kamikazi pilots, men prepared to pilot flying bombs to knock out vital targets. The Americans were falling back and the powerfully armed and extremely mobile King Tiger tanks were punching big holes in the American front lines. Heavy rain and cloying ground mists had grounded the Allied bombers and rocket-firing fighters, and the Germans grasped the opportunity for a counter-attack. The enemy's surprise counter-punch had caught the Americans off balance and set the alarm bells ringing in Eisenhower's headquarters. No one doubted that it was only a temporary setback. In the east the Germans were retreating before the seemingly invincible Russians and the Allied supremacy in men and equipment was bound to bring the Fatherland to its knees. Nevertheless, the heavy toll being exacted by the V and VI Panzer units was something that had to be stopped, and it was this which had brought about our period of hectic training; we were to be flown into the Ardennes where from ditches we were to knock out the Tigers.

The weapon selected was the bazooka, a cumbersome and somewhat crude piece of equipment, and very early on in our training we agreed that it was not the ideal contraption with which to challenge the Panzers. Too many of the missiles bounced off the trees which were supposed to represent enemy tanks and failed to explode. What was worse, once fired, your position was fully exposed to immediate counter-attack. It promised us as much future as Skorzeny's "suicide pilots".

One evening in a pub near our training base, I decided to make my Will on the sheet thoughtfully provided in the Army paybook. "Will" Fyffe, who was sitting opposite me, wondered if I had been keeping something from him and hoarded away a little nest egg, for he asked if I had much to leave. "Nothing," I replied, "but I want to make sure Doris gets it." "Will" downed his pint and remained silent, clearly bewildered by my perverse logic. We had all shown we were prepared to tackle any job no matter how hazardous, and no one was going to admit openly that this operation was a little too one-sided, and so any apprehension was passed off as a joke. As one of my mates said, "We're being sent to the Russian Front. That's why we're learning Russian roulette." Fortunately for us, the weather dramatically improved and the Top Brass cancelled the operation, preferring to leave the task to the Allied Air Forces who made a much better job of it than we could have hoped to do. We still went to Germany though, and took part in the race for Berlin.

By March, 1945, the last nails were being hammered into the coffin of Nazi Germany, and on the night of the 23rd Montgomery's 21st Army Corps crossed the Rhine at four points and fanned out into the heart of the Ruhr. We were in the vanguard and I personally experienced a sense of elation at standing on the home soil of those who had killed so many of my pals, and not all in battle. Many had been executed without mercy or trial. Our job was to penetrate the German fluid line, locate the eighty-eight millimetre gun emplacements which were causing such havoc to our armour, and knock them out. Although the writing was on the wall, I was amazed at the fanaticism with which so many Germans fought; it seemed as if they still clung to the vague hope that the Führer would perform some last-minute miracle and turn the tables. Although I had a healthy respect for their martial qualities, their discipline and courage, I was amazed they were prepared to die for such an evil cause, for by then they must have known about the atrocities committed in the name of National Socialism and the deliberate extermination of the Jews.

Although we had not been trained for it, we found ourselves engaged in a lot of street-to-street and house-to-house fighting, and I built up an unstinting admiration for the poor bloody infantry who took the brunt of it. It was a form of warfare totally different to anything we had experienced. We had become accustomed to a highly mobile hit-and-run style of fighting, and this duck-and-dodge stuff had nothing at all romantic or noble about it. We had to flush out the enemy who were holed up like trapped rats in the rubble of houses which were pockmarked with shell and bullet holes. It was estimated that they had a ten to one advantage over us; the pursuers had to expose themselves whereas they did not. In a short time we learned the art of survival which was to run like a bloody whippet between the buildings making use of every scrap of cover. We also learned that a well-lobbed grenade through a half-barricaded window was the best way of making this invisible army take a tangible form. It was a form of battle which confronted you with two options – kill or be killed.

One day our troop was flushing out some last-ditch fanatics in a village and I was crawling through some particularly soft and smelly cowpats in order to reach a farm outhouse when I thought I heard a noise coming from inside. I charged forward, firing as I did so, then burst down the door, still firing. On the floor was a dead German, but my bullets had not hit him. A huge pig was eating the soldier's head and its snout was covered with his brains. From time to time it paused to shake the corpse. I was violently sick, but when I had recovered I closely inspected the body and decided his skull had been smashed by a shell splinter. Yet there were no shell holes in the building. Then I realized to my horror that the farmer had dragged the soldier in to feed his pig. I thought, "If that's what they think of their own people they're not going to give us any quarter, and I'm bloody sure I won't spare any I come across." It was a sensible philosophy as events proved. Soon afterwards one of the squadron's jeeps rounded a bend to be confronted by a Tiger tank. Its first shell exploded in front of the jeep blinding the driver. His pals managed to pull him

113

free and dive for cover before the tank rolled forward flattening the jeep under its massive tracks.

It was rough, tough, dirty fighting with no holds barred and made me rather envious of the fighter pilots who still retained some semblance of chivalry in their man-to-man gladiatorial combats.

During one of these bitter hand-to-hand encounters, I experienced a repeat of the ghastly error in the forests of Central France when my jeep had nearly knocked out Sergeant Young's by mistake. Only this time I was on the receiving end.

Lieutenant Lord John Manners, the 22-year-old son of the Duke of Rutland, who had taken over as troop leader when Hugh Gurney was killed, was beside me in a ditch pouring Bren gun fire at some Germans who had dug in round a farmhouse. The jeep with "Will" Fyffe on the wireless was not far away. We had dismounted in order to set up the Bren which is more accurate for long-range work.

For some reason or other the SAS seemed to attract more than its share of aristocracy, although one would have expected them to prefer a regiment where spit and polish and due deference to rank were high on the agenda. Instead they seemed to favour the swashbuckling informality of the SAS, and Lord John was no exception. He slotted in perfectly, without sacrificing an ounce of respect; he mixed and drank with the lads while his barrack room vocabulary could make old sweats nod approvingly. Our admiration and affection were boundless, and thanks to his nonchalant bravery we owe him our survival.

In the early morning mist, as we poured fire into the Germans, our ears caught the sound of a vehicle to our right, followed almost immediately by the staccato chatter of a Vickers. But it wasn't firing in support, but at us.

We did not know it then, but the gun was being fired by Sergeant Laurie Brownlee, a most formidable operator of a twin Vickers. His first burst ripped through the side of the jeep forcing "Will" to dive head first into the ditch with the seat of his pants burning. It was like a scene from a Mack Sennet comedy. In the swirling fog and smoke Laurie had mistaken us for the enemy. We couldn't really blame him for the Generals invariably blamed their own cock-ups on "the fog of war".

One jeep was soon burning brightly, providing the Germans with an iluminated target, and Spandau fire from inside and outside the farmhouse was poured at us as we lay eating dirt in the bottom of the ditch. Lord John cautiously raised his head to peer over the rim, and exclaimed, "Good God, it's a jeep." "Will", living up to the famous comic who bore the same surname, remarked dryly, "Do we owe them money, sir?"

Our jeep, full of petrol, ammunition, grenades and explosives, was a mini arsenal and I knew with leaden certainty that any moment it would go sky high and take us with it. Lord John realized it too, and knew we could not make a run for it hemmed in by Laurie on one side and the enemy on the other. He turned to me and said with irritating calmness, "Keep down. Wait and don't do anything silly." I couldn't think of anything to do – daft or sensible. He then clambered out of the ditch, and ignoring his own advice under tremendous fire and waving his beret, strolled towards Laurie's jeep as if he was taking a Sunday morning stroll to church. His language, as foul as any I've heard, would have made any vicar stop his ears. I watched with mounting horror as he walked towards the jeep; any moment I expected to see him topple over, but he bore a charmed life and walked unscathed through what was literally a curtain of fire. Then the mist lifted and Laurie recognized him and stopped firing, although the Germans did not. Lord John bent double and sprinted back to the ditch shouting, "Run for it, you bastards." We leapt out of the ditch risking the German fire, and before we had travelled a hundred yards our jeep exploded with a deafening roar.

Safe from Jerry's withering fire I wondered how I, a ruddy corporal, could recommend a Lord for extreme gallantry in the face of the enemy, but then I realized that he had also saved us from our own side and that would take a lot of explaining. So I abandoned the idea, leaving him an unsung hero.

By then several more jeeps had arrived and were hitting the farmhouse with the full weight of their combined gun power, and we joined in with our personal weapons. One of the jeeps passed and I saw my pal Sergeant Vickers semi-conscious from a bullet which had completely shattered the bone in the upper part of an arm. Why, I wondered, did the best men always seem to get hurt? We had been through so much together, and right at the last knockings he had to catch one. Then as I averted my eyes I saw a young German weaving and bobbing his way across an open field towards us, the bullets pocking up little puffs of dust around his feet. He had clearly decided he wanted to take no further part in the war. Miraculously he survived the relentless hail of bullets from our side and his own, and dived into a gully alongside Major Mackie's vehicle. I surprised myself, still shocked at seeing Sergeant Vickers; instead of killing the lad I pulled him into cover and pressed his head down. He was my first and only prisoner. Maybe it was the sudden realization that miracles can come in pairs – first Lord John walking unscathed towards gunfire, then the terror-stricken youth running away from it – that I acted as I did. He put his trembling hand on my arm and thanked me and I shrugged him aside. "Don't push your luck," I snapped. "If you'd been SS I'd have blown your bloody head off." He obviously did not understand because he grinned. I pointed in the direction of the farm which was now burning and silent. "Piss off the way you came. You deserve to make it." As he shambled away he paused and waved back before disappearing. I glanced hurriedly round to make sure no one had observed my uncharacteristic behaviour, but if anybody had they did not say anything. We had seen so much death we had become skilled at concealing our emotions, and when someone did something totally alien to their normal conduct we kept silent. Criticism might have provoked an unexpected and unwelcome reaction.

By this stage in the war the regiment had a distinct cosmopolitan flavour about it for we had acquired several Frenchmen, Poles, Belgians, German Jews and a Russian whom I called "Gooski". He was a strange man who spoke reasonably good English although he normally preferred his own company. But he did enjoy wrestling, and occasionally he and I engaged in a rather hectic rough and tumble. In battle he was totally ruthless. Once while working through a small village I was standing behind him when an unarmed German ran out of a house with his hands aloft in a gesture of surrender. Gooski's first bullet hit him in the stomach and he slumped to his knees, the second smashed into his head. The Russian turned to me with a smile of satisfaction on his face, looking for all the world like a small child who is looking for a prize for a job well done. Remembering my recent experience with the German youth I remained silent. For the first time I accepted that men react differently when confronted by the same circumstances. Perhaps he could not forgive the rape and plunder of his own country, similar in a way to how I had found it impossible to forget what the SS had done in Italy.

All round us houses were ablaze and a terribly burned cat emerged from one, mewing piteously. I put it out of its misery with one well-aimed shot. When I looked at Gooski tears were streaming down his cheeks, and I said, "I'll never understand you, you bastard."

I could, however, understand the young American whose body I found when we were flushing out some woods soon after crossing the Rhine. In a small clearing I saw the bloated corpse of a German in a pool of stagnant water, and nearby were the bodies of two of his comrades. On the far side of the clearing lay a dead American paratrooper who had been hit by a burst of machine-gun fire which had disembowelled him. He looked terribly young, still in his teens, and his eyes, which seemed to be still alive, were gazing at a bird singing in the branches above. I instinctively knew what had happened; his 'chute was dangling from some bushes, and it was obvious he had drifted away from the rest of his group and, after releasing himself, been jumped by a party of Germans. Instead of surrendering he had made a fight of it, killing three of the enemy before dying himself. I remember thinking at the time, "You're the lousy bastard who picks fights with Yanks in the pubs and dance halls."

I tidied up his body as best I could, and covered him with his 'chute, leaving his face exposed. I could hear the drumming of artillery in the distance and gazing through the branches I could see the clouds scudding away as if in flight from such inhuman scenes. The bird was still singing, and unable to check myself I yelled out, "Spring – the time for bloody love." Then I checked my gun and crept off into the trees looking for more Germans to kill.

But after the incident with the cowardly young German I found myself in a troubled state of mind. I was more afraid of cowardice than I was of death, yet here I was suddenly starting to question things. Soon afterwards, during a foot patrol, I found myself detached from the rest of the unit when three Germans suddenly broke cover and raced along the road, clearly intent on saving their skins. I fired instinctively, dropping the first man. Then something snapped, like an overtaut wire breaking, and I ran after the others shouting at the top of my voice and firing blindly. As I passed the immobile German I paused just long enough to fire another bullet into him. A red haze of blood lust or a mere precaution, I did not know.

The two Germans ran into a small house, and when I caught up they had bolted the door. I had now lost all control and I repeatedly smashed my carbine against the panels, completely shattering the butt. After what seemed an eternity, but could only have been seconds, the door opened and a visibly terrified old man gestured towards the back door which was swinging open. A bewildering feeling of calm and peace swept through me. Apart from the occasional shot there was an uncanny silence, and peering through the open back door I saw everything in the most vivid colours, every object seeming unnaturally clear. Tears were streaming down my face and the old man gently put his hand on my arm, but I pushed him roughly away, saying, "Piss off, Kraut," and, dragging my useless gun, I staggered back to the jeep, clambered on and lit a cigarette with trembling fingers.

After a while my mind cleared and I was left with the eerie feeling that something strange had happened to me – something I could not comprehend but which frightened me immensely. For a brief spell I had lost my sanity.

When the others came back I said nothing about my traumatic experience and explained the ruined gun by saying I had shattered it when breaking a door down. In the SAS you did not wear your conscience on your sleeve like chevrons. Just then Lord John came up and I had no time for further self-questioning. There was, he said, an eighty-eight millimetre gun in action about a mile away and we had to put it out of commission. We encircled it but found the crew had fled. It was with a profound sense of relief that I found I had conducted myself in a perfectly normal manner, without any recurrence of the incident which had caused me to doubt my own sanity.

After a lot more fighting we reached the Elbe. Berlin was not far away and I experienced a feeling of profound relief. The war was virtually over and resistance was at a minimum. No way, I reasoned, am I going to cop it at this stage of the game. Most of the lads must have felt the same, for a sense of euphoria overcame us.

It was an excess of wishful thinking. We drove the jeeps onto armour-plated amphibious "Buffalo" transporters and quickly crossed the last natural barrier to our ultimate target. My jeep was first off and was greeted with a barrage of shellfire. Germany may have been dead, but it just wouldn't lie down. The air was filled with the whine of shrapnel and the jeep directly behind us was hit and Parachutist Dance was killed.

We roared through the bombardment, heading for what appeared to be a cluster of farmhouses, but before we could reach them the Germans started to demolish them with gunfire and we were forced to leave the jeep and seek shelter under an old wooden cart. As one of the shafts cartwheeled through the air, Lord John remarked laconically, "This bloody thing won't stop anything." I agreed, but reminded him of the famous Old Bill cartoon of the First War; there just didn't appear to be a better hole.

When the German guns had been knocked out we drove in the general direction of Berlin, and there was a perceptible slackening off of enemy opposition and we became quite accustomed to seeing the bodies of soldiers and animals lining the side of the roads. I was leading the column of jeeps one morning when a group of German soldiers ran in front with their hands above their heads. I got down and went up to them, and the only one who could speak English said the Third Reich was finished and they wished to surrender. I pointed due east and told them to head in that direction, and when they reached Moscow they would get the treatment they deserved. The last thing we wanted at that stage was to be lumbered with prisoners, and as we drove off we saw them standing in a dejected and bewildered huddle.

Not long after this incident the Regiment was assembled in a small village and told the war was all over bar the shouting, but a quick end depended on Hitler and his associates signing a peace agreement.

Charlie Hackney, a battle-hardened Scot (despite his name), and two of his pals decided they did not want to hang around, and they thought up an incredibly audacious plan to speed things up. They "borrowed" the car which Lord John Manners had "acquired" from a German and set off for Berlin. As Charlie later told me, "We wanted to get there before the Russians, and perhaps get someone from the Führer's bunker – Hitler himself if possible."

The plan broke down when the car did – in the middle of Lübeck. Charlie and his self-appointed team of peacemakers made enquiries of the locals who were only too anxious to tell them that several high ranking officers were in a large house nearby.

"When we got there," said Charlie, "the place was in darkness and I climbed in through a window. Then I heard a noise and found a trap door in the floor. I lifted it and fired a few rounds, and three men came out with their hands up. They were in civilian clothes and wearing long black leather overcoats. While we were searching them, one pulled out a pistol from beneath his coat and I kicked it from his hand and picked it up. Later, when the tension had eased, the man asked me for it back, and when I asked him why it was so important he replied that they had just come from Hitler's bunker in Berlin and the pistol was the one the Führer had shot himself with. At that time we didn't know he was dead."

Charlie said the man claimed to be a doctor.

During the night one of the prisoners escaped and Charlie was convinced he was Martin Bormann. He was equally convinced that the other two were Hitler's personal surgeon and Goebbels' driver.

Charlie and his pals had no opportunity to check it out because they were arrested by the military police and an officer was sent to Lübeck to bring them back. They were given a real roasting for their madcap scheme, although the officer who administered the rollicking secretly admitted that it was the kind of thing expected of the SAS.

Charlie was subjected to some rather hectic leg-pulling, but he was

119

adamant it was true and produced the gun to prove it. The pistol, a Walther 7.65 mm. self-loading automatic, was made around 1918 and was engraved with a swastika and an eagle.

(Many years after the peace which Charlie had tried to precipitate, he handed the gun over to the SAS Regimental Association, still convinced that it was the one Hitler used to commit suicide. He even approached Lord Dacre – the former Hugh Trevor-Roper, the distinguished historian who chronicled the Führer's last days – and asked him for his opinion. Lord Dacre told him it could well be Hitler's gun, but there was no way of proving it. The last time I heard of Charlie he was still trying to find conclusive proof about the gun and the three mysterious men.)

Berlin was taken and newsreel pictures were shown of Russians and Americans greeting each other in the moment of final victory. It was all over bar the shouting, and we were told that if we could make it to Brussels in time for VE night we were officially on leave from the moment we entered the town.

We were able to celebrate in style and without worrying too much about our wallets. Before leaving Germany we had acquired quite a selection of weapons from dead Germans, who were now either harping or stoking. They fetched a good price from American soldiers who wanted to take them home as souvenirs. It was a night to remember, but one which is distinctly hazy in my recollections. However, I can recall "Will" saying at around 3 a.m. that wine was pouring out of my ears, and me reminding him acidly that it was brandy. Whilst debating the cause of my inebriation we both fell asleep over the table.

When orders came for us to return to England aboard a Tank Landing Craft, we needed all our guile and cunning to get our own souvenirs past the customs officer awaiting our arrival at Southampton. We rubbed our hands in anticipation of a long leave in which the souvenirs could be converted into ready cash for a monumental binge before we headed for the Far East to sort out the Japs. But our hopes were dashed when we were told we were being flown to Norway, along with our jeeps, to complete the final operation – the rounding-up and disarming of the U-boat crews.

A fleet of Dakotas flew us to Stavanger, and I'll never forget my first sight of the U-boat pens which had been built into the sides of the mountains lining the fiords. No wonder the RAF had not been able to knock them out. They were amazing feats of engineering, and the sleek submarines housed inside them really did look like seawolves. I know a lot of people had a grudging admiration for the

8. Tanky and jeep in the village of L'Isle-sur-Sereine (p.97).

9. "Several of the local Maquis clambered aboard
brandishing their guns and clapping us on the back" (p.97).

10. Tanky and Doris, Watford, 1944 (p.87).

11. "I won the half-mile running in bare feet" (p.121).

U-boat crews, but I had nothing but loathing. I could not, and never will, forget the convoy which took us out to the Middle East and the shipful of nurses which went down without a single survivor. To me it was a cowardly form of warfare. At least I could stand up and be counted and say with some degree of pride that although I had killed a lot of the enemy it had been done face to face, with them having an equal opportunity to get me.

When we got the crews together I found them extremely arrogant, as if they were cast in some heroic mould, but even worse they seemed to think they had not lost the war. In good no nonsense SAS style we quickly dispelled that delusion.

Major Mackie, who knew of my experiences with the SS in Italy and of my intense hatred of them, gave me the opportunity to settle a few old scores. Some Gestapo personnel had been rounded up, and he considered they would benefit from some hectic exercise and there was no better PT instructor than Corporal Challenor. They must have felt I had missed my vocation and should have been one of them, because what I put them through would have made an army glasshouse seem like kindergarten. They were in a stable when I first met them, and one made the mistake of smiling at me. The gaze I returned had him backing away. Then I took them out one by one and exercised them with some stiff fisticuffs at which I was no mean performer.

Not surprisingly we were all doing a fair amount of boozing, but we were fit and hard and kept ourselves in that condition. An athletic meeting was arranged at the Bergen Sports Arena and I won the half-mile running in bare feet – long before Zola Budd made it fashionable.

The local girls took a fancy to the lads of the SAS whose exploits were for the first time being made public, and naturally enough this caused a great deal of resentment among the Norwegian boys. Three of our lads were beaten up, and this sparked off a mammoth punch-up with the police being called out. I could sympathize with the locals because I knew the resentment the Americans had aroused when they first arrived in the UK. "Over paid, over sexed, and over here," was a remark that summed up our frustration. Peace was restored when a ship sailed into Bergen and took us all back home. We had been in Norway three months. It would be a travesty of the truth to say there wasn't a dry eye among the crowds of Norwegian boys who lined the quay to wave us bon voyage.

Back home I was promoted to Sergeant, but the pleasure was dimmed by the announcement that the 1st and 2nd Regiments of the SAS were to be disbanded. Saddened though we were, there was unanimous agreement that there should be a combined officers' and sergeants' mess party to which our wives were invited. Before the party there was an athletics meeting, and again I won the half-mile in my bare feet. Some empty barracks nearby were commandeered as married quarters, and I was able to enjoy a second honeymoon with Doris.

We had some choice as to which unit we wished to transfer, and I opted for the 17th Parachute Battalion, then at Bulford camp in Wiltshire, to serve out the remainder of my time. The Paras were a great bunch of lads and I received a really splendid welcome in the Sergeants' Mess. Although the ordinary infantry-style training was far removed from the SAS knife-in-the-back training, I soon settled down and enjoyed it. I entered wholeheartedly into the sporting life of the battalion and represented my company in a boxing tournament and knocked my opponent out. I had developed quite a liking for the noble art and had visions of making my mark in the Army, but I was sent on a Quartermasters' course and promoted CQMS. I returned to find my first job was to prepare the company for shipment to Palestine.

Life aboard the troopship was one of unmitigated boredom with each day an exact replica of the one which had preceded it. To relieve the unremitting monotony the Regimental Sergeant Major organized a boxing tournament and knowing I was a useful performer matched me against an officer. I had no idea what prompted the pairing, but every ranker was clearly delighted at the prospect of seeing an officer get a belting. It wasn't that they disliked him, he was very popular, it was just a natural instinct. Afterwards I wondered whether the RSM wasn't trying to cut me down to size, because the officer turned out to be very good indeed. After two rounds of stylish boxing it developed into a toe to toe brawl before he caught me with a terrific right that put me out for the count. Unfortunately, in going down my head hit the canvas with a terrible clout and I have often wondered whether the blow might not have contributed, along with my other injuries, to my later troubles.

After the oven-hot heat and foul smells of the troop ship, Suez was like a breath of fresh air with its bum-boats, dirty postcard vendors, and gilly gilly boys who miraculously produced live chickens out of your ears. From there we moved into a wire-encircled camp in Palestine where we were kept penned in like animals. I had never been a political animal except for an intense loathing of Nazism, and in Palestine I was utterly confused. I had fought to defeat Germany and frequently there had been Jews alongside me. Now we were being killed by people of the same faith as those we had sought to liberate. True they were described as terrorists, but we were left in no doubt that our presence there was detested.

Looking back, I suppose our role could be compared to that of the Army in Northern Ireland today. Doing a thankless task as tactfully as possible, and being abused by the bulk of world opinion. But soldiers can't do the job of politicians, and it was the one part of my military service I disliked intensely.

In most other parts of the world the terrorists were seen as martyrs with a legitimate cause which could only be achieved through violence, much as the IRA are seen today. We felt we were the pig in the middle, obeying orders and heaping abuse on ourselves from nearly every corner.

When the lads were off duty they were forbidden to carry arms, although they were being shot down in the street. When in camp, unless actually training, they had to hand in their weapons to me in the armoury where they were recorded in a special book. It was very frustrating, and I frequently wondered what would happen if a full-scale terrorist attack was mounted on the camp. The extremists seemed to have everything in their favour with a seemingly special dispensation to shoot down off-duty soldiers without fear of reprisal.

In a fit of frustration I teamed up with another company sergeant major and formulated a private plan to deal with the terrorists. We had no grudge against the ordinary Jewish citizen, but were fed up to the back teeth with our pals being murdered, so we made shoulder holsters to carry a .45 colt and slings to hold grenades under our armpits. On every available opportunity we went into Tel Aviv acting drunk in the most dangerous areas in the hope that we would attract the attention of gunmen. It was strictly illegal and we were inviting a Court Martial. Thank God it was all to no avail; not once were we fired at. When the State of Israel was founded no one was happier than the British soldier. Sadly that part of the world is still in a state of civil war with the Arabs demanding what the Jews had sought and got.

Unhappy as I was in my role, I was delighted when I was posted to Brigade HQ and put in charge of the stores and made treasurer of the Sergeants' Mess. It was what old sweats called a "cushy number", and I was glad to be out of the firing line because the strange occurrences which I had experienced in Germany, and which I thought I need never worry about again, began to return with worry frequency. I began to indulge in fantasies in which I had been selected to take part in special SAS operations and I was constantly on the look-out for agents who were determined to kill me, and I knew that my personal war against the extremists was just one more symptom in my increasing instability. Although I was aware of what was happening I did not seek any help but resorted to exercising great cunning in keeping it from others. I also developed an irresistible urge for what I thought were harmless practical jokes, although none of my victims were in the least amused. Bob Taite, the Brigade Sergeant Major, was a particularly close friend of mine, having served with me in the SAS. He lived in a small brick-built hut in the middle of the compound, and one night as I was passing I stumbled over a very large stone. "I'll make a present of this haggis," I said to myself and hurled it through his window. There was a fearsome crash of shattering glass, and I ran off into the darkness. Someone was bellowing, "Call out the guard," as I slipped under the blankets and pretended to be asleep.

Bob sent for me next day and, pointing to the stone on his desk, said, "Tanky, we've got to get to the bottom of this." I kept a deadpan expression as he spoke, but I could tell from his eyes that he knew I was the culprit. Without openly accusing me, he said there was to be no repetition or there would be hell to pay. He was such a nice chap I knew he would take it no further. He even joined me for a drink later in the evening. (Looking back after the Brick Case which brought about my disgrace, I can't help feeling that that stone through the window was some sinister portent.)

Despite the warning, I was unable to curb my zest for practical jokes which were anything but funny; they were stupidly dangerous. Shortly after the stone escapade I captured a scorpion and, ignoring its sting, which can sometimes be lethal, I picked it up and put it in a cigarette tin. I went into the mess that evening and casually asked if anyone would like a cigarette. I then took out the tin and tipped the scorpion onto the table. The mess emptied in seconds. I was convulsed with laughter.

At this stage I was drinking more than was good for me, and one night, soon after I had nearly become a victim of an assassination squad, I decided to get hold of some explosives and make a big bomb, then find out from the Intelligence Officer the whereabouts of known terrorists and leave the bomb there. I would cover my tracks by wearing civilian clothes.

In the cold light of dawn I realized how demented I must have

124

been, and I was deeply relieved when the Orderly Room Sergeant informed me that papers for a rehabilitation course in plumbing prior to my demob had come through. The course was in Cairo, and I left the camp with no regrets. I was sick of Palestine, worried about my mental condition, and looking forward to a return to civvy street and normality.

In Cairo I enjoyed a happy month playing cricket and swimming, in between learning how to repair broken cisterns and seal fractured pipes. I also cut down my drinking and worked some of the hate out of my system.

The war had been a terrific adventure, but now it was over and I wanted to hear no more about killing. The slow voyage back to England did me the world of good. I felt totally relaxed and not once did I have the slightest reason to fear I was potty.

Chapter Twelve

In England I was issued with a smart demob suit, a trilby and a raincoat, and paid my war service gratuity. It was good to be back in civvies, although the demob suits were so alike they might just as well have been uniforms. It would have been nice for Doris and me to have had a place of our own, but that was out of the question in England where, because of the bombing, there was an acute shortage of housing and it would need a massive rebuilding programme to fill the gap. Doris was living with her parents in a requisitioned house in Cheam, their own home having received a direct hit during an air raid. Doris had sustained a fractured skull, her mother's legs had been crushed and broken, her father escaping with no more than a cut arm. Until their own home was rebuilt there was nothing else to do but muck in and make the best of it. (It was not until 1949 that they were able to move back to their old home.)

The course in Cairo had been too short and sketchy for me to find work as a plumber, and as I lacked any other special skills I was more than grateful when my father-in-law got me a job as a trainee iron moulder in the foundry where he worked at Beddington. It was hard physical work in extremes of temperature, but I learned quickly and enjoyed it. After four years there I moved to a steel foundry in Staines, Middlesex, where I increased my knowledge and experience. It was a pleasant enough life, and though the work was rather monotonous there were always the weekends to look forward to when I played football for a local side. There may have been faint murmurings of inner discontent; I really did think I was capable of better things, but I suppressed them, happy in the knowledge that apart from a couple of bouts of malaria there had been no repeat of the symptoms which had so terrified me in Germany and Palestine.

Then from out of the blue I received a letter from Roy Farran asking me if I was interested in joining him in an anti-terrorist operation in Palestine. I would be enrolled in the Palestine Police to provide me with the necessary cover for what was an obviously clandestine venture. I showed the letter to Doris, and she said, "If that's what you want I won't stand in your way." Her answer was enough to indicate her disapproval.

The letter had sent the adrenalin coursing through my veins and I badly wanted to relive old SAS days. I was like an old cavalry horse which has been put out to grass and hears the call of the bugle, but I sensed that Doris was deeply unhappy and I wrote back reluctantly declining Roy's invitation.

The enterprise in Palestine was to culminate in Major Farran's arrest for murder and the subsequent death of his brother who was inadvertently killed by a parcel bomb sent to him in error by Jewish terrorists. Doris must have sensed that I needed something more out of life than to emulate her father in the foundry. (Even with two artificial hips he continued to work there until he was 87.)

But I managed to suppress my discontent until 1951 when we were on holiday in Cornwall. Doris and I were stretched out on a sandy beach soaking up the sun when she suddenly put aside the newspaper she was reading and said, "The police are looking for recruits. It's a varied, open-air life. Why don't you give it a try? It might be what you need."

My reply was non-committal, but when we returned home I applied to join the Metropolitan Police and was invited to attend a medical examination. I was given a thorough going over and asked a lot of questions about previous illnesses, and I mentioned only my malaria and the eye wound I had received in action. I deliberately withheld everything about my weird lapses into a near fantasy world and the examining doctor could find nothing abnormal in my mental state. With my military background I was ideal material for the Force. So five years after the end of the war in the Far East I found myself back in uniform.

The initial period of training, during which I lodged in Peel House, lasted fourteen weeks and was extremely hard – but the work in the foundry had made me tough and fit and I found the physical side a piece of cake. With my lack of formal education I had to work twice as hard as anyone else at the paper work and I burned the midnight oil studying Criminal Law and Police Procedure. I revelled in the mock arrests and battles of wits which took place during the very life-like trials at which every effort was made to shake the evidence you produced. Occasionally I was sharply rebuked for using my ready wit when giving evidence at a make-believe trial: policemen are expected to retain a solid humourless demeanour. I still had a lot to learn.

In between the long periods of intensive study, I fought for the boxing team and did extremely well, although my ring tactics were not always appreciated in a Force where the emphasis was on the sporting aspect of the battle. One night I was fighting at Hendon Police College, and there I met ex-SAS Sergeant Bob Young whom I had nearly killed in France with his own guns. He had joined the Hampshire Police and was at Hendon on a CID course. When he learned I was fighting he said, "This I must see," and he warned me that the chap I was scrapping was very useful indeed. I digested his words and thought very carefully about my tactics. I watched the time-keeper's bell, and as soon as it rang I was out of my corner and across the ring almost before my opponent had time to leave his stool. He was taken completely by surprise and my solid right-hander put him out for the count. I happily accepted a case of silver fruit spoons. But, over a drink, Bob said, "You haven't changed at all, Tanky; typical SAS tactics." There was a faint hint of disapproval in his voice. I ignored the voice of caution and, during the next tournament, won three fights in a row and collected a very fine canteen of cutlery. Few people could have had so much pleasure in furnishing their home.

I took to police work like a fish to water, and at the end of my training my report said: "A very good recruit, aged 29 years, exceptionally willing, keen and hard-working. Seeks diligently after knowledge, and at times needs someone to keep the brake on his excess of energy."

My first posting as a very keen but fledgling constable was to the Mitcham Division – invariably called the manor – where I pounded a beat, played soccer and pulled my weight in the tug-of-war team. I studied on the bus to and from work, and passed my first two qualifying exams with marks of 85 per cent and 93 per cent. But I knew I was never going to be a policeman in the publicly accepted sense. I was always going to be a maverick, and this came to me when I was crossing through a factory area and I spotted a young man who had been posted as a deserter from the Army. As soon as he saw me he set off like a hare who has spotted the lurchers. But I was extremely fit and he couldn't shake me off, and I finally cornered him in a deserted corner of the factory complex. "You bastards," he yelled in frustration, "are all right in uniform but you haven't got the guts of a louse without it." That was like a red rag to a bull to me, and I replied, "That mean you want to fight?" and he sneered, "You haven't got the guts."

I took off my tunic, hung my helmet over a convenient post and squared up to him. I floored him twice, but he was a game little bastard and got up each time and caught me with a haymaker which brought me to my knees. He stood off while I got up, and when we went back into action he said breathlessly, "I'll call it a day if you're willing." I was, and that was the end of the scrap. I had a huge swelling on my cheek and he had black eye. "I'll come in quietly," he said, and as I put on my tunic and helmet I casually asked him if he had any problems. "Yes," he said, "but I need time to sort them out." I knew where my duty lay, but I ignored the rule book. "Look son, sort things out, then report back to your unit under your own steam. That'll be much better than being nicked and taken back." Having expounded that pearl of wisdom I invited him to join me in a pint.

At the Bath Tavern, situated in the middle of a gypsy camp near Mitcham Common, I put my helmet on a hatstand and called for two pints. The landlord, Charlie Monk, dipped his handkerchief in my pint and bathed my cheek. I reported back at the nick at the end of my tour of duty and told the sergeant I had tripped and banged my face on a gate post.

Some weeks later I saw the young deserter back in uniform and quite content to soldier on, having sorted out his domestic problems. I thought: There's nothing like a good punch-up to make an assessment of a man's character.

My beat covered such a wide area that I needed a bicycle to cover it, and I was subject to some good-natured banter about being Mr Plod on wheels. Although I did not mind sharing a good laugh, I demanded total respect for law and order and the uniform I was wearing, but that wasn't difficult because then a London Bobbie was part of the community in which he worked.

Those were the days before licensed betting shops and anyone who wanted to have a two-bob each way bet on the Derby or the Grand National had to rely on the street-corner bookie. A blind eye was turned on their activities because it struck most policemen as being rather incongruous that a gentleman could pick up the telephone in his club and phone his bookmaker without committing an offence, whereas a punter who palmed a street-corner bookie a bet was breaking the law. I was happy to go along with that providing the bookies were reasonably discreet and didn't take an obvious enjoyment in flouting the law, and on my patch that meant me. What the eye did not see did not exist, and that was a pretty good maxim for the bookies to adopt. They all had lookouts and when I appeared on the scene there wasn't a bookie or a betting slip in sight.

One morning, just before the off for a big race, one local bookie saw me and gave me a two-fingered salute which broke our unwritten code. I was so angry I cycled home and changed into my old gardening gear: cloth cap, grubby jumper and patched trousers, and pedalled back.

The bookie was doing a thriving business and, leaning my bike against a tree, I strolled up and said, with, I must admit, a touch of the Old Bill, "You are nicked, my old darling." I led him by the arm to the police box at Rose Hill and telephoned for the van. At the station he was searched and found to be in possession of a considerable sum of money and a lot of betting slips. But that wasn't the problem confronting the Inspector: he had to find some means for explaining why I, a humble police constable, had made an arrest in civilian clothes, for according to the book, which ruled our lives, no officer was allowed to leave his beat without authority, and in no way was he allowed to disguise his role by donning civilian clothing.

No one seemed to know how to deal with this infringement and I was left to stew in a juice of my own making before a senior officer summoned me before him and solemnly pronounced that there was a paragraph in Police Regulations which stated that in police work it was impossible for all contingencies to be covered by hide-bound rules, and situations could arise where an officer must rely on his own initiative. The incident with the bookmaker, he said with all the solemnity of a judge commuting the death sentence, applied in my case. Then, in language that would not have been approved of in higher quarters, he told me not to do it again. I readily promised that I would not err again and there was no need to, because when I rode around my patch again there were no reverse V-signs.

By this time I had decided that my future lay with the Criminal Investigation Department which seemed infinitely preferable to pounding a beat in sleeting rain and trying door knobs of shops to make sure there had not been an illegal entry. And so I applied to become an Aid to the CID, although I was still in my probationery period as a uniformed constable.

My application was approved, subject to a period of what was called "suitability", but I soon discovered that the role of an Aid was not that much different to being a constable on the beat. It still meant loitering around in the bitter cold in the hope of spotting someone about to break into a shop or house. Instead of being in a nice warm uniform I was in civvies. I made many arrests. Few required any great skill or powers of deduction, but it was all part of the vital job of cutting down the crime rate. There were occasions when an arrest gave a satisfaction that was out of all proportion to the relatively minor nature of the offence, because I knew I had brought to an end something much bigger. Let me quote an example. I arrested a man for loitering with intent to commit a felony, namely break into houses. He was given three months, but with his imprisonment a whole series of robberies which had been plaguing the area came to an abrupt halt. There was no praise or pats on the back for that kind of thing, because it was pointed out to me that it might have been sheer coincidence – when you knew damned well it wasn't.

Prior to that I had been loaned to Battersea sub-division which was suffering from a spate of burglaries. My job, along with that of a number of other Aids, was to find a convenient spot from which to keep observation in the hope of spotting the culprit. In the early hours of one particularly icy morning I heard footsteps approaching me through the swirling fog which seemed a feature of London at that period, and I found myself looking at the biggest man I'd ever seen. As he passed the doorway I thought, "Jesus, I've got to stop and search him, and he's big enough to eat me."

I stepped out, tentatively put my hand on his shoulder, and he said, "Hullo mister, I'm cold." His face and eyes looked strange and rather frightening, and I realized he was mentally ill. My mind was working overtime because I was afraid he might suddenly become violent. "How would you like a nice cup of tea at the blue lamp cafe round the corner?" I said, and he eagerly replied, "Yes please, mister." I walked him to Battersea Police Station where it was discovered he had escaped from Rampton Criminal Asylum. I considered that just as much a part of my duty as catching thieves.

I made the next rung up the ladder of promotion when I was posted to a Q-car – a plain unmarked vehicle – as a member of a three-man crew. Again our role was as much concerned with the prevention of crime as with its detection. We were a very successful team and we made a lot of arrests and built up a formidable list of informants. The prevention of crime is a thing that many members of the public are rather hazy about and often see it as bloody-minded harassment: stopping innocent people going about their lawful business and asking them to empty their pockets or the bag they are carrying. But people who have been subject to a burglary in their own home are never among the critics. The invasion of a home when everything is ransacked leaves a feeling that is akin to that of a rape victim. A home is never the same place again. It is useless to deny that innocent people are not sometimes stopped and questioned and not all policemen are very polite about it, but a good copper usually has a nose for the wrong 'un. I certainly developed that sixth sense.*

I also built up a memory bank of a rogues' gallery of faces. I took the view that if I did spot someone who was acting suspiciously and whom I knew had form, I would be failing in my duty if I did not question them. Sometimes that paid unexpected dividends. During the patrol of Tooting Broadway during a day when the shops closed early, I saw a man who had 14 previous convictions emerge from the rear of a parade of shops. I shot out of the car and collared him, and he said resignedly, "I know you, Challenor, and I know I'm nicked, but you are dead wrong. I went round there for a slash."

"Show me where," I said, and he led me to a spot by a fence which showed signs of having recently been watered. I still searched him but found nothing, and wrongly reading my intentions he said resignedly, "You're still going to nick me." In fact I was going to tell him to bugger off. He turned and said, "Write down this name and address. There is a nicked motor bike there being stripped."

"All right," I told him, "you are now un-nicked," and I gave him the name of a pub and told him to be there at eight o'clock.

I went to the house, and sure enough there was the motor cycle. I met my informant at the pub and told him I would try and get him some money from the Information Fund. I did, and later handed him £10. It must have been the first honest money he had earned for a long time because he was over the moon and subsequently provided me with a lot of valuable information. He apologized for not being able to give me anything really big, but, as he explained, he was no longer running with the big boys because the thought of doing any more bird terrified him. He admitted, however, that he still drank in a public house which was frequented by some very hard criminals such as bank robbers, but when I suggested it might be useful if I visited the place with him he shied off. Simply being seen in my company was a risk he wasn't prepared to take. They could be very violent. Then I had a crazy idea: I would repeat my Italian stunt and go dressed as

* Today nearly all Police Forces have special Crime Prevention units which lecture to the public on the importance of making their homes burglar-proof. A copy of the old adage about the horse and the stable door should be a compulsory item in every home and stood in a prominent place on the mantelpiece because most people only take precautions *after* they have been burgled.

a woman. He burst into gusts of laughter, and said, "It's crazy, but count me in."

I got hold of a woman's wig, borrowed one of Doris's longest skirts, a roll neck sweater, high heeled shoes, nylon stockings and a cloak-like coat and handbag. A close shave and a heavy application of make-up completed my disguise, and when I looked in the mirror I hardly recognized myself. I hoped no one would get fresh with me.

When we entered the crowded pub I sat on a stool at the end of the bar while my "boy friend" walked round chatting to customers. Every now and then he would look in my direction and discreetly nod. Each nod indicated a villain, and I mentally registered each face in my personal dossier, although there was one face already known to me. It belonged to a villain who had been suspected of being involved in a bullion robbery at London Airport and whom I had previously arrested for being in possession of a firearm outside Wandsworth Prison. None of it was of any immediate practical use, but if I saw them on the manor they would certainly have their collars felt.

As I was drinking my gin and tonic and thinking how much I'd prefer a pint of bitter, I was joined by an attractive young woman who confided she was on the "game" and I had to listen with feigned interest as she told me the most intimate things about herself and the oldest profession. I did not know it then but that little heart-to-heart about the tricks of the trade was to stand me in good stead when I worked in Soho which was a hotbed of organized prostitution. Occasionally I forgot to talk in a high-pitched voice and she commented on my bad cold. She bought me a drink and I returned the compliment. I then felt an urgent need to visit the toilet, and without thinking I walked straight into the Gents, but before I had time to rectify my mistake I heard someone coming in and I locked myself in one of the cubicles and waited till he had gone. But when I came out I bumped into another man who apologized profusely saying, "Sorry, I thought it was the Gents."

I said, "Don't worry, you're right. I've recently had a miscarriage and must still be a bit light-headed."

"You poor old dear," he said, "I'll buy you a drink."

He bought me a large port saying it was a very good pick-me-up for anyone who had recently lost a lot of blood. When he had gone a bloke who was old enough to be my father asked, "What's a nice girl like you doing in a dump like this?" and he took my arm saying he would take me to his flat which was much better and just round the corner.

My "boy friend" – whose face bore a vivid chiv (razor) scar –

joined us and grabbed the man by the tie. "If you don't leave my girl alone I'll cut you up." The man disappeared through the door like a scalded cat.

We left the pub and outside had a really good chuckle, and before we parted my "fiance" said, "Your left one's slipped and you're deformed, you silly old cow."

We kept in touch for a long time, and later in my career when I was with the Flying Squad he continued to provide information which was not confined to any particular area.

Sometimes I failed to see the humorous side of incidents which convulsed my colleagues. On one occasion I was in charge of a Q-car because the senior officer had been taken ill, and as we cruised around Tooting Bec Common late at night I saw a cyclist with a very heavy load hanging over the rear wheel. I told the driver to stop because the man could not have been shopping at that late hour. When I started to talk to him and got no response, I realized he was deaf. When I looked into the kit bag I found a lot of tools including a large electric Kango hammer, capable of going through solid concrete. He was invited to come to the police station. There I made a more thorough search and wrapped up in cloth were steel-cutting tools, a big torch with spare batteries, a jemmy and other housebreaking implements. The tools were spread out on a table in the CID room and he was given a chair and asked to explain all the gear, but he declined to answer. If he had he would no doubt have said they had fallen off the back of a lorry.

A good detective never loses his patience when a suspect refuses to answer questions, and I carried on the interrogation until, without warning, he leapt off the chair and knocked the Kango hammer off the table which hit my shins before landing on my toes. I let out a bellow of pain and pushed him back towards his chair. Wham! He smashed his right fist into my mouth splitting my lips which swelled up like a couple of bananas. When my head stopped spinning and my eyes watering I drew back my fist, then saw the tears streaming down his cheeks. I thought: Poor bastard, he's not only deaf, he knows he's got a lot of bird coming his way, and a lot more if I give evidence of having been assaulted. I'll swallow it. (I was particularly sensitive to his deafness because I was experiencing the first signs of trouble with my own hearing.) I held out the hand which a few seconds before had been clenched into a fist and said, "No hard feelings on my part." He shook my hand, then burst into tears again and said he would like to make a statement.

134

Adjoining Tooting Broadway Underground Station, he said, was a bank from which could be heard the rattle of passing trains, and a good climber could gain access to the bank and the strong room by jemmying open a window. Before doing this he had broken into a store on a building site and stolen the Kango hammer and some other tools.

The massive steel door of the strongroom was built into a cement wall, and he planned to attack this as trains pulled in and out of the station, thus deadening the noise. When he had broken in he found, to his dismay, that the Kango was wired for DC current whereas the bank was AC and he had been forced to give up, leaving only the jemmied window as evidence of his forced entry. I had no hesitation in charging him, but when the other CID officers asked me what I had done to my mouth I said I had tripped over the tools and banged my face on the table.

Next morning when I gave evidence at South Western Magistrate's Court, I had difficulty in speaking and the magistrate asked if the prisoner had given me any trouble. "None whatever, sir," I replied.

I was allowed to remain in charge of the case although I was still only an Aid, and by the time he appeared on trial at the County of London Sessions I found he had a long record of serious crime. He was sentenced to nine years' imprisonment, and as he was led to the cells below he turned and smiled at me. I thought: My God, you took that like a man. Nine bloody years!

That was my first really big job, although just before it I had been commended by the Commissioner of Police for my part in catching a dangerous criminal. The trouble was *that* success had been pure luck. I had been detailed for night duty with instructions to keep observation on the house of a man wanted for questioning about a big wages snatch in case he visited his wife. At about 3 o'clock in the morning I spotted a man walking slowly along the road peering carefully at houses, then walking on. Although he looked reasonably smart he was acting in a furtive manner for when he stopped outside an empty house he went into the garden to look through the front windows, whereupon I decided to approach him. He spoke in a well-educated voice, but was unable to satisfy me that he was just being curious, and I told him I was arresting him. He became extremely annoyed and threatening, and I drew my truncheon and told him that if he did not come quietly I would be forced to use it.

When he appeared at Mitcham Magistrate's Court next day, one of the magistrates announced that there was a valid reason why he should not preside and promptly left the bench. It was not a rare occurrence, but it usually happened when a magistrate had a vested interest in the case he was trying which might suggest to the accused he was incapable of being impartial, such as the theft of cigarettes from a tobacco company in which the magistrate had shares. But I had never heard of one standing down in case of a person loitering with intent.

The prisoner stoutly protested his innocence, but was found Guilty and sentenced to three months, and the magistrate commended me for my diligence. I was as surprised as my colleagues.

Later I learned that the magistrate who stood down had earlier received a letter from the accused's mother which led to a detective interviewing her son in prison where he confessed to burning down an hotel, a bungalow, and setting fire to a Rolls Royce in the Croydon area.

A report by the Divisional Detective Superintendent described me as being conscientious, efficient, and able to conduct my cases in court in an extremely able manner, adding that I had the capacity to work very long hours and was methodical and very competent in dealing with the paper work. During my time as an Aid, I made 105 arrests, and he strongly recommended me for permanent appointment to the CID and I officially became a Detective Constable and was sent to Hendon Detective Training School where I passed with high marks in all but two subjects.

On the completion of the course I went to Croydon where my star continued to rise, especially after I had secured the conviction of a crook nicknamed Fagin because he recruited a lot of youngsters to steal for him. He protested at his trial that I had "verballed" him – an underworld term meaning I had put words into my evidence which he had never uttered. I was shocked at the time but quickly discovered that the allegation of a "frame up" was the automatic recourse of the criminal fraternity. It did not help in his case.

I heard on the grapevine that I had been dubbed "The Bastard", but that did not worry me in the least, neither did it bother my superiors who noted that "he has made his presence felt by his initiative and drive".

I *was* a bastard when it came to case-hardened crooks, but there was also a bit of the marshmallow in my make-up. Once I received a call to take a car to the grounds of an hotel situated in extensive grounds where it was reported a man armed with a knife was lying in wait for his wife who worked there. I found the man and quickly overpowered him, and when I relieved him of the knife I saw tears coursing down his face. I was reminded of the time in Germany when I had broken down and wept when chasing two soldiers, and I realized the man was mentally ill. I told him I was arresting him for his own good and would explain his condition to the Court. I was relieved when he was remanded for mental and medical reports.

Hard I may have been, but I had enough compassion to know that a mentally sick man was not always responsible for his actions. I had no idea that in the not too distant future someone would have to make the same decision regarding my conduct.

Chapter Thirteen

My annual reports in 1956, 1957 and 1958 contained the phrases "a magnificent worker", "continues to forge ahead", "Excellent", and "Very hard working".

On 5 August, 1958, I received my happiest posting. I was attached to The Sweeney, Scotland Yard's famous Flying Squad which has a worldwide reputation for its successful operations against major criminals and organized crime. Television has given "The Sweeney" a glamourised image which bears little resemblance to the truth. We were a bunch of dedicated professionals who pitted our wits against equally dedicated professionals. We did not cut corners and certainly were not a law unto ourselves; neither did we race through the streets, tyres screaming, indifferent to the fate of anyone or anything that stood in our path. Nor did we beat anyone insensible to obtain a confession: a man in the dock sporting a black eye is pretty sure to get an acquittal, because the average jury is only too willing to listen to defence counsel's warnings of corrupt and brutal policemen. As far as we were concerned the best way to arrest crooks was to catch them red-handed.

In my day the official designation of The Sweeney was C.8 and it consisted of a small headquarters unit and eight teams of the same number of men, each of which operated under the direction of a Detective Inspector. We all came from different police districts, had our own informants and an encyclopaedic knowledge of the criminal element on our own patches. We pooled any information we received as we did that which came in from other Divisions and County forces. We operated like a good soccer team with no one trying to hog the ball. Normal working hours were out of the question because crooks don't work office hours.

Like most police work it required more perspiration than inspiration. Let me give you an example. As our night shift was coming to an end I received a call from an informant who wanted me to meet him and discuss a van load of stolen whisky. (Crime like the calendar goes in seasons. Around Christmas there is always a big increase in the hi-jacking of spirits, cigarettes and turkeys. In summer it is holiday clothing, beachwear and photographic equipment.) As my informant insisted I would need an observation van, I speedily acquired a clapped-out old vehicle and the three-man team wearily made our way to Croydon where my contact put me in the picture. At the end of the road to which he directed us was an open yard behind business premises, and parked there was a very large container lorry packed full of scotch. The two men who had driven the hi-jacked vehicle to its destination were off somewhere negotiating with a potential buyer, and, as my informant had pointed out, if we held our horses and waited for the container lorry to drive off and we followed it, we would be led to even more stolen property.

The jackpot is always better than a single cherry, so we waited. "It might be a long wait, Harry boy," said my informant, and he was right. The hours passed interminably. We went without breakfast, lunch and tea, and the air in the observation van became foul with the fumes of chain-smoked cigarettes. Fortunately there was an aperture in the floor of the vehicle through which we could urinate, and when I splashed the well-polished shoes of a chum there was surprisingly little anger. "Wave it about, Harry," was all he said in protest, and someone else shouted, "Man the lifeboats." You needed that quirky kind of humour to put up with it.

It wasn't until around 6 p.m. the next evening that two men arrived to drive the lorry away. Immediately our tiredness vanished because we all knew our vigilance would have been wasted if we lost sight of it in the ensuing "tail".

The juggernaut rolled through crowded streets with our dilapidated van following behind at a discreet distance. It followed a circuitous route and I knew the lorry driver had twigged that we were following and at any moment they would abandon the vehicle, which was exactly what they did. Right in the middle of Thornton Heath High Street. The occupants legged it through the back streets and we piled out and set off in pursuit. One man was quickly apprehended but the one I was chasing took to the back gardens, taking the fences like a Grand National steeplechaser. It was so ludicrous I burst out laughing, and thought: One of us silly buggers is going to come a cropper. At that precise moment the man ahead of me planted his feet in the middle of a cold frame and when I caught up with him he held his hands up in a pitiful gesture of surrender. One of them was bleeding profusely, and I said, "Don't worry, me old darling, I'll see you get the best medical attention possible."

He was driven in the van to a nearby hospital where he was stitched up before being taken to South Norwood Police Station where he and his accomplices were charged. It was several hours later that I was able to clock off. We had been on duty non-stop for nearly forty-eight hours.

When I arrived home in the early hours of the morning, Doris was still sitting up. She said, "You're early. Forgotten your keys?" Then she smiled, gave me a big hug and a kiss and said, "You look tired. Off you go to bed. I'll bring a tray up." Lovely, adorable Doris made those hours in the stinking van seem like a minute. Here I'll digress to point out that few people realise how important the role of a good wife is to a policeman. In most other professions a woman would insist on a husband having a word with the boss over the ridiculous hours her spouse is working.

As I lived closer than anyone else to Croydon Court, I was first up in order to be there and give evidence of arrest and requested that the two men be remanded in custody pending further enquiries. This was agreed to and investigations revealed that the whisky had been stolen in the Victoria area, and this led to further arrests. My informant was rewarded for his efforts with a sum which bore no resemblance to the value of the goods recovered.

I had only been with The Sweeney a month when Tommy Butler, one of the Yard's most famous detectives and ruthless pursuer of the Great Train Robbers, wrote, "He continues to apply himself strenuously to the job in hand. Is capable and willing, but is inclined to noisy tactlessness." A year later he was less harsh: "He is capable and fearless in his dealings with criminals. Has improved in general bearing . . ."

Doris saw less and less of me as home became a place to call in to snatch a couple of hours sleep. The phone in my office at the Yard was constantly ringing with informants anxious to give me a tip off – a van load of tape recorders would be on offer in a pub near the Elephant and Castle, a greengrocers' shop was being used as a warehouse for stolen property, a hi-jack was planned on a security van.

Once an informant had established his reliability I gave him my home number, and early one morning one telephoned to tell me about a consignment of stolen lamb which had been hidden in a Croydon yard. I broke all records getting from my home to the yard where I arrested the receiver of stolen property. After charging him at Croydon

Police Station, I made arrangements for the meat to be delivered to a cold storage depot and had some breakfast in the canteen before going to court to arrange for a remand in custody. And the day had hardly started.

By the very nature of their work, policemen lead a rather solitary social life. Apart from the fact that they are often working when others are sleeping, they find it difficult to make friends; people just do not want to invite them into their homes, unless they have been burgled. I once read of an experiment where several people were wired up with special equipment which would record their heart and pulse rates whilst driving their cars, and it was found that the pulse rate of a perfectly honest citizen jumped alarmingly at the sight of a police car through the rear mirror. Despite numerous campaigns, the police still retain an unpopular image, and no one really knows why, because the average person's only contact with a policeman is through a motoring offence and their normal reaction when stopped for speeding or parking illegally is, "Why aren't you out catching criminals?"

I was doing precisely that when I was beaten soundly over the head with an umbrella wielded by an irate City gentleman who called me a thug. It happened when I was investigating a particularly serious and vicious crime. Two men armed with sawn-off shotguns had broken into the home of the manager of the American Express Bank and savagely beaten him and his wife before stealing the keys to the deposit room.

A tip off reached me that one of the gunmen was meeting his girl friend next morning at Liverpool Street Station and the two of them would then meet the girl's mother who was arriving on another train. I passed the information on to my Guvnor and soon afterwards we had very good descriptions of the two bank robbers. Several detectives took up position at different points at the station and, while Detective Inspector Reg Roberts discreetly positioned himself near the platform where the mother was expected, I went upstairs to the buffet. There I immediately recognized one of the robbers who was talking to a young girl. He fitted the description I had been given: hard, mean, and very strong. As I drank my tea I thought: What must it be like to be asleep in your bed when two wicked bastards like him burst in with shotguns and knock you about? It must have been a terrifying experience for the manager's wife.

I went downstairs and reported to Inspector Roberts who said we would stick to the original plan and arrest the man when he and his girl friend went to meet the mother. Hardly were the words out of his mouth than the train arrived. The man and woman from the buffet appeared on the platform and I thought: It's a racing certainty he is armed, and even if he isn't there's going to be one hell of a fight and innocent people could get hurt. Old Reg is due for retirement and he is likely to get injured.

I decided to do it my way, and without Reg's approval because it was a trifle unorthodox. I strolled ahead of him, and when I drew level with the man I hit him with a straight arm commando blow across the throat. When he hit the ground I sat astride him until Reg ran up and held his arms.

I said, "You are nicked, my old darling, and my boss will tell you that formally in a minute."

Suddenly I felt blows raining down on my head and I looked up to see a well-dressed gentleman hitting me with his furled brolly and shouting, "Stop it, stop it. You thug."

The arrested man was taken to Scotland Yard where he was searched and in his wallet we found an address in North London, and there under the floorboards were two shot guns and a quantity of ammunition. As we were leaving the other man arrived and he was quickly arrested. Both were sentenced to long terms of imprisonment.

For some time I had been experiencing a loud ringing tone in my ear which the blows from the umbrella had done nothing to improve. Apart from the ringing I was becoming increasingly deaf, a considerable handicap to a detective who has to appear in court. I went to St Thomas's Hospital and explained my problem. I was subjected to a thorough examination and a specialist thought that it had been brought about by the massive overdoses of quinine I had been given in Italy to treat my malaria. A deaf aid was suggested, but that did not help because my main trouble was in hearing high tones.

I still continued to work extremely long hours, but the work was so varied I had no time to worry about over-doing it. No two jobs were the same. One of them was a real teaser. Agatha Christie could have aptly named it The Case of the Vanishing Lorries, although we gave it a more mundane tag, "The County Job". Over a long period of time, lorry loads of high value cargoes were being stolen from numerous places north of London. The puzzling feature was that the vehicles were never found abandoned, they just disappeared. I was detailed to work under a Detective Sergeant and we sat down and tried to devise a plan of action which was not easy as we had so little to go on. Eventually we drew a circle on a map which enclosed possible hiding places and set off to investigate them, pretending that we were car rally or treasure hunt organizers. We visited pubs and cafes frequented by long-distance drivers in the hope of picking up some information, but after several days we had drawn nothing but blanks. But the weather was fine and the beer good.

One morning I was sitting in a pub idly passing the time of day with an old gentleman when I remarked, "At least you don't get the roar of bloody great lorries in this lovely village." He looked askance at me. "You must be joking. What about all the lorries that go down the lane at night? Some of them are so big I don't know how they make it."

I pressed him further and learned that the narrow lane led to a big building which was obscured by trees and a high hedge. I signalled to my boss that it was time to go, and we soon found the lane. However, we decided to delay a closer inspection until it was dark. An enormous guard dog put an end to our nocturnal visit and we returned again in daylight. As soon as we spotted one big lorry we wirelessed for reinforcements and the rest of the team arrived. Several arrests were made and a considerable amount of stolen property recovered. We also solved the mystery of the lorries; they were cannibalised and the parts sold all over the country.

Not all our jobs were successes. Too often weeks of work, much of it spent in the most intolerable conditions, ended in what we called "blow outs". But they were part and parcel of a detective's life and one learned not to brood over the failures. I even deliberately blew one job to protect an informant I valued highly. Her name was Lilly and she was a well known Tom (prostitute), as hard as nails and at times a real bitch. I got to know her when I was leaving court one afternoon when a wise old uniformed officer pointed her out and told me she was worth cultivating as she mixed with a lot of villains. She was remonstrating with a Greek and I guessed, rightly as it turned out, that he was trying to ponce off her (live off her immoral earnings). I took him aside, and told him there was little future for him if he did not leave her alone. Then I took her for a drink and she said, "Even though you're on the Sweeney you must like a bit of the other. Seeing as you've done me a favour I don't mind obliging." I told her I had given it up for Lent, but if she really did want to do me a favour she could help me put away some of her crooked friends and in return I would pay her from the Information Fund. She met me half way, saying she would help me put away one or two of them, but only when she felt like it.

She turned out to be an excellent informant and I was surprised what villains would tell her when they literally had their pants down. I stressed that I only wanted information, and on no account was she to become involved in any crime herself. I pointed out that if the villain was arrested and she was not, I could be accused of being an agent provocateur, as a defence counsel could allege that she had set up the job with my knowledge and on my instructions, which meant I had committed an offence by encouraging a crime to be committed.

Lilly just did not get the message. She phoned me and tipped me off about a proposed safe-blowing and I staked the place out for two whole nights in the freezing cold. Just as I was about to turn it in the cracksman arrived with Lilly in tow. I knew that I had to "blow" the job because I couldn't arrest her, so I shouted, "Police" at the top of my voice and they ran off. When Lilly rang me I told her I would see her at her place of business, and when I got there I shook her like a rag doll, calling her all names under the sun. She was so astonished she burst into tears. I thought: Christ, I've never seen a Tom cry!

Lilly wiped her eyes and said, "When that dirty bastard was screwing me I was doing it for you, Harry. I wanted to put him away for you. I don't care about the money you give me, I can earn all I need. He was going to put it off yet again so I took him there because I couldn't bear the thought of you spending another night in the cold. You treat me decent, Harry, like a woman should be treated. I only did it for you."

I gave her a hug and told her not to be so bloody daft in future, but she went missing for a time and it was only when I was reading a police circular that I learned she was wanted for escaping from Holloway Prison. I was worried that she would get tied up with the Mob and end up with a heavy sentence, so I called on her mother and asked her to get Lilly to contact me. She did, and when I met her I talked to her like a Dutch uncle, "Go back and finish your bird, then come and work for me again."

"Harry," she said, "you're a bastard, and I must want my head seeing to, but can I have a good drink before I go back?"

I took her to the dive bar of the Red Lion, not far from the old Scotland Yard building on the Embankment. Several of the lads from the Squad were there off duty, and everyone bought Lilly drinks and she asked me one final favour before I took her back. "Harry, can we go somewhere and have it off?"

144

I explained that I just had time to run her back to prison before going out on a job. After a tearful farewell in the pub I took her to Holloway where she was greeted like a long lost child.

I spent three and a half years with The Sweeney, and although the work was hard and often dangerous, I enjoyed it. The special camaraderie that existed among us was unique and lasting. Even when off duty we sought each others' company. In the dive bar of the Red Lion someone would put a trilby hat on the bar and everyone would chip in an "Oxford" (five shilings), which in those days was enough for all the beer we wanted. And when the bar closed it was not unusual for us to go on to places where the criminal elements met and where information could be obtained. It might not have met with the approval of those who judge others by the company they keep, but by God we got results.

Chapter Fourteen

In March, 1962, I was promoted to Detective Sergeant Second Class. It had not been easy passing the exam because I had so little time in which to study, working as I was on difficult cases, appearing in court and preparing mounds of paper work. My only disappointment was that I had to leave The Sweeney, but it is a custom in the Met that on promotion an officer is posted to another Division. It is on a par with the Royal Navy's custom that a man who is commissioned from the lower deck never returns to a ship in which he served as a rating. It is a sensible and practical means of ensuring that a new man's authority is not undermined by old friendships. My base was Southwark Police Station, and the new manor embraced the notorious Elephant and Castle area and a chunk of South London renowned for its dangerous gangsters, and the first serious crime in which I was involved gave me a good idea of what I was up against.

A young girl had fallen out with her mobster boy friend, and one night as she was leaving a club he drove at her, knocked her down, then reversed back over her again before driving off. Then he disappeared, and despite the most diligent enquiries he could not be traced until one of my informants told me that he was still driving the same car but he knew no more. Even so, it was of vital importance because first-rate forensic samples had been obtained at the scene of the crime: specks of paint, blood and other items which could prove it was the car which had nearly killed the girl.

My Guvnor – Detective Chief Superintendent "Nick" Carter – learned that the suspect often visited Brighton which in those days had a far from salubrious reputation, and was still very much as Graham Greene depicted it in *Brighton Rock*, and he sent me there to try and track him down. I did not see him in the Regency seaside resort, but I learned a lot about his movements and soon after I returned to London I caught sight of him patrolling one of his favourite patches. He also spotted me and drove off at high speed. I failed to catch him, but when he was arrested I was able to give evidence that ensured he went away for a long time.

I left the Old Bailey at the end of the trial when I noticed the girl he had tried to murder; although she had a heavy limp she was working a beat in the West End. I stopped and asked her how she was, and she replied, "Making a living." Like so many others I encountered in my work, the sleezy world that existed under the bright lights had a magnetic attraction that was irresistible.

Television and the cinema have given the gangster a gloss of romance and I often wished I could bundle some of the film-makers into my car and take them out on some of the investigations I was involved in. Then they might not have glorified violence and excused themselves by claiming it was all in the sacred name of realism. Realism is blood, broken bones, and disfigured faces, and evil bastards who procure "rent boys" for equally sick men and put under-age girls on the streets.

I was called in to investigate an attack on an eighty-year-old woman who had been savagely beaten about the head and body for the pitifully small amount of money she kept hidden in her flat. I sat beside her bed in Guy's Hospital and patiently obtained a description of her attacker, whom she described as big, strong and aged about thirty. I thought: If I catch the bastard I'm going to give him a real belting. I realized my emotions were not quite in keeping with those of a well-disciplined policeman and maybe my volatile nature did not make me ideal material for the job. Even so, I knew if I had found him I might well have put my thoughts into action. I put more work into the investigation than I would have done into a full-scale murder inquiry, and I had photographs of the old lady and her injuries circulated throughout the country, and with her assistance I had an Identikit description of her assailant made up which was also circulated. But he was never arrested because I was taken off the case as it was considered I would be more useful in Soho and the West End of London where crime was escalating at an unprecedented scale. I may have failed on that case but it certainly gave me the necessary zest for what lay ahead.

On 9 July, 1962, I was transferred to C Division attached to West End Central Police Station which in those days was referred to as "The Mad House" because of the amount of work the CID was involved in. The station included the districts of Mayfair and Soho – the two most disparate areas in the capital as the majority of the former's residents seemed to have been drawn from Debrett's and Burke's Peerage, and a considerable number of the latter's from the Yard's CRO (Criminal Records Office.) It was decreed that I would concentrate on Soho, "the square mile of vice", because my robust and unorthodox approach to the war against crime was considered unsuitable for the more rarefied atmosphere of Mayfair. The pressure of work was such, however, that I often found myself working in that refined district where there were more coronets than kind hearts.

I was, for lack of a better word, happier in Soho, because there I honestly believed I could be of greatest use. Without wanting to sound too emotional, I had a sense of vocation, and nowhere did I feel this more than when I was dealing with cases involving young junkies; the youngsters who had become hooked on drugs and would resort to anything to get money for a fix. I had a lot of sympathy for the kids who used public lavatories to give themselves a fix with filthy needles but none at all for the "pushers" who were responsible for their descent into total degradation and eventual death.

I also developed a near obsessional hatred for the "mobsters" who ruled by a reign of terror, threats and incredible violence. They waxed fat and rich with their protection rackets, and there were times when I turned a blind eye on the police's Disciplinary Code to bring them to justice. By that I don't mean I bent the rules; I simply consorted with the non-violent elements of that twilight world and made it clear that if they were prepared to help me bring the big fish to book I wouldn't lean too heavily on them. Setting a sprat to catch a mackerel isn't all that immoral. At least it wasn't in my book. And so I drank and mixed with prostitutes, straight club owners, gamblers and good honest people who owned shops and ran restaurants. As Soho had quite a big Italian community, my knowledge of the language was a great help in establishing and cementing some valuable friendships. My target was the people who ran the organized crime: the big men who would burn someone out with a petrol bomb if they did not pay their "rent" – an aphorism for protection money.

The telephone seldom stopped ringing as more and more people rang to tip me off about every conceivable crime from murder to petty larceny. From a tip-off I helped to break a big fur-stealing gang which operated in the classier areas of the West End, and concentrated on titled women to whom a mink coat was a status symbol.

My reputation spread quickly, and despite the reservations of my superior officers I often received calls from Mayfair residents seeking my assistance. One came from a particularly famous Duchess whom I addressed as "Your Duchess" until the butler pointed out my faux pas. She could not have cared less because I got the result she desired. Another time I was called in by a very influential gentleman whose name was known countrywide. As he poured himself a hefty drink from a cut glass decanter he turned to me and said, "I don't suppose you drink on duty?" and I astonished him by saying, "I do all the time, sir." The copper who doesn't is a figment of the crime novelist's imagination and he has about as much chance of catching villains as a priest has of finding sinners in a nunnery. He too was a satisfied customer.

If variety is the spice of life then I lived it to the full at West End Central. No two cases were the same, and I quickly learned never to jump to conclusions. A senior officer walked into the CID room late one night and told me to accompany him to Middlesex Hospital where a man had been admitted after dying suddenly in a Mayfair house. On examination we saw distinct ligature marks around his neck which suggested manual strangulation. What had seemed a coronary was now a murder investigation. We went to the house where he had died and it turned out to be a pervert's paradise. One room was filled with the paraphernalia of flagellation and sadism: masks, whips, weird costumes and the inevitable shiny thigh-length boots. The establishment was run by a lady wearing high-heeled shoes. None of which accounted for the ligature marks until I peeped through a spy hole and saw a room equipped with a wooden frame complete with straps and a hangman's noose. It transpired that the dead man could only find sexual gratification by being strapped into the frame and the noose adjusted when he was standing on tip toes. He was then left alone and he could only climax when his legs started to give out and he was in dire danger of strangulation. Unfortunately, on this occasion observation had been rather lax and he strangled himself.

The case was taken over by a senior officer, and not being particularly interested in the sexual peccadilloes of the upper classes I did not even bother to find out the outcome. I was more concerned with the "heavies" who smashed up clubs and other premises, then assured the owner it would stop if they paid for protection. Sometimes the owner of a club or betting shop would refuse and they were rewarded with a petrol bomb through the window.

I soon learned that the men – in fact they were mostly young men barely out of their teens – were the minions of the big timers who operated behind the scenes. The yobboes, as I called them, were so mesmerised by their flashy cars, sparkling rings, fat wallets and curvaceous blondes, they couldn't wait for the day when they would step into their hand-made shoes.

The trouble was that too many decent people were scared to death of reporting them and they became so arrogant they ordered the most expensive meals and wines without any thought of paying the bill, although they were generously paid for their terror tactics.

The extent to which fear enforced silence cannot be imagined by anyone who has not experienced it at first hand. I often met people who lived happy, untroubled lives who assured me that no matter how grave the threat they would consider it their bounden duty to tell the police if they knew a criminal offence had been committed.

I would have loved to have taken them to the home of a woman who telephoned me one night saying she had been forced out of business. I went to her flat where she removed her blouse and showed me her breasts which had been terribly disfigured by burning cigarette ends. Her back had also been mutilated. The injuries, she said, had been inflicted by a bunch of young tearaways, all in their twenties, who had demanded money, but rather than pay she had decided to retire. The sad thing was that she would not make a formal complaint or give evidence in a court of law although she was prepared to identify her attackers. She even refused to have her injuries photographed, and so the incident was recorded in the "Unreported Crime Book", officially a non-existent volume which I had introduced to West End Central.

Although the gang had got away with their cowardly attack, it meant the CID would keep a sharp eye on their activities, and in due course they all received heavy prison sentences for crimes which did not include the attack on the woman. At least she had the satisfaction of reading they had been put out of circulation for a long, long time.

I recall another case where a big-time crook was able to avoid arrest by threatening potential witnesses and provoking convenient bouts of amnesia. I was determined to bring him to justice and decided to keep tabs on him, knowing that the leopard doesn't change its spots and sooner or later he would do something that would enable me to move in. The opportunity came when a club owner told me that this particular crook, who specialized in "protection", prostitution and pornography, was putting the arm on him and it occurred to me that if I could keep him under observation it might help as corroborative evidence. My problem was how to do that without my presence being spotted; I was so well known in

Soho I couldn't walk down the street without the whistle being blown.

Then I remembered a "Tom" I had helped out of a spot of trouble and who was particularly well disposed to me. She had business premises in the room on the second floor of a house which overlooked the club where the owner had been "fingered". I took her out for a drink and explained without going into detail that I had to keep observation on the place. As most of my mornings were spent in court I could only keep vigil from late afternoon until midnight, a suggestion which did not meet with her wholehearted approval for, as she pointed out, that was when she did most of her business and her "gentlemen callers" would not take too kindly to performing with a copper standing at the window. As her room contained only a bed and a bidet, I could not keep popping out whenever a client called; the obvious answer was for me to slip under the bed. Although it had the flavour of a French farce, I thought it might work and I made arrangements for an "overlap" watch to be made on the club when I was in court in case a team of "heavies" turned up to wreck the place.

That sordid little room also became my office because I took a lot of paperwork along with me, as I was working on several other cases at the same time. On an average I worked 14 hours a day, and if I waited until I returned to the nick to do my paperwork I would have been giving myself an impossible burden.

I kept observation for several nights and learned a lot about the oldest profession and a lot more about the men who patronise it. I remember one particularly heavy man, he must have weighed eighteen stone, who did his utmost to drive me through the floorboards. But he was never in any hurry to leave and he would remain on the bed chatting away while I was mentally pleading with him to leave. Perhaps he was aware of the enormous pressure he exerted on my lady friend because he always paid her double. One vicar who was a regular caller called her his Mary Magdalen.

One evening I was standing at the window when a regular called and I was forced to dive under the bed where I was overcome by an urgent need to relieve myself. I squirmed out and used the bidet and slipped back without the customer even noticing. After several excrutiatingly uncomfortable nights I called it off, the crook did not turn up. Maybe he had been tipped off. Apart from that, I had been told by an informant that a murder may have been committed on the manor, and that was a crime that took precedence over anything else.

Acting on his information I went to a small courtyard behind some business premises and found a blood-stained axe with human hairs adhering to it lying on the ground below the window of a first floor "spieler" (gambling joint). The "spieler" was deserted.

In view of the serious implications, I passed on the information to Detective Superintendent Ron Townsend who organized a full-scale investigation. Everybody connected with the "spieler" was traced and questioned. Typically none of them had seen or heard a thing, although I observed the give-away shocked look of fear in their eyes. There was no trace of a body, nor was there any hospital record of anyone having been admitted with serious injuries consistent with having been attacked with an axe. Soho could cocoon itself in silence when the message was spread around of what would happen to anyone who grassed. That is an aspect of police work which the public who are always demanding results never hear about.

Neither was it an isolated case. Often days, sometimes weeks, of work ended up with nothing to show for them. A typical example was the occasion when I was called in to investigate a double shooting in a clip joint. On the surface it looked simple: the owner had shot his partner, then turned the gun on himself. Nothing, however, must be left to chance, and again Mr Townsend mounted a rigorous investigation for in Soho things are not always what they appear to be. In the early hours of a very grotty morning I stood by his side at Westminster Mortuary looking at the two corpses laid out naked on their respective slabs, illuminated by particularly harsh overhead lights. Superintendent Townsend wanted to retrieve the two bullets to make certain they came from the same weapon.

A post mortem is not the thing you want to attend on an empty stomach, but then it doesn't do to have a full one either. As far as food goes it is a no-win situation. It is a grizzly procedure and the sound of a saw cutting through a human skull is something that takes a long time to shake off. I looked across at the Superintendent who was impassively sorting through the dead man's possessions, and I thought: Old coppers are like old soldiers, there is nothing left to disturb them. He turned, caught my gaze and said, "Harry, when we've finished here we'll get some coffee and a bite to eat."

I liked Mr Townsend, a man of quiet authority with a vast experience of criminals, who, like so many good coppers, had learned to conceal his emotions. To an outsider his behaviour might have been misconstrued as callousness, but it was only a form of self-protection. Beneath the case-hardened exterior he was a kindly sympathetic man.

12. Doris, Tanky and Tanky's mother
at the Château Austruther (p.195).

13. "I was taken outside and to my astonishment shown an old wartime jeep
with . . . 'Little Tanky' . . . painted on the spare tyre" (p.195).

14. "During a visit to Granrupt Major Farran,
    Captain Stonehouse and I were decorated with the Resistance award
    of medaille d'argent de la Legion Vosgienne" (p.197).

15. "The next stop was the most poignant of all for me personally" (p.196)
    Tanky greeting the Mayor of Velorcey. Sgt. Robinson is on the left.

I had served under him in The Sweeney and I was very happy to be under him at West End Central.

After the bullets had been retrieved and sent to ballistics for checking, I managed to snatch a catnap in my office chair before attending a remand hearing at Marlborough Street Magistrate's Court, by which time the clip-joint affair had been confirmed as a murder and suicide.

Inevitably when one spent so much time in the company of villains you tended to talk their own jargon. Often it was the only language they understood. The Judges' Rules lay down the precise form of words to be used when a person is arrested, but few policemen ever adhere to them.

Let me give you an example. Donald was a con-man who lived on his wits and the gullibility of others, but who abhorred violence. When in funds he was generous to his friends, but he had a weakness for slow horses and fast women. When he was caught out he did not protest his innocence but accepted it as an occupational hazard. Once I went to a drinking club to arrest him and when I walked in he said, "Is it upon me, Harry?" I nodded and he asked me if he could finish a business transaction first. I agreed, bought a drink and waited for him to come over. When he did I said, "You're nicked, Donald, you don't have to rabbit and if you want to ring your brief (solicitor) you can do it from here." In effect I had formally told him he was being arrested, cautioned him and given him access to legal representation.

If I had used the Judges' Rules he would have asked me if I was drunk. When he went to ring his solicitor I did not accompany him, holding his arm as prescribed for an arrest. I knew he would not try and leg it.

On the way to the police station he said, "Can I talk to you about it, Harry?" and I told him, "Look Donald, you've got your bloody brief on the way to the nick, rabbit to him." According to the Judges' Rules I should have reminded him that he had been formally cautioned.

After the formalities had been gone through at the station I bought him a cup of tea and a newspaper and took them to his cell. He immediately settled down to the racing page.

Although I loved my work I knew I was overdoing it, for there were times when I thought it was hardly worth going home as I had to be in court early next morning. Doris was beginning to describe me as "the stranger".

Drug trafficking was rife in Soho and I developed such a loathing for the pedlars in death that I did my utmost to keep away from drug enquiries. I had seen too many young girls who would sell their bodies for a fix and teenage youths whose dead eyes reflected the hopelessness of their condition. I'll never forget the time when a policewoman asked me to accompany her to the women's detention room where I saw a most pitiful sight. A young woman in filthy rags, hardly any flesh on her bones, her face ravaged and the veins on her arms punctured by a multitude of injections. She was whimpering like an animal and had clearly given up the fight. She had been found in a scruffy disused basement in Soho. Enquiries had revealed she came from a very good class family. Victims like her had my sympathy whereas the bastards who waxed fat on their needs made me so angry I seriously doubted if I could control myself if I arrested any of them. But a detective can't pick and choose the type of investigation he goes on, and there was one occasion after I had helped break a very vicious ring that I visited the cells after they had been given hefty sentences. I told them that if they ever returned to the West End after finishing their terms, I would kill them and then assist in the investigation which would establish they were the victims of gang warfare.

No official complaint was made about my conduct which was in one respect a pity. It might have led to a full inquiry which would have spotlighted the growing menace of drug trafficking which in those days was not ringing the alarm bells as it is now.

Fighting crime in Soho was like trying to swim against a tide of sewage; you made two strokes forward and were swept back three. For every villain you put behind bars there were always two more to take their place. Most of them were professional crooks, and if there is any truth in the cliché crime doesn't pay they never got the message. If they were caught and sent down they carried on where they had left off as soon as they were released. They just were not interested in making an honest living, the pickings were not good enough, and they laughed themselves hoarse at the suggestion that they were what they were because of deprived childhood. They had nothing but contempt for the decent, hard-working people who were content to put in a good week's work for a wage packet that would not have kept them in cigars. In wartime they had cornered the black market in practically every rare commodity – petrol, cigarettes, spirits, nylons, clothing coupons – and anyone who put on a uniform in preference to living high off the hog needed to have his head examined. In peacetime they saw policemen in the same light: mugs who played cops and robbers instead of feathering their nest with backhanders.

They hated people like me whom they saw as meddling busy bodies, custodians of the law in a jungle that recognized no law. They resented police interference into what they considered was a personal domain. Any trouble there was should be left to them to sort out.

I had an experience of this when I went to a rather select Mayfair club which had been turned over to a bunch of "heavies". It looked like the scene of a pitched battle, chairs and furniture were overturned, broken glass littered the floor, and customers stood in terrified groups. Naturally the manager and his staff had not seen anything, although it was obvious to me that there had been a row over protection money. In one of the toilets I found a decent young man who had gone out for an enjoyable evening and been stabbed in the eye with a broken glass.

At a corner table I spotted a well-known gang leader looking pathetically innocent and deeply incensed that one of his men had been arrested for being in possession of a flick knife. He invited me to search him, but I knew that would be waste of time. In any case, I had no power to search everyone in case I offended genuine customers.

I took the injured man to Moorfields Hospital where I was told he had lost the sight of his eye.

The next evening I received a message from the gangster saying he would like to meet me in the club where he had been responsible for so much mayhem. He gestured me to a seat beside him at a corner table, and I leaned forward, brushed his lapel and said, "I thought I saw some porridge on your suit." (A message, conveyed in words he could understand, that he was due for a spell in prison.)

He ignored the taunt and said, "Sergeant, my boy who got nicked last night complains he got a belting and was fitted up and verballed."

I replied, "I'm a very busy man, would you take this unfounded complaint to the proper quarter?" I was not at all worried by his allegation; crooks invariably called foul when they were arrested. Looking back I wish I had not been so blasé.

He then called for drinks and said, "Let's be friends, Sergeant. There is just the two of us here so we can talk." By that I knew he meant that whatever he said could not be used as evidence because there was no one else to corroborate it. "Last night another team tried to move in and we stopped them. We are men of the world so why don't you leave us to sort out our own problems? I'll see that you get a good drink from a safe source."

I told him I was not interested in the bribe, simply in the rival gang, but he shrugged and said, "We can look after little people like them."

I wondered who would look after the young fellow who had lost an eye. The gangster would have been appalled if he could have read my thoughts. I was thinking back to the SAS when dangerous enemies were removed with a well-aimed bullet.

I left him under the false impression that he had got his message across, whereas I visualized him wearing a prison uniform with porridge down the front. I may have lacked finesse, but I was strong on tenacity and I knew it would not be long before I booked him. As far as I was concerned he had simply been remanded on bail. I had no doubt that when he appeared in court he would have what we called in the Met a fit of dock asthma. That was how we described the often histrionic behaviour of a hardened criminal when a police officer went into the witness box to give evidence. The accused would fix his eyes on the jury, breath deeply and roll his eyes in disbelief that a servant of the public could invent such wicked and evil things about an innocent person. The trouble was it often worked.

Perhaps I was turning my work into too much of a personal crusade, but no one could say I did not get results and that in my book was all that mattered. I had received numerous commendations and passed the exams which would lead me to bring promoted to Detective Sergeant First Class. I toyed with the idea of refusing it, because it might mean having to leave Soho.

If my success rate was high I also chalked up some failures, but they were inevitable and I never cried over spilled milk, although I cursed my own ineptitude. I lost one big case of demanding money with menaces because I made a slip up in my interpretation of the Judges' Rules. But as the accused was already serving a term of imprisonment not too much was lost. It happened like this: A Turkish gentleman who owned a Soho club told me he had been beaten up for failing to pay his "rent" (protection money), but instead of being intimidated he had come to me for help. I started to make enquiries and found that one of his attackers was beyond the reach of the law; someone had shot and killed him. I shed no tears for him. The other, I discovered, was in custody at West London Court where he had been sentenced on an entirely separate matter. I decided to interview him in the cells below the court. I was aware that the Judges' Rules required that a person in custody should be cautioned before being questioned, but I wrongly assumed that this referred to the matter for which he was being held. My business was completely detached from that. I submitted the results of my interview to the Solicitor's Department at New Scotland Yard for consideration of a charge of demanding money with menaces, and this was agreed to. When the prisoner appeared at the Old Bailey the club owner who had been beaten up gave his evidence and I gave mine. An astute defence counsel spotted my failure to administer a caution and submitted that my evidence was inadmissible. The judge upheld him and the prisoner was acquitted, and he was returned to prison to serve out the sentence imposed at West London Court. Often there is a too fine distinction between justice and the law.

The club owner was not too depressed. "One is dead, the other is in prison. I have nothing more to fear. I won't be intimidated by others because they'll know I'm prepared to go to the police." That was the kind of co-operation I had been working so hard to establish, so I wasn't too deflated either.

With crime escalating at a terrifying rate – offences were up fifty per cent while arrests were up only twenty per cent – some new approach had to be made. The senior officers just could not handle more work, and so special night squads were set up consisting of young Aids to the CID. They were put under my wing and that of Detective Sergeant Ken Etheridge, a highly skilled operator. The Aids were very keen young men who had been carefully chosen for their enthusiasm and aptitude for detective work. They were an immediate success, but soon there was considerable concern over the amount of work they were putting in. I wasn't very old, but I looked upon them as my family and I was the Old Man they could come to with their problems, not only workwise but domestic. It was the same close relationship which had existed in the SAS between officers and soldiers barely out of their teens. Those young Aids were doing a difficult job in extremely harrowing and dangerous conditions: they were threatened, often assaulted, their existence hardly acknowledged by the outside world, yet they were human, sensitive beings with homes and families of their own – whom incidentally they seldom saw.

Unknown to me there was mounting concern about my health and fear that the underworld was working out the best way of getting rid of me – and they would not be sticking to any rules. In their own jargon they were preparing to "stitch me up".

During one thirteen-day period I had worked 187½ hours and the strain was clearly showing. I was also having more trouble with my hearing, and it was noticeable that I was becoming noisy and boisterous. Detective Superintendent Townsend told me to ease up on my activities and limit my cases to those already in hand; on no account was I to undertake any fresh investigatioons and I was not to exceed an eight-hour day. He had also heard that attempts would be made to discredit me in order to get me out of the way, and he spoke to the Deputy Commander, the late Reg Spooner, and suggested to him that for my own good it might be best to move me to a quiet station and give me a desk job. When I heard about it I pleaded with him not to transfer me; that seemed to be playing into the hands of the crooks. A move was what I dreaded more than anything; Soho was my manor, and so much still remained to be done. And so I remained silent about what I was dying to confide to someone: that I believed I was going mad, and getting worse. If I did, that would not mean just a move but departure from the Force. I kept quiet, telling myself it did not affect my work.

After a routine meeting with an informant, I casually remarked that we would soon be embarking on a thought transference operation. He looked at me and said, "I always thought you were fucking mad, Harry." I got up and angrily walked out. He was the nutter; there was nothing wrong with the operation I had hinted at.

Then came the Brick Case and what I had been so skilful in concealing from my superiors and Doris was publicly proclaimed in blazing headlines throughout the country.

Chapter Fifteen

I have only the vaguest recollection of the night I was escorted into Netherne Mental Hospital, although it had an indelible impact on the staff. I signalled my disapproval by smashing my fist through a large window and breaking the glass cover of a fire alarm which brought out the internal fire brigade. This was followed by a hectic period of persuasion with members of the staff trying to impress on me the need to go to bed and rest while I attempted to convince them that that was the last thing I wanted. Eventually they succeeded.

When I awoke next morning in a locked ward, I experienced a strange feeling of remoteness and lurking dread. Only those who have been mentally ill will know what I mean, because it is a feeling that cannot be put into words. From the rather disjointed fragments of conversation I gathered we were scheduled for "treatment", and when I asked what exactly that meant I received the emotionless reply, "Convulsion treatment". The leaden tone implied that it was not very effective, neither was it something to be looked forward to.

We were taken to an annexe where we waited our turn to go into the Treatment Room. After an injection in the arm I lost consciousness while electric currents were passed through my brain. When I came to I found I was strapped to the couch. Apparently the treatment lived up to its name for the patient's body underwent terrific contortions. I experienced an awful sense of despair and helplessness which took a long time to overcome. (I was to experience the same sensations every time I received the treatment during the three years I was in Netherne and my periodic detentions later.) The mere thought of it brought me out in a cold sweat. I felt as if each visit to the treatment room was a walk from Death Row to the electric chair.

When I had recovered sufficiently to be moved, I was allowed into the day room with the other inmates, and with a shock that was like a plunge into ice cold water I realised I must be considered dangerous. The room could only be entered and left by the use of a key which was

159

kept in the possession of a ward nurse or some person in authority. It was as secure as a prison.

I have mentioned earlier the sense of loss and desolation that led me to attempting suicide and how Doris rescued me from the abyss of despair, but my time as a young man in Leavesden Mental Hospital also helped. There I had worked alongside many hopeless cases and done my utmost to make life a little more tolerable. I had learned to accept their plight without being too shocked and treated them as far as conditions allowed as normal people. It was, I decided, merely a question of adapting.

As the weeks turned into months and then years, life became more tolerable. I found my sense of humour had not deserted me, and I discovered that at least I was an inveterate gossip. On reflection I thought this was what made me so at home with people of such contrasting backgrounds during my detective days.

Remembering how I entertained the patients at Leavesden, I became a rather amateurish forerunner of the talking library. I told my fellow patients about the old man with a lurcher who kept down the foxes on the sewage farm near my home, and the incredible cosmopolitan world I had worked in in Soho and the more rarefied strata of Mayfair. It was entertaining for them and a form of therapy for me.

I had never been one to tolerate fools gladly, but at Netherne I mellowed considerably. When you have been certified you are not in a position to be intolerant. Having experienced for myself the fantasy world that mentally ill people flit in and out of, I could sympathize and understand those who lived in a world of delusions and discovered how important it was not to scoff at them but to move into their strange world. The task of curing was down to the medical staff; I was simply interested in trying to make some of those leaden-footed hours pass more quickly.

I particularly remember a man of about forty who was seriously retarded and had no hope of ever being allowed to return to the outside world. He seemed at times to know this and his plight was made all the worse by the fact that he had no living relatives. He did a lot of the ward chores that others did their utmost to avoid, and I started to call him Boss, not in a derisory or patronising manner but simply because he enjoyed the title. Over the years he had built up a fantasy situation in which one of the male nurses, I'll call him Bob, figured strongly. Bob was cast in the role of the villain, but being a very kind and gentle person he entered Boss's makebelieve world. Gradually I was drawn into the game, and like the nurse became a fellow conspirator.

160

Boss confided that he owned a very luxurious flat outside London which was being looked after in his absence by his very beautiful girl friend, and Bob, a sex maniac, was trying to find out where it was.

It was more than wishful thinking on Bob's part; it was the one thing that made life tolerable, and I had no intention of disillusioning him. I even went so far as to claim that I had met the young lady and invented a story about being invited to coach at Watford Football Club where she had called out from her flat which overlooked the ground, "Give my love to Boss".

Boss made me swear not to divulge the whereabouts of the flat to Bob who would be certain to go there.

Bob and I kept it up like a long-running serial, and although there were times when the plot-making became ludicrous it kept Boss happy. I recall telling him that on one occasion when visiting Watford I had seen Bob being thrown out of a public house hopelessly drunk, and when he was arrested his pockets were found to be full of contraceptives. Boss was delighted. The nurse was all he claimed he was: a sex-mad alcoholic.

I don't want to give the impression that I was the one sane person in a ward of madmen, I was still a captive to my own weird little world where the SAS lurked in the background like ghostly spectres. The evening pills brought welcome sleep and escape into a total vacuum. (I must have taken millions of pills over the years, and I still have to. I ought to rattle like dice in a throwing cup.)

Madness, like most other things in life, has its degrees, and I was determined that one day, no matter how long it took, I would return to the outside world and resume a normal life. But for others I knew there was no such future. I well remember one young chap who had been a brilliant scholar who endlessly paced the ward with a large book under his arm, speaking to no one from the time he got up until he went to bed. (He was still doing it when I left.) Others sat and cried all day, while some were extremely noisy, bursting into raucous song or indulging in noisy bouts of totally incomprehensible conversation.

When I was eventually discharged from Netherne I was far from cured, and I had to make periodic returns when I was in a "high" state when it took five or six weeks to bring me down. I also had spells of treatment in Belmont and Chiltern Wing Mental Hospitals. I was extremely fortunate in having Doris as my buttress, for whenever my spirits slumped and I was in danger of throwing in the towel, she was always there giving me encouragement. I knew she had shared every minute of my suffering, and it would have been act of betrayal not to keep on fighting.

It was not without a feeling of trepidation that I prepared to resume life on the outside, for I was acutely aware that with my mental history I could never hope to obtain a job of any responsibility or position. I would have to content myself with surviving. This had occurred to me during my last year at Netherne because I studied everything I could get hold of on industrial radiography and the hospital helped me considerably by letting me borrow everything that might help from the library. My studies helped me to obtain employment in this field with a small firm in Croydon, and later I moved to A.P.V. (Metal Propellers) in the same area. I worked hard and enthusiastically, and no one made any comment when I had to pay a visit to what I jokingly called my Country Home. I remained with the firm for several years before the branch was closed down. With my knowledge of Criminal Law, court procedure, and my experience with legal paperwork, I got a job as a clerk to a firm of Solicitors in Norbury. But the past came to haunt me in a rather unexpected manner. I was sent to Brixton Prison to obtain a statement from a man who had been remanded in custody and whom the firm was representing. When I entered the prison I casually remarked to a prison officer, "I used to come here as a CID officer interviewing prisoners, then I came as a prisoner myself, and now I'm here for the defence. That's what you call bloody good all round experience."

The prisoner I was to interview took a different view. He declined to make a statement and said he wished to change his Solicitors. I attended Bow Street Magistrate's Court next morning and the client told the magistrate that the reason he wanted to change his legal representative was because he had been told that ex-Detective Challenor was a police informant.

I spent more than a year with the firm during which time I had two serious bouts of mental illness which entailed becoming an in-patient for spells which lasted several weeks. That clearly was a matter of grave concern for my employers who were dealing in delicate legal matters, and the time came when I had to think of finding fresh pastures. I had to find somewhere I could read-ily admit to being a "nut case" and go off for treatment without covering it with a tissue of lies. I thought of the foundry where I had worked after leaving the army and where my father-in-law still worked. He spoke to the foreman and I was offered a job as an iron moulder. It was in some respects a home-coming for me

162

as many of the old hands remembered me and really made me feel welcome.

After a long spell in hospital and the periods of sedentary employment, I was soft and flabby and the first six weeks nearly killed me. I still retained the old skills, but some of the materials and techniques had changed. But with the unstinted help of Harold, a first-class moulder who nursed me along like a child, I made good progress.

One day I astonished my work mates by a sudden outburst of unexpected hilarity. That summer was an extremely hot one, which did not make conditions in the foundry any better. I was ramming a mould, stripped to the waist and filthy dirty with black sand and dust. Streaks of sweat had made white rivulets down my coal black torso, and I traced one with a finger and shouted, "Good old Harry, always in the shit."

It wasn't a cry of despair, but more a bellow of contentment; for the first time in years I was leading a normal and happy family life. I had a loving wife, friendly neighbours, and the company of workmates who were kind and thoughtful. I now went to the pub for a social drink and not to pump someone for information or keep my ear to the ground.

The lads in the foundry were a wonderful bunch, who in their down to earth fashion made it clear that they did not in the least care that I had been insane. In fact they encouraged me to make a joke of it. I even drew up plans for what I called my last operation and titled it, "Operation – Preserve Insanity". It was a send-up of one of the fantasies I had indulged in. I prepared it as if it was a real job and I gave vital roles to nearly everyone in the works. It was a long paper which took me hours to type without a single error in spelling. I gave as the reason for the operation:

Information has been received that the German SS and the Russian KGB have joined forces in an endeavour to take over the world. The organisation is codenamed "Sanity" with headquarters situated near Berlin. We know that the Nazi forces exterminate Jews, coloured people and those who are mad and this could pose a threat to Pullen Foundry as we come under this last mentioned category. However, on a happier note, it is known that the KGB secure sane people in mental institutions. If they can be induced to put *all* sane people in mental institutions, there is a strong chance of survival for the world.

It was a mixture of the Goons and the Benny Hill show, filled with zany situations and a lot of red-blooded sex. The finale was the assassination of the heads of the SS and KGB by means of poisoned *News of the World* Championship darts. I ended the Secret Operational Order with: My signature is in invisible ink.

My mates entered into the spirit of it and I know it did me the world of good. Having reached the stage when I could laugh at myself I knew I was on the road to full recovery, albeit a long and winding one.

Chapter Sixteen

When I was committed to the mental hospital, the name of Sergeant Harry Challenor was not allowed to vanish into peaceful obscurity. Complaints about my handling of criminal cases flowed in and what started as a snowball threatened to develop into an avalanche. After the conviction of the three CID Aids, the National Council for Civil Liberties said there should be no further delay in Scotland Yard's study of cases in which I had been involved over the previous 18 months. In fact, Chief Superintendent John Du Rose, one of the Yard's most brilliant detectives, had been ordered to carry out an investigation.

At the conclusion of the Brick Case trial, Mr Justice Lawton had added further fuel to public disquiet by summoning Mr Du Rose before him:

"Chief Superintendent Du Rose, I would be very grateful if you would bring to the attention of the Commissioner my grave disturbance at the fact that Detective Sergeant Challenor was on duty at all on 11th July 1963. On the evidence which I heard from the doctors when he was arraigned, it seems likely that he had been mentally unbalanced for some time, and the evidence which I heard from Superintendent Burdett in this case has worried me a great deal. It seems to me the matter ought to be looked into further."

On 18 August, 1964, Mr Henry Brook, the Home Secretary, ordered a Public Inquiry and appointed Mr Arthur Evan James, a distinguished QC, to "inquire into the circumstances in which it was possible for Detective Sergeant Harold Gordon Challenor of the Metropolitan Police to continue on duty at a time when he appears to have been affected by the onset of mental illness."

Appointed to assist him as Assessor were Commander William Willis, a retired naval officer and formerly one of Her Majesty's Inspectors of Constabulary, and Mr G.H. Baker of the Home Office who filled the role of secretary. The evidence was presented by Mr

Hugh Park, QC (later Mr Justice Park) and Mr M.L.M. Chavasse, who had been instructed by the Treasury Solicitor. Numerous Counsel were briefed to protect the interests of the 132 witnesses who were called to give evidence.

I was blissfully unaware of this dramatic turn of events because as I have said elsewhere all news of any kind that related to my conduct as a police officer was kept out of my sight and hearing.

Mr James heard evidence in public from 28 September until 26 November, 1964, but his report was not submitted to Parliament by the Home Secretary – by then Sir Frank Soskice QC – until August, 1965. No one could say there had been a rush to pass judgment; it was an extremely detailed and critical report.

Although the main purpose was to find out when I became ill, the Inquiry, so far as I was concerned, became a personal trial, for Mr James decided that in order to reach a fair conclusion he had to probe into cases in which it was alleged I had acted illegally and corruptly. As I was not allowed to appear it may have appeared to some as *Hamlet* without the Prince of Denmark, but when I was able to read the report I had no grounds for complaint. Many of the allegations that were made against me were proved to be unfounded. As Mr James commented: "Such allegations form part of the armoury of the criminal and are directed at any target which it wished to destroy."

I can only deal briefly with each case, for the Report of the Inquiry is a book in itself, but I will try and deal as fairly as possible with them and not leave out any salient point. Throughout the long Hearing there were big headlines and columns of copy chronicling my alleged wickedness. Most of the evidence came from people with criminal records. But it at least provided the reader with an in-depth picture of the murky world in which I and my colleagues worked.

First I will get out of the way the conclusion Mr James reached about my mental condition. After re-hearing all the expert medical evidence and that of numerous senior officers and that of Doris, he said that prior to the month of July, 1963, there were no manifestations or symptons which at the time could have been attributed to mental illness even by an expert in psychological medicine: only in retrospect could it be said that the mental illness was present and developing during this period. "I find that 6th September 1963 was the first occasion upon which Sir John Richardson had sufficient data to justify a diagnosis of mental illness, and that Detective Sergeant Challenor was removed from duties by Sir John Richardson at the first opportunity on which the information available justified his removal."

All the senior officers were absolved from any blame for not spotting it earlier than they did because ". . . Sergeant Challenor was particularly adept at concealing from others the emotions which he was experiencing, which concealment is a normal feature of the disease." There was no evidence to support the view that it commenced prior to April or May, 1963.

The first case reviewed concerned Lionel William King and David Lewis Silver whom I had arrested in Charing Cross Road at 4.30 a.m. on 25 April, 1963, and charged with being in possession of detonators knowing them to have been stolen, and possessing them with intent to cause malicious damage to a building by explosion, and conspiracy to cause damage to a building. Each was found guilty and sentenced to a term of imprisonment.

In November, 1963, after I had been found insane, King wrote to Mrs Joyce Butler MP and protested that I had planted the explosives on him and on 9 January, 1964, Mr Clinton Davis, a Solicitor, wrote to Mr John Du Rose who was investigating complaints against me requesting that the case be considered.

On 2 July, 1964, it was announced that Mr King and Mr Silver had been granted Free Pardons.

Mr King's story went back to the summer of 1962 and was related to matters concerning John Ford, Joseph Oliva, Ricardo Pedrini and Wilfred Gardiner, of whom more will be heard. King made no attempt to conceal his criminal background and admitted that he had been released from prison in 1961 for an offence committed with Joseph Oliva. He then took employment with a bookmaker who had betting shops in Greek Street and Percy Street, Soho, which were both damaged by explosives.

I was investigating attacks on betting shops, and in the course of my duty I had interviewed King. He claimed at the Inquiry* that I was rough and tough and threatened to plant something on him if he did not provide information, and at a second interview I had made the startling disclosure that I was "in charge of the protection racket." (That seemed in direct contradiction to the results of the investigation into my financial affairs.)

Luckily for me, Detective Constable Jay, who had been present at one of the interviews, was called to give evidence to the Inquiry which

* Any reader who wishes to study in greater detail the evidence given and the conclusions reached by Mr James should consult Report of Inquiry by Mr A.E. James QC, Her Majesty's Stationery Office. Command 2735.

totally contradicted Mr King's version of events. He recalled that King had been asked if he knew a Mr Wilfred Gardiner who alleged that he (King) and others had threatened him with violence. I had then told King that the facts would be reported and consideration given as to whether he should be charged, and I cautioned him. Jay said that King replied, "Don't you think I'm in enough trouble with all those bombs? I can't say anything – I will get my throat cut. I'm getting it all ways." (A telling feature was that the statement prepared by Jay had been submitted to the Solicitor's Department of the Metropolitan Police.)

Mr James then went back in time to the early morning of 24 April, 1963, when King and Silver were arrested. According to King he had been delivering literature to clubs in the West End when he by chance met Mr Silver who asked for a lift home in his car. But before doing that they went to some clubs where they were joined by two girls. (They too figured in one of the other complaints investigated by the Inquiry.) After taking the girls home they returned to the West End and as they were leaving Leicester Square they were stopped by a police car which contained myself, Jay, and Detective Sergeant Etheridge. Silver was ordered out of the car and searched and taken by Sergeant Etheridge to the police vehicle while I was said to have leaned into the stopped car and removed a cushion. I was then said to have taken it to the police car, slit it open and produced two small objects with wire attached, saying to King, "I've got two detonators here. You're nicked."

Silver, however, claimed that I borrowed a knife from Sergeant Etheridge, slit open the cushion, and that my hand seemed to move towards my pocket before the detonators were produced.

Detective Constable Jay's evidence to the Inquiry was that I earlier told him I had information that King was in the West End and his car contained explosives. He confirmed that I borrowed a knife and produced two detonators from the cushion, but I could not have "planted" them because I did not have the opportunity to do so.

Sergeant Etheridge's evidence did not differ all that much, although he recalled me getting out of the car before the arrests and returning to say I had seen an informant who told me that King was in a car containing explosives. They returned to the station where various officers were detailed to carry out patrols for Mr King. He then went out on a separate search with me and Jay. And referring to notes made at the police station, he said that when the explosives were produced King said, "Don't look any further, Sergeant. There's no "gelli" here now. You could score all this down to aggravation. We're unlucky; that's somebody else's gear."

Mr James recalled that at their trial neither of them alleged that *I* had "planted" the detonators, although King said they must have been put there by somebody else. In explanation, King told the Inquiry that that had not been the defence he had wanted, but he had been advised that an attack on the police would mean his previous criminal record could be produced. But papers produced by Counsel revealed nothing to indicate he had made any allegation of being framed, although Mr James did point out that his Solicitor's Clerk may have pointed out what the effect of any such allegation would have.

Mr Silver took a similar line saying his Solicitor had told him there was insufficient evidence to support an allegation of "planting", and secondly it was bad tactics to make an allegation which would permit his criminal record to be produced. He also claimed that the oral statements he had made were false, but he had not challenged them again on the advice of his Solicitor. The admission he had made under oath at his trial that the statements were true was a lie.

Mr Norman Beach, his legal representative, told the Inquiry that Silver had suggested the detonators had been planted, but after this was carefully examined he told Mr Silver that he did not think the police were involved and he specifically asked him if he had seen me put my hand in my coat pocket, but he could not recall that and did not want to put forward an allegation that could not be justified.

But, as Mr James pointed out, in a statement Silver made to Chief Inspector Green on 17 January, 1964, he described how I had put my hand into my raincoat pocket, taken it out, placed it in the cushion and withdrawn the detonators. He preferred Mr Beach's evidence to that of his client.

Mr James solved this conflict of evidence by saying he preferred that given by Detective Constable Jay which was supported by a statement submitted to the Solicitor to the Metropolitan Police, and made before any allegation had been made against me.

Mr James stated that he felt unable to regard Mr King as a witness of truth, and went on to say, "Upon the evidence of Detective Sergeant Etheridge and Detective Constable Jay there was no opportunity for Detective Sergeant Challenor to place the detonators in the cushion."

And he rejected as "inaccurate and deliberately untrue" the passage in Mr Silver's statement that he saw me put my hand in my raincoat pocket.

There was a possibility that someone else had placed the detonators in the cushion and then taken steps to ensure that I was in the West End at the time to search the car.

"On the other hand the reliable evidence strongly points to the conclusion that Detective Sergeant Challenor did not place the detonators in the cushion but did make a genuine discovery thereof, and that is my conclusion."

That was of more importance to me than his finding that there was nothing to indicate I was mentally ill at the time.

The next case which alleged corruption on my part also centred around the sleazy world of Soho's clubland which only comes to life when most decent people are fast asleep in bed. It illustrates yet again the difficulties facing the police in an area like Soho. Organized crime is big business and it is pursued with the relentless determination of a business tycoon who is hell bent on building an empire; the great difference, however, is that violence replaces brains, and truth is something that just doesn't exist.

At 12.20 a.m. on 25 May, 1963, at the request of the owner, Detective Sergeant Etheridge, myself and Police Constable Robb went to The Establishment Club in Greek Street and arrested Ernest George Pink, Robert Joseph Brown, William Francis and Frederick Steven Bridgeman. Each was charged with possessing an offensive weapon, namely an open razor, a flick knife, a hatchet and a knife. They were tried at the Old Bailey and each claimed the weapons had been planted on them by the officers concerned, but the jury found them guilty and Pink was jailed for two years, the others for twelve months. The judge commented adversely on their defence which he described as a baseless attack on a number of police officers. Later the Court of Criminal Appeal quashed the convictions on the grounds of misdirection of the jury by the judge.

Later Pink wrote to the Commissioner asking for his complaint of wrongful arrest to be investigated. Pink at first declined to give evidence before the Inquiry on the ground that he was frightened because he had been threatened by a police officer, but this turned out to be no more than a suggestion from an officer friendlily disposed towards him that he should keep away from a certain club.

Mr James commented that he did not think Pink would be scared of anyone. It was an observation which Pink, a "strong arm man" at a strip club, more or less invited, for he said in evidence, "I don't have trouble because most people are afraid of me. I am deaf and dumb and use exaggerated signs and they think I am mental." He was also a powerfully built man who admitted to having a criminal record for offences involving dishonesty and violence.

Mr Pink said the four had gone to the club where they had gained admittance after he had threatened to black the doorman's eye, but he had said it as a joke. He was surprised that as he was leaving with Brown he was arrested. At West End Central he claimed that I produced an open razor and accused him of having it in his possession. Through the night, he said, he had repeatedly claimed he had been "framed".

The others also claimed that the weapons had been planted on them. Brown's version was that Detective Constable Robb had struck him before "planting" a flick knife on him. Francis claimed that Detective Constable Smith produced the axe he was accused of having in his possession. He also alleged that I had offered to let him free on payment of £150. Mr James said that under cross-examination Francis showed himself to be "an unreliable witness".

The four men were detained in the cells for five hours before being charged and the long delay was adversely commented on by Mr James.

Later Pink and Brown complained to Detective Superintendent Townsend that they had been framed and he (Townsend) explained that because of the impending criminal proceedings their complaints could not immediately be investigated, but they were fully entitled to make their allegations at the trial. Detective Sergeant Etheridge who had been in charge of the operation by virtue of his seniority, told the Inquiry that I took the razor from Pink's pocket when he was in the police car. Soon after arriving at the police station I assumed charge as he (Etheridge) left to raid the Roaring Twenties Club. Later I took part in the raid and was away from the station for the period covered by Pink's allegations.

Detective Sergeant Walker, a Detective Constable at the time of the arrests, said he was the driver of the car and corroborated what Etheridge had said in evidence.

Detective Constable Birch, who was with Robb at the time, said Brown violently resisted arrest and the flick knife was found when he was searched in the street outside the club.

Inspector Champion, the officer who actually charged the four men, said that none of them made any complaints about the conduct of any of the arresting officers although they refused to sign the charge sheets acknowledging the offensive weapons as being part of their property.

It was not until 26 June, 1964, that Solicitors acting for Francis and Bridgeman wrote to the Solicitor's Department of the Metropolitan Police claiming damages for wrongful arrest, malicious prosecution, and false imprisonment. The letter said that I had committed perjury at their trial and the evidence against them had been fabricated. The delay in making the claims, the letter went on, was due to waiting for the conclusion of the investigation being carried out by Chief Superintendent Du Rose.

As Mr James noted in his report: "That claim for damages has not yet been met."

Mr James's conclusions were not uncritical of me for he accepted that I had rubbed my hands and expressed delight when the weapons were produced. But he cleared me of "planting" a razor on Pink, and he went on to record, "I find no evidence to support a contention that Detective Sergeant Challenor instructed or countenanced the 'planting' of evidence by any other officer. Indeed on the evidence at the Inquiry I am not satisfied that any weapon was 'planted' on Mr Pink, Mr Brown, Mr Francis or Mr Bridgeman."

He made what, to me at least, was a very interesting observation. "If the conduct of fabricating evidence or tolerance of the use of violence is contended to be evidence of the onset of mental illness in the case of Detective Sergeant Challenor, then it is evidence of the onset of mental illness on the part of the other officers concerned."

Despite all the allegations made against me, including those of boisterous enthusiasm, there had been nothing to indicate to those present at the station that I was mentally ill.

The next phase of the report dealt with what Mr James called "The episode concerning Ronald William Braggins, Frank Matthews, Clifford Ireland and Frederick Steel."

The four men had been arrested within the precincts of Marlborough Street Magistrates's Court on the morning of 22 June, 1963, charged with using insulting words and behaviour, and at my request were not released on bail for some hours when I withdrew my objection. They appeared at Marlborough Street on four different occasions before being committed for trial at the Old Bailey, the main charge being one of conspiring to pervert the course of justice by the intimidation of witnesses. On 18 September no evidence was offered by the prosecution and all four were acquitted. The reason given to the court was that a few days earlier I had been diagnosed as being mentally ill, and had to be regarded as an entirely unreliable witness.

All four claimed compensation for unlawful arrest and Braggins

172

received £750 from the Metropolitan Police, Matthews £574, Ireland and Steel who were deaf mutes, £250 each.

As Mr James wrote in his report: "The story unfolded by the evidence is a strange one."

A fight had broken out at the Limbo Club in Wardour Street at which a man named Bates had been injured. Arising out of the incident Ernest George Pink, then on bail for being in possession of an offensive weapon at The Establishment Club, was charged with assaulting Bates and occasioning him bodily harm. His bail was withdrawn and he was due to appear in Court on 22 June alongside Brown, Francis and Bridgeman who had also been charged with possessing offensive weapons at The Establishment Club. (Readers will recall this case has been previously dealt with.)

On the day of the Hearing Braggins, Matthews, Ireland and Frederick Steel also turned up at the court. They explained to the Inquiry how this came about, but Mr James had reservations about their explanations which revealed a marked consistency with each other. Even a benevolent view of their evidence, and the manner in which it was given, "stretched credulity to its limit".

A fair but very condensed version for their reason for being present at court was that Steel had wanted to see how his friends were getting on and the others joined him.

They claimed I had been talking to the injured man, Bates, but when they appeared I left him and approached them with Detective Constable Robb and an interpreter in deaf and dumb language who at my request asked them their names and addresses. Then, according to Braggins, I said, "I heard there was going to be trouble up here." (My conduct may have seemed brusque but I had good reason for behaving as I did, although at the time I could not say so. In the very early hours of that morning there had been more trouble at the Limbo Club which had involved the use of a firearm, and I connected the appearance of the four men with the incident.)

They were then taken to the cells where they insisted that they had not intimidated anyone and did not know any of the witnesses in the case about to be heard.

That did not tally with the evidence given by Detective Constable Robb. According to him when Braggins entered the court building he said, "Wait until they see the other mob tonight," and Matthews said, "He'll want a bigger piece of plaster than he's wearing now." Both men denied they had used such threats. Mr James said that he and Commander Willis had been impressed by Robb as being a completely honest witness and an officer of ability and promise, but without any reflection on his conduct or credibility they had to treat the incident on the basis that there was no evidence before the Inquiry that the words had been spoken. (It sounds complicated, but I can only assume that this was because no evidence had been offered at their trial.)

Not that it mattered because Mr James found there was nothing in their conduct which justified me taking them into custody, and this was a manifestation of the onset of mental illness.

I was not called to give evidence at the Inquiry for obvious reasons, but I can recall the incident at court with great clarity and what I heard and saw made me disagree with Mr James's decision about the arrests, although I do not quarrel with him about his assessment of my mental condition. I would have been failing in my duty if I had acted differently.

The next case investigated by the Inquiry was one in which the victim might well have been said to have got all that he deserved. A young Swiss visited the Boulevard Club, a "near beer" or "clip joint", in Frith Street where he met Jean Browne who told him that if he bought sufficient drinks he could have sex with her later on. He bought the drinks and arranged to meet her in a coffee bar, but she did not turn up. Most young men would have left it at that, not wishing to advertise that they consorted with prostitutes, but the Swiss gentleman preferred to go to the police and register a complaint. As a result of his allegation, I made investigations into the conduct of Sydney Harold Dacosta Padmore, Patricia Violet Hawkins, Jean Browne and Broulio Dario Oliva.

To start with I went with the Swiss gentleman and Detective Sergeant Etheridge, something of an expert on "clip joints", to the club where the victim of the deception identified Miss Browne. She denied she was a prostitute but explained, "I have to earn a few pounds somehow. We kid the punters that they can have a bit of the other and then send them down to Wardour Street where friend Padmore speaks to them about his girl. They don't come back. Have a word with Mr Oliva; he is the real boss here."

The implication of her words was that Padmore would frighten off any customer by suggesting he was outraged at the idea of his girl friend being mistaken for a tart.

The next person we spoke to was Mrs Hawkins who was employed as a "waitress" but whose duties included the supervision of the hostesses employed at the club. According to her she was asked if she was "Big

Pat" or "Fat Pat", and if Oliva was the owner, but before she could answer I abused her and knocked her to the ground. She also said I was drunk, and when she offered to pay £9 to the Swiss gentleman I ordered him to hand back the money.

Detective Sergeant Etheridge painted a completely different picture of what had occurred. With the aid of his notebook to refresh his memory after such a lapse of time, he said he asked her if she was the woman who had assisted Browne to defraud the Swiss on the false promise of sexual intercourse, and she replied, "Yes, but don't take the girl, she takes her instructions from me. I told her to send him down to Wardour Street, and if a man had been there as he should have been this wouldn't have happened. Why don't you talk to Mr Oliva?" When he told her a warrant would be applied for to secure her arrest, she became hysterical and her conduct alternated from pleading to threatening. She had fallen to the ground when I had prevented her from handing back the money to the Swiss. He said that I was not drunk at the time, neither had I abused Mrs Hawkins.

Although I did not give evidence, my own notebook filled in at the time was produced which confirmed what Etheridge had told the Inquiry.

When warrants were obtained for the arrest of the two women for obtaining money by false pretences, I returned to the club with Detective Constable Robb and several other officers, both male and female. Browne was not there but Hawkins, who was, became so hysterical I had to call for the assistance of a policewoman.

Again Mrs Hawkins offered the Inquiry a different version of events. She claimed that both I and Robb assaulted her, and that I swore and threatened her with two years' imprisonment. She also said I was drunk.

Police Constable Powell who drove the police van said he saw no abnormal behaviour on the part of any officer, but he had a clear recollection of Mrs Hawkins being hysterical and crying and saying, "I'm rather a sick woman."

Of vital importance to me and the other officers was the evidence given to Mr James by Mrs Maureen Holland, a former woman police officer who had been in the party which went to the club. She said she had been instructed by me to go along as I feared Mrs Hawkins might make allegations against me of improper conduct, and she therefore watched events very closely. She said no violence was used against Mrs Hawkins, neither was she sworn at.

"This witness," wrote Mr James, "impressed me as a person who would have had no hesitation in reporting any misconduct by a male police officer towards a female prisoner, and who would have remembered any such conduct as Mrs Hawkins complained of in her evidence."

At midnight on the day Hawkins was arrested, Mr Padmore arrived at West End Central asking to see me. He was a native of Barbados, weighed 16 stone and was well over six feet tall, with an athletic build. He was shown into the CID room where I was with Detective Constable Robb, Constable Bridge and Detective Sergeant Cruse. From time to time other officers entered and left the office.

Padmore said he shared a flat with Mrs Hawkins, and after a certain amount of evasion admitted they were lovers; although he knew where she worked he knew nothing about the club and never went there. He strenuously denied playing any part in offences of obtaining money from customers by false pretences.

He said that he went to the police station after hearing of Mrs Hawkins' arrest in order to arrange bail, and when he was shown into the office I said, "What does a black ponce like you want in a white police station?" When he said he had not come to be insulted and intended to leave, I then ordered the door to be closed saying, "We'll have some fun with this coon; he looks big enough." After being told to empty his pockets he was grabbed by Robb and some other officers, whilst I struck him in the mouth breaking a tooth on the right side. He was still held while several more blows were struck. I then said to Robb, "Take that black bastard out of my sight. I wish I was in South Africa. I'd have a nigger for breakfast every morning," whereupon I started to sing, "Bingo, Bango, Bongo, I don't want to leave the Congo". The other officers present thought it was all a huge joke.

From time to time, said Padmore, Robb and I drank whisky which was on the desk, and I was showing signs of being affected by the drinks. He further alleged that I said I would think of something to charge him with and he would get seven years.

At this point, Detective Sergeant Cruse told me that Mr Dario Oliva had also arrived at the station and Padmore was moved to a typist's cubicle.

From there Padmore said he saw Dario Oliva go into the CID room where I struck him and abused him. (The condition of the door through which Mr Padmore saw the assault was to be the subject of some interesting and conflicting evidence, as were the broken tooth and other injuries Padmore alleged had been inflicted on him.)

176

Padmore said he was released at 7 a.m. and told to report back the following Thursday. At that stage he had not been charged with any offence. Oliva was released at the same time.

Padmore said that as soon as he could he went to the offices of Bernard Solley & Co., Solicitors, where he handed a written statement to Mr Stoller, a legal executive with the firm. On the Thursday when Padmore returned to West End Central Police Station, he was accompanied by Mr Stoller who was told that his client would be charged and kept in custody. Padmore alleged that soon after this I struck him again, breaking another piece of the already damaged tooth.

When Padmore appeared at Marlborough Street Court, he found himself in the company of Mr Rooum who had been arrested the previous evening in circumstances already described. Rooum gave the Inquiry details of Padmore's injuries and what he had said about the assault, but Mr James rejected his evidence.

Padmore was represented in court by Mr Claude Allen who told the Inquiry he noticed that his client's lip was swollen, he saw some blood on his shirt sleeve and had a vague recollection of being told about an injured arm.

Mr Stoller, who was also present, then instructed him to apply for a summons alleging I had assaulted his client, but this was refused. After the Hearing, Mr Allen said he saw me in the charge room with my head in my hands saying, "I must have my Guinness", or "I must have my beer".

Mr Stoller's evidence about Padmore's injuries was greatly different from that of his legal colleague. He said his client showed him a gap in his mouth from which a tooth was missing and his lips were swollen, one eye blackened and one arm was in a blood-stained bandage. The arm was held across his body and dangling as if broken. He too had heard me say I wanted my beer, and he formed the opinion that I "was either under the influence of alcohol or drugs".

He was quite emphatic at one stage of his evidence that Padmore showed him a piece of broken tooth and said it had been damaged the previous night (11 July), but later he was equally convinced that it could not have been so and the tooth had been broken on 6 July. The difference in the dates was of considerable importance.

Dr Hassan Bayoumi told the Inquiry he had been called to the court for the purpose of examining Mr Padmore's injuries, and he found a small contused wound on the inside of the lower lip on the left side and the second premolar tooth on the left side was broken. In his opinion the wound had occurred within 24 hours of his examination. Mr Padmore also complained of pain in the left side of his jaw, but he saw no sign of injury. Neither did he observe any eye or arm injury. As Mr James observed, "This evidence was a striking contradiction of that given by Mr Stoller."

The doctor went on to tell the Inquiry that the wound was consistent with a person biting the inside of the lip, and the damaged tooth had been substantially filled in the past and could have broken under the slightest pressure. The damage was also consistent with a blow, and this he regarded as the most likely cause. Such a blow would not require a lot of force.

Mr James found it confusing. "This witness's evidence refers to a broken tooth on the left side, whereas Mr Padmore had asserted that on 6 July the blow broke a tooth on the right side. The broken tooth found by the doctor had been subjected to dentistry, and the portion of 'broken tooth' which Mr Padmore said he had preserved and which he produced at the Inquiry was in fact, as Mr Padmore admitted, not a portion of tooth but a piece of dental filling."

Mr James then dealt with Mr Dario Oliva, stressing that he was in no way connected with Mr Joseph Oliva who had also made a complaint against me. The witness described himself as a professional gambler and admitted to having a criminal record for offences involving violence. Each of them arose out of his activities at clip joints and three of them involved violence towards customers. He denied that the promise of sex was ever made at the Boulevard Club. He only knew Padmore as a friend of Mrs Hawkins, and although he had seen him outside the club he had never seen him inside.

The reason he had turned up at West End Central Police Station was because he knew Mrs Hawkins was suffering from heart trouble and he wanted to arrange bail. When he saw me he found me very excited, insulting and aggressive, and I threatened to put him away for five years. He was also struck by me and he noticed I had blood on my hand which I described as "black blood" or "poncey blood".

He was released without being charged, and outside he saw Padmore who complained of his treatment. The report quoted the following extract from his cross-examination:

"Had Padmore got any mark on him?"

"Yes he did."

"What mark did you see on him?"

"A hanging tooth, a few loose teeth. He had a mouth bleeding and swollen."

"A hanging tooth?"

"Literally hanging."

"This description cannot stand square with the evidence of Mr Padmore nor with the object produced as being the 'broken tooth'," said Mr James.

Mr Oliva said that he "didn't like the whole tenor of things" so brought forward his holiday and left the country for Spain, not returning until late in January, 1964, by which time he learned no proceedings were to be taken against him as I was in a mental hospital. His reason for going away was that he feared I would "frame" him.

Mr James then dealt with the evidence of Detective Constable Robb, a very important part of which was that the door to the CID room could not be closed because it was damaged, and this was confirmed by others, including Detective Inspector Taylor. Robb also denied that Padmore had been struck. The same applied to Mr Oliva. Neither had he or I been drinking.

Robb was strenuously cross-examined by Leading Counsel, appearing on the instructions of the Treasury Solicitor in an attempt to discredit his evidence, and Mr James recorded, "The manner in which he dealt with the questions and his answers were of assistance in establishing him as an honest and truthful witness in respect of the events of 6 July, 1963."

Detective Sergeant Cruse, who was in the CID room in charge of the switchboard when Mr Padmore was brought in, said he was invited to listen to what was being said and he left his post to hear more clearly. He told the Inquiry he heard Padmore say to me, "I'd like to speak to you about Pat, the woman you took from Frith Street; she is my friend," and I replied, "What do you mean, your friend?" Padmore then said, "Well Sergeant, I think you know my friend Dario Oliva who has the clip at Frith Street. Now this is rubbish and only a few pounds owing. If I could have been at Wardour Street when the Swiss boy turned up you would not have this trouble." According to Sergeant Cruse I then said I did not understand what Padmore meant and pointed out the amount of work the incident had resulted in, and he said by way of explanation, "Look, I know that Sergeant. That is why Dario asked me to come and see you. Leave it to us, man. Dario will pay the Swiss boy, and when the punters come to Wardour Street I will make sure that if they are still unhappy I will take them to Dario and he will pay them and you will get no more trouble."

I was, said the witness, taking notes and when I finished told

Padmore that he appeared to be part of a conspiracy to obtain money by false pretences and a warrant for his arrest would be applied for. Padmore said in reply, "Very clever, Sergeant, but you forget we have the girl (Browne). You won't get her, and where is your case then?"

Sergeant Cruse's evidence was given with the aid of his notebook in which he recorded his notes on the night of the alleged conversation. My own notebook written at the same time was also produced and it confirmed the Sergeant's version of events.

The Sergeant also recalled my interview with Mr Oliva, again refreshing his memory from the notes made at the time. One most significant entry was a remark made by Oliva. "What can I say? I know you know the routine, and there is no answer to it if the Swiss boy goes the whole way. We have got the girl, and if the big spade had been doing his job at Wardour Street the boy would not have troubled you. I will be generous to the Swiss boy, and I will tell you Sergeant that there will be no more complaints."

Evidence was also given to the Inquiry by gaolers at West End Central and other officers on duty at the police station and Marl-borough Street Court who all said they saw no sign of injuries to Mr Padmore's face. They were officers whose duty it was to record such things.

Students of crime fiction are accustomed to the dramatic appearance of a mystery witness, and although it seldom happens in real life it did in the case being described. Mr James Ralph Rodriguez was serving a term of imprisonment at the time he gave evidence to the Inquiry. It was not his first prison sentence but when not in gaol he worked as a "leg man" for Fleet Street reporters and it was through this connection he came to be giving evidence. He wrote from prison to a reporter relating certain events which concerned Oliva and Padmore on 6 and 7 July, and the letter was sent to the Treasury Solicitor who submitted it to the Inquiry, and Mr Rodriguez was called as a witness.

On the night of 6 July, he said, he was in Frith Street and Mr Oliva whom he knew and like himself was a Gibraltarian, Mr Padmore who was Hawkins' boy friend, Mr Mario Requena and Mr Ralph Lopez. The conversation turned to who was the best person to seek the release of Mrs Hawkins, and Padmore left the group for that purpose. When Padmore did not return, Oliva announced that he would go, but he also failed to return. He (the witness), Requena and Lopez then went to West End Central and Rodriguez who knew me, having helped with information about a protection racket, volunteered to go in and speak to me.

The witness said I told him that Padmore and Mrs Hawkins were in the station and I wanted information about the missing Miss Browne. He left the station and had a conversation with the two men waiting outside and they took the view that if the girl could be kept in hiding it would not be possible to charge anyone. They then adjourned to a club and returned to the station to see if Oliva was to be released, and the witness said that he again spoke to me and promised that if Oliva was released he would provide information about the missing girl. Shortly afterwards Padmore and Oliva were released and they joined the witness and Requena and Mr Lopez.

Mr Requena, continued Rodriguez, who was regarded as the legal adviser to the group, said it had been a big mistake not to have charged the two men because when they returned to the station as requested they could claim they had been beaten up. Requena then suggested that as Padmore had no previous convictions he should return with a Solicitor and if he was charged and kept in custody over night, he should harm himself by biting his cheek and pinching his cheek bone.

Rodriguez said he saw Oliva the next evening who said he was going to see someone to get information about Challenor. He returned looking very worried and said his informant had told him that Challenor would not accept any money and his advice was to leave the country.

Understandably, Rodriguez was vigorously cross-examined and it was suggested he had said what he had in order to secure an early release from prison, but that did not seem sufficient reason as he was shortly to be freed anyway. He stoutly denied the suggestion, insisting that the sole reason was that he considered an injustice was being done to me by persons who were trying to "frame" me.

The next thing Mr James dealt with was the statement Padmore had written and given to Mr Stoller, and another dictated by the Solicitor in his office and entitled, "Statement of H.D. Padmore".

Mr James commented, "Comparison of the two revealed changes of words and substance which could have arisen either through Mr Padmore giving further instructions to Mr Stoller, or by alteration of the content in the course of dictation. The typed statement was the more adverse to Detective Sergeant Challenor."

Examples of the changes were "a voice" became "a loud voice"; the word "said" was changed to "yelled" and to "snarled"; "I could smell his breath and noticed an open bottle of whisky" was changed to, "his breath could be smelt from a distance and to confirm it he took

the bottle out from the desk and relaxed after his so-called exercise".
But the most striking of all was, "I saw he could not concentrate as he
was wiping his eyes and yawning" became "he could not concentrate
due to his heavy drinking".

When Mr Stoller was cross-examined with a view to ascertaining
whether Padmore had given him further instructions leading to an
"improvement" or "strengthening" of his statement, Mr James found
his replies "were in some respects contradictory and were entirely
unconvincing".

Mr Stoller said that he may have altered "said" to "yelled" to make
the statement read more legibly and that Mr Padmore had given him
oral instructions which had been incorporated in the typed version.

Mr James found his evidence regarding the alterations "completely
and utterly unreliable" and he was driven to the conclusion that the
typed statement was a "hotted up" version designed to carry more
weight against me. He concluded that the statement taken to Mr
Stoller by Padmore contained false allegations against me and the typed
statement made at Mr Stoller's dictation contained embellishments not
of Padmore's invention but ones he was prepared to adopt. "I am
satisfied Mr Stoller had no knowledge or means of knowledge that
the allegations made by his client in the manuscript statement were
false . . ."

In September, 1963, Miss Browne was arrested and she with
Padmore and Hawkins were committed for trial at the Old Bailey; but
at the trial the jury could not agree and a new trial was ordered. But the
Swiss gentleman who had already made several visits from Switzerland
declined to attend, and the prosecution offered no evidence and all
three were acquitted.

Padmore's Solicitor then wrote the letter to the Commissioner of
Police which has already been mentioned, and Padmore received
£750.

Mr James in his report found that Mrs Hawkins had not been
assaulted, and he reached the same conclusion about the alleged
assaults on Oliva and Padmore on 6 July. I was strongly criticised
for holding them in the cells for so long without being charged,
but this was due to my enthusiasm for work which had become an
obsession. I was out looking for the elusive Miss Browne. He also
accepted the evidence of Mr Rodriguez.

He did find that I lost control of myself on 11 July and struck
Padmore in the mouth, but he did not accept that the extent of his
injuries were as Mr Stoller described them.

182

Although no officer could be blamed for not recognizing my conduct as symptoms of mental illness, it was possible in retrospect to say they were.

I would not refute that because I was aware of my own worsening condition, but I would like to put the record straight on one thing. I did strike Padmore, but not for the reasons he claimed. I was alone with him in the CID room – I'm not sure if it was on 6 or 11 July – when he said, "Why should I talk to the son of a back street whore?" (My mother at the time was supplementing her pension by working as a tea lady in a Watford office.) I caught him on the temple with a right hander and knocked him down. I had never before hit a man in custody, but in the circumstances I think most people would have done the same. He had no need to make a false allegation because I would readily have admitted it if I had been able to attend the Inquiry. But my blow did not damage his tooth.

Mr James also dealt at considerable length with another case concerning Soho's clubland which took place during the months of July, August and September, 1962. He had done so because it had been suggested that there was some evidence that I was mentally ill at the time, but this he rejected entirely, saying his decision to investigate the incident fully was because attacks had been made upon the character and conduct of several people and in fairness to them ought to be investigated.

In December, 1962, five men – Ricardo Pedrini, John Ford, James Fraser, Joseph Oliva and Alan Cheeseman – had been found guilty at the Old Bailey of demanding money with menaces and of possessing an offensive weapon.

Pedrini was sentenced to seven years, Cheeseman three years.

John Ford, accused of demanding money with menaces – five years.

James Fraser, for possessing an offensive weapon – fifteen months.

Mr Oliva, for conspiring to demand money with menaces and possessing offensive weapons and receiving stolen property – six years.

In underworld jargon they had been involved in protection.

In July, 1964, the Court of Criminal Appeal quashed their convictions on the ground that my subsequent mental illness may have led the jury to reach a different conclusion.

I was extremely relieved that Mr James took the line he did because I was accused of assault, planting weapons and accepting bribes to show favour to the accused.

I became involved in the case following complaints by Wilfred Gardiner who was the owner of two striptease clubs. Again it was a tortuous case of conflicting evidence, outright perjury, and allegations of innocent people being hounded by crooked coppers.

The dramatis personae, as they might have been called in more sophisticated society, were dealt with one by one by Mr James.

Pedrini said he was a waiter employed in a restaurant owned by his parents, and he spent some of his spare time dancing and drinking in West End clubs with Ford whom he had known since childhood. He had been introduced to Cheeseman in 1961, but did not know Fraser or Gardiner. He admitted that at his trial he had lied by saying he did not know Oliva. The evidence against him was fabricated and the only way he could think of getting out of something he had not done was to tell lies. He now realized it would have been better to have told the truth. (Such was my corrupting influence on hapless citizens.)

Ford, a 26-year-old waiter who was also a frequenter of night clubs, said Oliva was a close friend although he had denied this at his trial. He did this because he knew Oliva had twelve previous convictions. He also pursued this line because I, some other officers, Gardiner and a woman called Evans were trying to frame him.

Fraser, aged 23, said in testimony that before their trial they had all agreed to say they did not know each other.

Oliva, aged 26, was a docker who also frequented clubs and had been jailed for being in possession of house-breaking implements and for assaulting an attendant at a Turkish bath. He also admitted that he had lied at his trial as to which of the accused he knew.

It was then suggested to him that he was someone who fancied himself as being capable of running "protection rackets", which he denied. Then an article, published in the *Daily Sketch* in 1959, was produced and handed to him. He tore it up and denounced it as "lies and filth", although he had signed the original and initialled the corrections.

I reproduce it in some detail to give some idea of what I was up against in Soho and the complexities which faced Mr James at his Inquiry:

"Joseph Francis Oliva, age 19 of 6 Radcliffe Buildings, Bourne Estate, Clerkenwell N., says, 'I was shot in the chest as I stood in the doorway of Carlo's Restaurant, Theobald's Road, Holborn, last night.' "

He then went on to describe his religious schooling and his criminal record which included one for causing grievous bodily harm.

" 'In the shooting last night I got about 16 lead shot in my chest. My mates picked them out with a knife. This is what happened. Ten of us were drinking tea when a black Austin pulled up outside the cafe. A man stuck a single barrel shotgun through the window when I went out to see them. When I was two yards from the car the man fired. The car raced off before I could get at the man. I am not disclosing his name to anyone, not even the police. I know who it is and I am out to get him myself. I will settle this my way. . . . The reason for the shooting is because I am the leader of a gang four hundred strong. They call me King Oliva.

" 'The shooting was in retaliation for a fight which took place in a dice speiler in a Camden Town club three weeks ago. It was a revenge attack because six of us cleaned up all the money, about £80. We just did it to show I was the "Guvnor". The money has gone on a car – a big Buick car, big enough to hold the lot of us.

" 'I am going to be boss of the night clubs – and run the night clubs around the West End. I have got to shift one or two big gang leaders to do it. But I have got a man behind me financing me. . .' "

It went on in the same vainglorious fashion saying how he operated a protection racket on behalf of a businessman who owned property and had a big house outside London.

" 'I command about four hundred people. I can get them all at 24 hours notice just by fifteen to twenty 'phone calls to individual top men in each gang. Then I am Governor of them all . . . They worship me – King Oliva.' "

The article continued:

" 'We do not value our lives because without money we are nothing.

" 'I am not worried about jail. If you do these things you have to expect "bird". It is one of those things. I am not afraid of prison or afraid of anything or anybody. When I am dead, that's it. I am not afraid of serving as much time as Billy Hill* but I am not going to jail for nothing.

" 'Look at Billy Hill. He was like us when he started. We admire him and look up to him. He's living easy. He is respected – feared if you like. I am going to be like Billy Hill one day . . . I am going to be boss because there are some rich pickings. All a fellow needs is guts and backing – and I've got both. We are going to live good

* Billy Hill was the self-described boss of London's underworld.

with cars and fine clothes. A big showdown for power is coming and when it does come it will be a bloody battle.'"

Mr Oliva, all injured innocence, said that none of it was true and he had only done it for money.

Mr Cheeseman, a 22 year-old salesman, also protested his innocence.

Mr Wilfred Gardiner was the owner of two strip clubs which had been closed for a while following threats of violence. He made no secret of his own criminal background which included offences of violence and obtaining money by false pretences. But he denied there was any conspiracy between him and me and other police officers to obtain the conviction of innocent men.

A precis of the vast amount of evidence heard by Mr James was that Gardiner was being subjected to pressure over protection money and had been assaulted. Other acts of intimidation followed, most of which were marked by a reluctance to complain to the police. One incident concerned damage to Gardiner's car and nothing would have been heard of it unless Detective Inspector Bruce had not read a newspaper article saying the club owner was the victim of protection racketeers. As a result he saw Gardiner who confirmed he had been assaulted but refused to give names.

Further incidents occurred involving Mr Gardiner and demands for money which culminated in him coming to see me at West End Central Station, where he made a written statement. Later information was received that seven men led by Oliva were running a protection racket, and soon afterwards Pedrini and Cheeseman were arrested outside the Phoenix Club, with Ford, who later ran away. An officer had heard Pedrini say to Gardiner, "You are going to give us £100 . . ." Gardiner confirmed that they had threatened to close his club if he did not pay them. It was noticed that his ear was bleeding and he said Ford had nicked it with a knife.

It was at this stage that I entered the scene. Pedrini in evidence to the Inquiry said he was taken to a cell and I entered carrying a length of iron bar. I asked him about his friends and mentioned the name of Oliva. I then threw the bar on the floor and said, "That's yours, my old darling," and when he refused to pick it up I struck him.

(People have often asked me about my habit of addressing criminals in terms of Cockney endearment when I was born well beyond the hearing of Bow Bells. It was not an affectation but something that began as a joke. During my time in Mitcham I arrested a young villain who repeatedly referred to me as "Me old darling". For some unaccountable reason I began to use the phrase myself, and then my colleagues started to employ it when they were talking to me, and before I knew it it had become a habit of speech.)

At his trial, Pedrini had said I assaulted him because he was Italian and another officer had said to him, "That man is mad. He was a prisoner of war by the Italians and he hates Italians." (My only comment to that is, "Read of the great debt I owe to the Italians who sheltered and befriended me.")

Cheeseman also claimed I had assaulted him and planted a knife on him.

Ford said that on arrival at the police station he was seen by me and falsely accused of being involved in a protection racket.

The evidence of PC Wells was of importance because he said he found the iron bar in Pedrini's pocket and when asked what it was Pedrini replied, "My cigar holder." Likewise PC Legge said he found the knife on Cheeseman who said he carried it for self-protection.

Joseph Oliva was not arrested until 23 September, 1962. Detective Constable Jay and PC Laing, both Aids to the CID at the time, said they had been detailed to keep observation on Oliva as I had received information that he intended setting fire to the Phoenix Club. He was seen in a coffee shop, and I was informed.

I waited outside with Jay and Laing in a police car, and when Oliva drove off with two women, Miss Ryan and Miss Murray, we followed his car and stopped it.

PC Laing removed Oliva who was shouting and struggling while I went to the nearside of his car. Jay detected the smell of spirit in the car, and on searching it found an oval-shaped bottle, two-thirds full of a colourless liquid smelling of turpentine and near where Oliva's right foot would have been.

The bottle was plugged with a piece of towelling. The officer told the Inquiry it was impossible for me to have placed or thrown it into the car. At the police station a flick knife was found in Oliva's pocket.

The Inquiry was told I informed Oliva that I believed the bottle was intended to start a fire and I had received information that the target was the Phoenix Club. According to DC Jay, Oliva replied, "If I don't burn him somebody else will."

At his trial Oliva had made no claim that the police had planted the bottle and the knife, but he did claim he had loaned his car to somebody and it was during that time the bottle was put there.

Although I was unable to give evidence in person, a statement signed by me at the time was submitted which included a report from a forensic officer saying the piece of cloth used as a plug matched in colour, texture and design a piece of towelling found in Oliva's home, and both pieces fitted perfectly together.

Oliva told Mr James he had never seen the bottle until it was shown to him by one of the officers sitting in a rear seat and then it had a screw cap on it. When he asked me what it was I replied, "It's for you. You were just going to blow Gardiner's Club up."

At West End Central Police Station he saw an officer tear off a piece of towelling and put it in the top of the bottle. He recognized the towel as the cloth he used for cleaning his car. The knife was also "planted" on him.

Miss Murray, against whom no charges were preferred, had given evidence at Oliva's trial when she said on oath that she had not seen the bottle in the car. But at the Inquiry she admitted that her evidence was deliberately false. She told Mr James that prior to the trial she had visited Oliva in prison and discussed the evidence she would give, and he had told her not to call the police liars as that would enable them to produce his criminal record. She admitted she deliberately gave false evidence but asserted she was telling the truth to the Inquiry.

Miss Ryan, the other passenger in Oliva's car, told the Inquiry that the towel was used for cleaning purposes and she had not seen the bottle until it was produced in the police car, then it had a piece of white cloth in it. Oliva had said to her, "Look what they are putting on me." Neither had she seen the knife in his car.

Later, at the police station, she noticed the bottle standing on a table with a piece of towelling acting as a stopper; the rest of the towel was also on the table. She was certain I had put the piece of towel into the bottle because it was different to the cloth she had seen in the car.

Although she had not given evidence at the trial because she wished to avoid being described as a prostitute, which she was not, she knew Oliva was going to give false testimony, but her attitude was that while she did not favour giving false evidence on oath, she did not see why the defence should not resort to it if I and other police officers were going to do so.

As I read Mr James's report, I was reminded of the familiar quotation: Oh, what a tangled web we weave, When first we practise to deceive. I certainly did not envy him the gigantic task of sifting the true from the false.

The evidence of Mr Berrill, the club doorman, was a typical example. He had made a statement about Oliva's arrest, which was submitted to the Appeal Court as fresh evidence, in which he said, "I knew the day before the bottle was found on Oliva that it was going to be found. Gardiner told me. He told me, rubbing his hands, 'There's going to be a gun, a bomb and tools'. He made it very clear to me they were going to be 'planted'. It had cost him a lot of money to get them put away but he didn't care if he had to pay forty policemen to come to the Old Bailey to swear their lives away. Those were Gardiner's own words."

At the Inquiry he did not refer to his statement until questioned about it by Counsel, then he said the words were not quite accurate but were roughly what Mr Gardiner had said, adding that they might have referred to a different occasion to that referred to in his statement.

Mr Gardiner denied he had said any such thing to Berrill. The doorman had, however, said to him that Pedrini had told him he would burn the club down but for the fact that people were living above it.

Fraser was arrested by Detective Constable Gibson and PC Edwards who were keeping observation outside the Phoenix Club. On 15 September they saw Fraser approach Gardiner at the corner of Greek Street and Old Compton Street. Gibson searched him and found a cutthroat razor in his jacket pocket. Edwards confirmed this. Fraser said, "I suppose he (Gardiner) put you on me, did he? He doesn't know what's coming to him," and when told he was being arrested replied, "He'll have to get more than you lot to look after him. His days are numbered."

Gardiner's version to the Inquiry was that Fraser went up to him and said, "I have been looking for you, you bastard," and it was then he nodded to DC Gibson whom he knew to be keeping observation.

At his trial Fraser did not dispute the evidence of the two officers, nor that of Gardiner, and although he admitted possessing the razor he said he used it at Convent Garden where he worked. It was only when investigations were being made into my conduct that he claimed the razor had been "planted" on him.

He told the Inquiry he had been advised not to allege the razor had been planted because that would enable the prosecution to produce evidence of his criminal record, and as a result the defence he had put forward was pure invention. But as he claimed privilege in respect of any further communications being revealed between him and his Solicitors, Mr James was unable to pursue the matter further.

Mr James's conclusions which were based on the evidence of witnesses and their demeanor and the documentary evidence submitted were, in my opinion, extremely fair, because he stressed that a man with a criminal record might resort to lying on oath in order to prevent evidence of his character being introduced.

Having said that, he accepted that no weapons had been "planted" on Cheeseman or Pedrini. The evidence of Constables Legge and Wells was accepted without reservation. Directly concerning me was the conclusion, "I reject as false evidence the testimony of Mr Pedrini that Detective Sergeant Challenor produced the iron tube to him in a cell saying, 'That's yours', and threatened and assaulted him."

He also acquitted me of the allegations of framing Cheeseman and striking him.

Mr James also dismissed Oliva's claim that the fire bomb was planted. "In the witness box Mr Oliva revealed himself to be a young man of anti-social instincts and of violent temperament. I reached the conclusion that he had no regard for the truth and the taking of an oath to tell the truth meant nothing to him. I find it impossible to rely on his evidence."

The two girls were dealt with in more generous terms, although their evidence was rejected.

Fraser he found "to be a witness of utter unreliability" who was "prepared to invent and to swear to the truth of a pack of lies when it served his interests or those of his friends."

The Inquiry had to sift through a mass of oral and written evidence, some of which had been submitted to the Court of Criminal Appeal alleging that I received regular payments from Mr Gardiner and had accepted bribes to show favour to people I had arrested, but Mr James rejected them all.

I would like to state here that these allegations were particularly trying for Doris who had to suffer the implication that she had benefited by my alleged wrong doing. I was in hospital at the time when Detective Superintendent Williams of the Wolverhampton Police, who was assisting his Chief Constable into the spate of allegations made against me, made thorough and detailed investigation into my financial affairs. Doris fully co-operated and made available everything that would have revealed concealed savings or any abnormal expenditure or a standard of living not possible on a Detective Sergeant's salary. But she did it with quiet dignity, although Mr James's verdict that we "lived simply and almost frugally" was not a thing she would have liked advertised.

Mr James also found that there was no evidence to suggest that I was mentally ill at the time. My only comment on this aspect of the Inquiry was that there had been a rather hasty decision to exonerate the men who had done so much to blacken my character, especially when it was known that £1,000 was readily available to any person without a criminal record to come forward and testify against me.

As you may imagine, the part of Mr James's report which most interested me was that dealing with The Brick Case, and although I have no criticism of the manner in which he dealt with me, I honestly think it was inconsistent not to have allowed the three convicted officers to give evidence. I know that Mr James's terms of reference were limited to finding out why I was allowed to remain on duty when it appeared I was suffering from the onset of mental illness, and by then it was common ground that I was mad at the time of the case. Even so it did not make a lot of sense to me to probe into the case without hearing the views of the three convicted detectives. Working under my direct supervision they would have known as much or more about my condition as anybody else.

I am not a lawyer and find it extremely difficult to put my thoughts into words, but anyone reading the report and its conclusions will realize that despite its terms of reference it was as much about justice as my mental condition. As I have said elsewhere, and I make no apology for repeating it because I consider it so important, I think it was virtually impossible for the three officers to have been tried by a jury that was totally unbiased. And as others found themselves unable to accept the guilty verdict, I think it would have been fairer to have heard the convicted men. After all, evidence was given by people who had been awarded damages and had their convictions quashed because of my alleged corruption, and yet Mr James had dismissed their allegations. It suggested that the Police and the Home Office had been overanxious to support the allegations made against me. However, nothing Mr James said could alter the decisions that had been taken, but his report made it abundantly clear that what was said in court was not always the whole truth and nothing but the truth. At the same time it was conceded that the defence an accused person put forward at his trial was not always the one he preferred. That could well have been so in the case of the three policemen. I do not say it was, I simply suggest it as a possibility.

After all, a great many people had depicted me as a tyranical boss who scared the living daylights out of those working under me. I don't agree, but supposing it *was* true!

I know it is hypothesizing, but just assume that the three men had been allowed to give evidence. Nothing they might have said could have altered the jury's verdict, but their reputations might have been restored. They could have claimed that I was solely responsible for what happened and they acted as they did out of fear and under duress. As I have so little recollection of that night I would have been in no position to deny it even if I had been allowed to appear before the Inquiry. The point is I would not have denied it, because I believe in their innocence. But this is wishful thinking, and I only hope they read this wherever they may be.

I do not pretend to be unbiased and maybe I am wrong in thinking that Mr James may have felt his terms of reference were too limited, for he wrote: "The terms of reference of the Inquiry did not necessitate any findings to be made as to whether or not Detective Sergeant Challenor was guilty of conspiring to pervert the course of public justice, or in particular as to whether or not Detective Sergeant Challenor fabricated evidence by means of "planting" bricks upon innocent persons who had been unlawfully arrested. I have therefore studiously avoided making any findings on those questions, and the Inquiry has not been conducted in any sense as a review of the verdicts of the jury or the observations of the learned judge."

I wish he had. Not, I hasten to add, for my sake, but for that of my three colleagues. After all he did investigate other cases in which I was accused of "framing" innocent people and come to the conclusion that I had not acted improperly.

Equally important to me was the criticism he made of Mr Rooum's evidence to the Inquiry because he had been a vital witness at the trial of the three Aids and at the Magistrate's Hearing in the case of the two youths.

He wrote: "By the time of the Inquiry he (Rooum) was well versed in his evidence, and his apparent enjoyment in the giving thereof detracted from its objectivity and the weight which could be given to it."

And later: "An important aspect of Mr Rooum's evidence was that, according to him, the first assault upon him was witnessed by five other officers, and the next three assaults were witnessed by the officer he believed to be Police Constable Goldsmith, and yet not one of those witnesses protested or reported the incident, and not one has subsequently admitted to witnessing any such incident. There is no corroborative evidence of Mr Rooum's allegations of assault. Despite the fact that Mr Rooum was small in stature and of a gentle disposition,

I find it very difficult to accept that a man so fervent in the causes which to him seem just and so hostile to injustice was assaulted as brutally as he described and yet made no complaint immediate thereof. In the light of the whole evidence before me as to the events of the night of 11 July, 1963, I find the probabilities to be that Mr Rooum was assaulted by Detective Sergeant Challenor but that his version is an exaggerated one both as to the number of occasions on which he was struck and the degree of violence used. I reject his evidence that he believed at that time that the whole Police Force was involved in a great conspiracy and he was a victim thereof."

It was not a vindication of my conduct, but at least I emerged less black than I had been painted. If the three young officers had been allowed to give evidence, who knows what Mr James's conclusions might have been!

Chapter Seventeen

Often as I look out of my window at the Atlantic I think it was inevitable that I should choose Cornwall as the place to spend what is left of my life. Nowhere could be further removed from Soho. The air is unpolluted, the scenery beautiful, and organized crime something the local people only read about or see on television. I play golf at the nearby course, drink in the locals, and join the theatre excursions to Plymouth. I have no idea if any of my friends know about my past because none of them has ever mentioned it. If they do know I certainly don't put it down to indifference, but to their inherent good manners and a deep belief that when the price has been paid past misdeeds should be forgotten. And for that I am extremely grateful. I'm just as grateful to those people in Italy and France who remember me from my SAS days and have always made me a welcome visitor, although there have been times when my recurring illness has not made me the ideal guest.

A great many of my former colleagues in the Met supported me in my times of trouble and sincerely believed that the good I did outweighed the bad. Understandably I did not retain many links with them because I felt it might be to their disadvantage; I did not want to expose them to the risk of taint by association. Too many villains might have jumped at the opportunity of using any friendship with me as a weapon with which to blacken a decent honest policeman. Many have now retired, but it is too late to reforge the links.

Thankfully I have had no such inhibitions about maintaining the many friendships I made in the SAS, and I am as welcome in their homes as I am in the Special Forces Club. Roy Farran, who has held many distinguished public offices in Canada, has no qualms about having me as a guest on his Calgary ranch, and Lord John Manners is the same when it comes to his stately home. I owe them all a debt that is beyond repayment. They showed me I still had a place in society and that Mark Antony was not entirely accurate in his funeral oration to Caesar. The good is also remembered.

Soon after leaving Netherne I decided to prepare myself for the future by returning to the past. I still carried the trauma of my disgrace like an invisible albatross, and I suppose I subconsciously felt that a return to some of the places in Italy where I had distinguished myself would have a purgative effect. So during the summer of 1967, I took Doris and my small son Andrew on a motoring tour of Italy in which I retraced the escape route I had taken in my Italian suit and later in my improvised woman's clothing. Everyone gave us a great welcome, especially those members of the Eliseio family who had not emigrated to Australia. To them and others, I was still Pietro the train-blower. It did a lot for my battered dignity and was the beginning of a long, slow period of rehabilitation.

Then some years later the SAS Regimental Association received a letter inviting all surviving members of Operation Wallace to attend a reunion with the Resistance fighters and the people in the areas in which we had operated. I was asked to organize it, and I was able to mobilize a fair number of old comrades together with their wives who wished to relive old times. I was a little tensed up as it had been a long time since I had been asked to organize anything, and my anxiety was not helped by the news that there was a strike at the ferry ports. Then just prior to our departure I received a telegram from Maurice Rouselet, one of the organizers, who had been a 16 year-old Maquis at the time of Wallace, which said, "Seamen's strike no problem to SAS". It was like a bugle call to an old charger which had been put out to grass. We justified his faith by arriving by air, hire cars and via a most circuitous route through Belgium.

We rendezvoused at the Château Anstruther near Montbard where we were greeted by Madame Blondell, the owner, and many other familiar faces including Maurice and Leon Gervais. Leon vividly recalled the time when he was temporarily recruited into the SAS to act as a gunner in one of Roy Farran's jeeps because we had lost so many men. After a sumptuous meal, Doris and I stayed at Leon's home and next morning we assembled at the Château where I was taken outside and to my astonishment shown an old wartime jeep with a large bouquet on the bonnet and the words, "Little Tanky" painted in white on the spare tyre attached to the radiator. My operational jeep had borne the same words.

The driver was a big man wearing a peaked baseball cap who greeted me with the words, "Get in buddy. You know more about these than

I do." He turned out to be an American who lived in the area and had a deep interest in veteran wartime vehicles. He had made enquires all over France in order to get hold of the ancient jeep.

At the wheel of the jeep I led a procession of cars on a grand tour of the towns and villages where we had operated. We received a tumultous welcome wherever we went and were showered with flowers, and wined and dined with a generosity that defies description.

At the Priory de Vause we relived the night when we hid our jeeps in the woods and the entire squadron were fed by the locals, and where Lieutenant Gurney had played the piano.

Then we motored on to Villaines where we had encountered the Afrika Korps and lost so many men. There we examined the proudly preserved bullet holes which pock-marked so many of the houses, and visited the graves of troopers Rudd and McEachen. In front of the church on each side of the entrance was the clutch housing and sump of a jeep containing growing flowers. We laid our own wreaths on the graves which were beautifully maintained and bright with flowers.

From there we travelled to the spot where I had laid McEachen's body. It was not far from the spot where twenty-three members of the Resistance were executed. There we paid homage to those gallant Frenchmen whose exploits are virtually unknown here. At L'Isle sur Sereine there were more joyous reunions and celebrations and I was profoundly moved at being feted as a liberator when I recalled that I and two other SAS men had got lost there and created sheer havoc. That was all forgotten; the locals were far more interested in having joy rides in "Little Tanky".

Then we travelled on to Epoisses to pay tribute at the grave of Lieutenant David Leigh whom we had carried mortally wounded to a house opposite the church.* The next stop was the most poignant of all for me personally. Buried at Velorcey is Lieutenant Gurney who died trying to save my life. He was the father I wished I had had, and a part of me is also buried there. I was sporting a silk handkerchief in my breast pocket bearing the name tag H.G. Gurney. It is one of my proudest possessions. When we returned to England after VE Day, I went to Northrepps Hall, near Cromer, to offer what comfort I could to Hugh's mother. She bore her loss with quiet dignity, and knowing how fond I was of her son gave me his handkerchief as a memento.

---

* I returned there with Mrs Leigh when she presented a lecturn to the church in gratitude for the manner in which the villagers had maintained David's grave. The room where he died had been kept exactly as it was when he was carried there, but Mrs Leigh could not bring herself to enter it.

Such visits became a regular form of pilgrimage, and later during a visit to Granrupt, Major Farran, Captain Stonehouse and I were decorated with the Resistance award of medaille d'argent de la Legion Vosgienne. I found it rather bewildering as we had brought nothing but tragedy to the village – the SS had devastated it and executed a large number of men and boys as reprisals for helping us and sent many more to concentration camps. Instead of treating us coldly the entire population, along with several prominent politicians, lined the streets to greet us while army and police bands provided a medley of rousing music. We in turn laid our own wreaths on the magnificent memorial to the Martyrs of Granrupt.

At Montbard we were presented with a Vickers gun and parts of Major Farran's jeep which was destroyed in one particularly hectic skirmish. They are now honoured trophies in the SAS museum.

During another trip we were invited to Chatillon sur Seine for the unveiling of a memorial to William Holland who was killed in the assault on the town, and among those present was Count Pinci whose son was killed in error by one of our own fighters. I was deeply moved to find he bore no bitterness. Sadly for all of us – French and British – our efforts to trace any relatives of Bill were unsuccessful.

It was during this trip that Major Farran invited me to join him on a visit to Italy, and I reluctantly agreed. My hesitation was due entirely to the fact that I was experiencing what I feared could be a recurrence of my illness. But I did not want to spoil things for him, and rather stupidly I flushed my preventive drugs down the toilet. I don't know why. Maybe I believed I was capable of coping without them, or perhaps I did not want to dull my senses. What transpired is a bitter reminder that I will never be one hundred per cent fit.

We set off by car and visited the La Spezia area before going on to the small seaside resort of Moneglia where we booked into an hotel. I began to think that my fear of a sudden attack was groundless until he and I went for an evening swim. Then suddenly, without warning, I believed I was swimming towards North Africa and loudly cursing the submarine which had failed to pick me up after an operation. Roy must have sensed something was wrong for he swam after me as fast as he could and when he caught up with me he said, "Come back, Tanky, and I'll buy you a beer." The inducement worked and I returned to the hotel with him.

Next morning I woke very early feeling perfectly normal and decided to go for a swim. We were on the third floor, but when I went down I found the front door locked and bolted and even though I made a heck of a din I could not rouse anyone to come and open it. I returned to the room where he was still asleep and went out onto the balcony where I found a coil of stout plastic-coated wire. I tied one end to the balustrade and abseiled down to the astonishment of the people below. One of them must have related my odd behaviour to the manager because when I returned he told me we had been kicked out.

We drove on to Reggio where we booked in to another hotel before going off for a reunion with some old partisans. That night I woke and looking out of the window I saw a full moon rising over a distant mountain and I had an overwhelming urge to climb it. As before I found the front door locked and bolted, but in addition there was a ferocious-looking dog keeping guard. I decided to wrestle with it, thinking in some confused manner that this would help me strike up a rapport with the beast. Unfortunately, during the ensuing tussle several pieces of furniture were knocked over and I looked up to see the owner in his dressing gown gazing down at me and looking thoroughly displeased. Aware that I was having an attack, I said the dog had gone for me while I was trying to open the door to go for a walk. He gabbled something in Italian, too fast for me to understand, then opened the door and slammed it behind me.

I went for a long walk, during which I fell over and cracked a couple of ribs, then I had a strange fantasy in which I was one of the robbers on a cross beside the crucified Christ who turned to me and said, "Go down and save the world."

The next thing I remember was battering on the hotel door and telling the proprietor that I had been sent to save the world. He anxiously crossed himself, then protested that his dog was terrified, his wife had nearly had a heart attack, and some of his possessions were beyond repair. Unruffled I asked him if he could let me have a room for the night, and he angrily pointed out that I already had one. When he took me to it I saw his wife was roundly abusing the Major. He said quite calmly, "Hullo Tanky. I'm afraid we've been kicked out again."

We packed our cases and drove until we were halted by thick fog and he was forced to pull off the road. He settled down to sleep in the car, but my attention was attracted by a haystack and I was transported back in time to when I had slept on piles of hay during my time on the run in Italy. I made a hole in the hay and settled down for the night. In the morning I woke Roy and said, "I've got a nasty feeling it was my fault we got kicked out," and he just smiled and said, "Not at all, Tanky, they just don't have our sense of humour."

Everything went smoothly until we reached Dijon where we booked into an hotel with a swimming pool. Early morning I decided to have a swim. I dived off the top board, and almost immediately Major Farran was informed that his friend had just dived naked into the pool. When I got back he was already packing.

When we reached Charles de Gaulle Airport, I had a strange feeling that the people all around were trying to read my thoughts so I wrapped my coat around my head and remained like that throughout the flight home.

Major Farran drove me home and handed me over to Doris. There were no words of recrimination, and he had no qualms about leaving me. He knew Doris could cope. She made a telephone call to the hospital, and packed my bag. I was away for six weeks before I was fit enough to return home. Doris said, "That'll teach you not to forget your tablets."

Without her support I don't think I could have survived. She never lost faith in my ability to do so, and she has no time for post mortems. She tells me to forget what has happened, it's all in the past. But I can't. Often when I walk down the steep hill to the sea I wonder why and how it was that a detective who had been an admired member of the police should have left in disgrace. I think it was Wilde who said that all men kill the thing they love, and I certainly did that. I was dedicated to my work and would no more have dreamed of tarnishing its image than I would do anything to dishonour the SAS. I accept that my illness may have resulted in me approaching my work with a crusading zeal, and it might have made sense if I had been found guilty of framing criminals, but I was not. Why was it, then, that I tried to convict innocent people? It just doesn't make sense to me, especially when there was no need to prove my worth, for I can honestly claim that I arrested more criminals in my period of service than any other officer. None of it was accomplished by unlawful acts, but by the cultivation and use of informants. They trusted me and knew I would never let them down. The men of violence were my target.

I know that with modern medicine I need never again see the inside of a mental hospital. If I feel an attack coming on I take my pills, go to bed, and in a few days I'm up and about again. However, mental illness is still very much a closed book, and although the experts are getting closer and closer to curing some aspects of it they are also very much in the dark as to what triggers it off. I hope that one day I will learn why it happened to me. I would hate to think my father was right when he said I was inherently bad. I would prefer my epitaph to be the following description which appears in Mr James's report:

"He was regarded as a man who was kindly and considerate to children and the elderly, and who was abhorrent of the bully."

INDEX